Revenue Patterns in U.S. Cities and Suburbs

Revenue Patterns in U.S. Cities and Suburbs

A Comparative Analysis

Susan A. MacManus

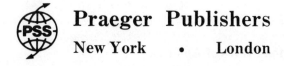

Praeger Publishers

New York   •   London

Library of Congress Cataloging in Publication Data

MacManus, Susan A.
    Revenue patterns in U.S. cities and suburbs.

    Bibliography: p.
    Includes index.
    1. Municipal finance—United States. 2. Revenue—
United States. 3. Local taxation—United States.
I. Title.
HJ9145.M33   336'.02'73   77-27499
ISBN 0-03-022846-8

PRAEGER SPECIAL STUDIES
200 Park Avenue, New York, N.Y. 10017, U.S.A.

Published in the United States of America in 1978
by Praeger Publishers,
A Division of Holt, Rinehart and Winston, CBS, Inc.

89   038   987654321

For My Parents

Preface

Most studies of municipal government finance have focused on the expenditure side of the budgetary ledger. This study, on the other hand, focuses on the revenue side of the municipal budget.

It has become increasingly apparent that fiscal strain occurs when a city's revenue-raising capacity is insufficient to meet ever-expanding expenditure needs. Many studies have shown that greater expenditures are necessitated by both growth (economic and physical) and public expectations, and demands for more and better services. Yet few studies have examined the impact of these same forces on the revenue-raising capabilities of U.S. municipalities. In fact, little is known about the various types of local government revenue other than the infamous property tax.

One of the purposes of this study is to describe the various types of revenues (external and internal) raised by municipalities. External sources of revenue are typically labeled intergovernmental revenues and include monies coming from the federal government and the state government. Internal, or locally raised revenues, are often labeled revenues from own sources and fall into two broad categories: tax and nontax. Tax revenues may be further broken down into property tax revenues (real and personal) and nonproperty tax revenues (sales, excise, income). Nontax revenues, often referred to as charges and miscellaneous revenues, typically include fees, fines, forfeitures, special assessments, charges for water, sewer, garbage, occupational licenses, and so on. It should already be apparent that very little is known about the extent of usage of these various types of municipal revenues. Even more critical is the fact that very little is known about revenue usage in municipalities other than the very largest central cities.

It is generally believed that fiscal strain is most severe and occurs most frequently among the largest cities in the United States. In contrast, suburbs are generally perceived as being healthy and wealthy, with surplus revenues in their coffers. Could it be that this general perception is grossly inaccurate?

Another purpose of this study is to contrast revenue patterns of 243 central cities and 340 suburban municipalities from the Standard Metropolitan Statistical Areas (SMSAs) existing in 1970. Specifically, the relationships among various demographic, socioeconomic, and governmental characteristics, and use of each of these revenue types by cities and suburbs, are compared. Demographic, socioeconomic, and governmental data for each city were collected for 1960 and 1970 from the U.S. Census of the Population, the U.S. Census of Housing, FBI Uniform Crime Reports, and Vital Statistics of the U.S. Revenue data were collected for three time points (1962, 1967, 1972) from the Census of Governments and City Finances publications of those years.

The study goes beyond a mere comparison of the types of revenues used by cities and suburbs and compares various revenue-related measures: levels (per capita), reliance, tax burdens, effective property tax rates, and tax efficiency structures of cities and suburbs. To be tested is the notion that the intensity of usage varies significantly between cities and suburbs as a result of differing demographic, socioeconomic, and governmental characteristics.

The study would be incomplete if it did not attempt to comment on what all this means in terms of the ability of cities and suburbs to raise revenues now and in the future. Thus, the study concludes with two specialized analyses. First, seeking to comment on what all this means now, is an examination of the impact of the current local government tax system on women and minorities living in the large metropolitan areas of the United States. Second, seeking to comment on future implications, is an examination of the changing revenue patterns of U.S. suburbs that attempts to predict their likelihood of financial crises in the near future.

Acknowledgments

Many people are to be thanked for their assistance in this study. Special thanks are due Thomas R. Dye, teacher and friend, for his guidance, training, and financial assistance made possible through the grant from the Center for Population Research, National Institute of Child Health and Human Development (Grant HD07629). I also wish to express my thanks to Malcolm B. Parsons, Norman R. Luttbeg, and William W. Rogers, who read the manuscript in draft. Nikki R. Van Hightower (coauthor of Chapter 7) deserves special mention for her suggestions and assistance in the preparation of that chapter. Others who made valuable contributions, administratively and supportively, include Elaine Riegler, Ricky Avriett, Betsy Mixon, Jeannie Mouton, and, of course, my very special parents.

Contents

		Page
PREFACE		vii
ACKNOWLEDGMENTS		ix
LIST OF TABLES		xv

PART I: EXAMINING CURRENT REVENUE PATTERNS

Chapter

1	COMPARING REVENUE PATTERNS: PROBLEMS AND PRACTICAL SOLUTIONS	3
	Types of Municipal Revenue	4
	Intergovernmental Revenues	4
	Tax Revenues	7
	Nontax Revenues	7
	Common Measures of Revenue Usage	8
	Revenue Level	8
	Revenue Reliance	9
	Tax Burden	9
	Effective Property Tax Rate	10
	Tax Efficiency	10
	Limitations of Existing Municipal Revenue Data	11
	Other Shortcomings of Previous Revenue Research	15
	Summary	16
	The Design of This Study	16
	The Data	16
	Methodological Techniques	20
	Notes	21
2	REVENUE LEVELS: HOW MUCH DOLLAR INTAKE PER PERSON?	27
	Previous Revenue Level Studies	28
	General Revenue Levels	29
	General Revenue Levels by Region	32

General Revenue Levels by Population Size   35
General Revenue Levels by Economic Base   37
General Revenue Levels by Governmental Character
   (Reformism)   39
General Revenue Levels by Functional Responsibility   44
Determinants of Revenue Levels   48
  Methodology   49
  Results   49
  Intergovernmental Revenue Level Determinants   50
  Tax Revenue Level Determinants   54
  Nontax Revenue Level Determinants   57
Significance of the Findings   59
Notes   59

3   REVENUE RELIANCE: WHAT PROPORTION COMES
   FROM EACH REVENUE SOURCE?   62

Introduction   62
Previous Revenue Reliance Studies   63
General Revenue Reliance Patterns   65
  Revenue Reliance Patterns by Region   67
  Revenue Reliance Patterns by Population Size   69
  Revenue Reliance Patterns by Economic Base   72
  Revenue Reliance Patterns by Governmental Character   76
  Revenue Reliance Patterns by Functional Responsibility 79
Determinants of Revenue Reliance Patterns   83
  Determinants of Intergovernmental Revenue Reliance
   Patterns   83
  Determinants of Tax Revenue Reliance   88
  Determinants of Reliance on Nontax Revenue   89
Significance of the Findings   92
Notes   93

4   TAX BURDENS: HOW MUCH STRAIN ON THE PERSONAL
   INCOMES OF MUNICIPAL RESIDENTS?   95

Introduction   95
  Defining Tax Burden   95
  Why Compare Tax Burdens?   96
  Framework of Analysis   96
Previous Research   97
  Weaknesses   97
  Earlier Studies: Findings   98

General Tax Burden Patterns   99
  Tax Burden Patterns by Region   100
  Tax Burden Patterns by Population Size   102
  Tax Burden Patterns by Economic Base   104
  Tax Burden Patterns by Governmental Character   106
  Tax Burden Patterns by Functional Responsibility   107
  Summary   110
Determinants of Property and Nonproperty Tax Burdens   111
  Determinants of Property Tax Burdens   111
  Determinants of Nonproperty Tax Burdens   115
Significance of the Findings   119
Notes   120

5   EFFECTIVE PROPERTY TAX RATES: COMPARABLE
     MEASURES OF PROPERTY TAX RATES ACROSS
     COMMUNITIES   122

Introduction   122
  Weaknesses of Nominal Property Tax Rate Measures   122
  Advantages of Effective Property Tax Rate Measures   123
  Types of Property Examined   123
  Framework of Analysis   124
Previous Research   124
General Effective Property Tax Rate Patterns   126
  Effective Property Tax Rates by Region   127
  Effective Property Tax Rates by Population Size   129
  Effective Property Tax Rates by Economic Base   131
  Effective Property Tax Rates by Governmental
    Character   133
  Effective Property Tax Rates by Functional Responsi-
    bility   133
Determinants of Effective Property Tax Rates   137
  Central City Effective Property Tax Rate Determinants:
    All Types of Real Property   137
  Suburban Effective Property Tax Rate Determinants:
    All Types of Real Property   138
  Central City Effective Property Tax Rate Determinants:
    Fully Taxable Single-Family Residential Property   139
  Suburban Effective Property Tax Rate Determinants:
    Fully Taxable Single-Family Residential Property   139
Significance of the Findings   141
Notes   142

6   TAX EFFICIENCY PATTERNS OF U.S. CITIES AND
     SUBURBS: DIFFERING PATTERNS OF COMMUNITY
     CHOICE   143

     Introduction   143
     Previous Research   144
     General Tax Efficiency Patterns   146
       Tax Efficiency by Region   148
       Tax Efficiency by Population Size   148
       Tax Efficiency by Economic Base   151
       Tax Efficiency by Governmental Character   151
       Tax Efficiency by Functional Responsibility   153
     Demographic, Socioeconomic, and Governmental Corre-
       lates of Tax Efficiency   154
       Correlates of Central City Tax Efficiency   154
       Correlates of Suburban Tax Efficiency   158
       Central City/Suburban Differences   159
     Determinants of Tax Efficiency   160
       Determinants of Central City Tax Efficiency   160
       Determinants of Suburban Tax Efficiency   160
     Significance of the Findings   161
     Notes   162

PART II: SPECIAL INVESTIGATIONS: PRESENT
AND FUTURE IMPLICATIONS OF
CURRENT REVENUE PATTERNS

7   THE IMPACT OF TAX STRUCTURES ON WOMEN AND
     OTHER MINORITIES: INEFFICIENCIES AND INEQUALI-
     TIES   167

     Introduction   167
       Framework of Analysis   168
       Types of Household–Status Groups   168
     Patterns of per Capita Personal Income   169
     General Tax Burden Patterns   172
       Tax Burden Patterns by Household Status   173
       Tax Burden Patterns by Race   174
       Tax Burden Patterns by Region   176
       Tax Burden Patterns by Population Size   176
     Tax Efficiency Patterns   176
       General Tax Efficiency (All Services)   179
       Tax Efficiency: Poverty-Related Services   181

Chapter   Page

  Significance of the Findings   183
  Notes   184

8 CHANGING REVENUE PATTERNS IN U.S. SUBURBS:
  A POTENTIAL FISCAL CRISIS?   186

  Introduction   186
   Framework of Analysis   187
  Previous Research   187
   Weaknesses   187
  Changes in Suburban Revenue Levels   188
   Changes in Intergovernmental Revenue Levels 194
   Changes in Tax Revenue Levels   195
   Changes in Nontax Revenue Levels   197
  Changes in Suburban Revenue Reliance Patterns 198
   Changes in Intergovernmental Revenue Reliance 199
   Changes in Tax Revenue Reliance   200
   Changes in Nontax Revenue Reliance   202
  Determinants of Changes in Suburban Revenue Levels
   and Reliance Patterns   202
   Determinants of Change in Suburban Revenue Levels 205
   Determinants of Change in Suburban Revenue Reliance
   Patterns   210
  Significance of the Findings   215
  Notes   216

SELECTED BIBLIOGRAPHY   219

INDEX   262

ABOUT THE AUTHOR   267

LIST OF TABLES

Table		Page
1.1	Demographic Independent Variables	17
1.2	Socioeconomic Independent Variables	18
1.3	Governmental Independent Variables	19
1.4	Dependent (Policy Output) Variables: Revenue Measures	20
2.1	Revenue Levels (per Capita): All Central Cities and Suburbs	31
2.2	Revenue Levels (per Capita) for Central Cities and Suburbs, by Region	33
2.3	Revenue Levels (per Capita) for Central Cities and Suburbs, by Population Size	36
2.4	Revenue Levels (per Capita) for Central Cities and Suburbs, by Economic Base	40
2.5	Revenue Levels (per Capita) for Central Cities and Suburbs, by Governmental Character	42
2.6	Functional Distribution for Central Cities and Suburbs	45
2.7	Revenue Levels (per Capita) for Central Cities and Suburbs, by Functional Responsibility	46
2.8	Determinants of Federal Aid Revenue Levels: Central Cities	51
2.9	Determinants of Federal Aid Revenue Levels: Suburbs	52
2.10	Determinants of State Aid Revenue Levels: Central Cities	53
2.11	Determinants of State Aid Revenue Levels: Suburbs	54
2.12	Determinants of Property Tax Revenue Levels: Central Cities	56

Table		Page
2.13	Determinants of Property Tax Revenue Levels: Suburbs	57
2.14	Determinants of Nontax Revenue Levels: Central Cities	58
2.15	Determinants of Nontax Revenue Levels: Suburbs	59
3.1	Revenue Reliance: All Central Cities and Suburbs	66
3.2	Revenue Reliance for Central Cities and Suburbs, by Region	68
3.3	Revenue Reliance for Central Cities and Suburbs, by Population Size	70
3.4	Revenue Reliance for Central Cities and Suburbs, by Economic Base	74
3.5	Revenue Reliance for Central Cities and Suburbs, by Governmental Character	77
3.6	Revenue Reliance for Central Cities and Suburbs, by Functional Responsibility	80
3.7	Determinants of Federal Aid Revenue Reliance: Central Cities	85
3.8	Determinants of Federal Aid Revenue Reliance: Suburbs	85
3.9	Determinants of State Aid Revenue Reliance: Central Cities	87
3.10	Determinants of State Aid Revenue Reliance: Suburbs	87
3.11	Determinants of Property Tax Revenue Reliance: Central Cities	89
3.12	Determinants of Property Tax Revenue Reliance: Suburbs	90
3.13	Determinants of Nontax Revenue Reliance: Central Cities	91

Table		Page
3.14	Determinants of Nontax Revenue Reliance: Suburbs	91
4.1	Central City and Suburban Tax Burdens, 1972	100
4.2	Tax Burdens for Central Cities and Suburbs, by Region, 1972	101
4.3	Tax Burdens for Central Cities and Suburbs, by Population Size, 1972	103
4.4	Tax Burdens for Central Cities and Suburbs, by Economic Base, 1972	104
4.5	Tax Burdens for Central Cities and Suburbs, by Governmental Character, 1972	107
4.6	Tax Burdens for Central Cities and Suburbs, by Functional Responsibility, 1972	108
4.7	Determinants of Property Tax Burdens of Central Cities and Suburbs	112
4.8	Functional Responsibility Determinants of Property Tax Burdens of Central Cities and Suburbs	113
4.9	Determinants of Nonproperty Tax Burdens of Central Cities and Suburbs	116
4.10	Functional Responsibility Determinants of Nonproperty Tax Burdens of Central Cities and Suburbs	117
5.1	Effective Property Tax Rates: All Central Cities and Suburbs, 1972	127
5.2	Effective Property Tax Rates for Central Cities and Suburbs, by Region, 1972	128
5.3	Effective Property Tax Rates for Central Cities and Suburbs, by Population Size, 1972	130
5.4	Effective Property Tax Rates for Central Cities and Suburbs, by Economic Base, 1972	132

Table		Page
5.5	Effective Property Tax Rates for Central Cities and Suburbs, by Governmental Character, 1972	135
5.6	Effective Property Tax Rates for Central Cities and Suburbs, by Functional Responsibility, 1972	136
5.7	Determinants of Central City Effective Property Tax Rates: All Types of Real Property, 1972	138
5.8	Determinants of Suburban Effective Property Tax Rates: All Types of Real Property, 1972	139
5.9	Determinants of Central City Effective Property Tax Rates: Fully Taxable Single-Family Dwellings (Median), 1972	140
5.10	Determinants of Suburban Effective Property Tax Rates: Fully Taxable Single-Family Dwellings (Median), 1972	140
6.1	General Tax Efficiency of Central Cities and Suburbs: All Services and by Specific Service Area	147
6.2	Tax Efficiency for Central Cities and Suburbs, by Region	149
6.3	Tax Efficiency for Central Cities and Suburbs, by Population Size	149
6.4	Tax Efficiency for Central Cities and Suburbs, by Economic Base	152
6.5	Tax Efficiency for Central Cities and Suburbs, by Governmental Character	152
6.6	Tax Efficiency for Central Cities and Suburbs, by Functional Responsibility	155
6.7	Demographic, Socioeconomic, and Governmental Correlates of Tax Efficiency: Central Cities and Suburbs	156

Table		Page
6.8	Determinants of General Tax Efficiency (All Services): Central Cities and Suburbs	161
7.1	Per Capita Income of Employed Persons Living in SMSAs over 250,000, by Household Status, Race, and Gender	171
7.2	Tax Burdens of Employed Persons Living in SMSAs over 250,000, by Household Status, Race, and Gender	175
7.3	Tax Burdens of Employed Persons Living in SMSAs over 250,000, by Region, Household Status, Race, and Gender	177
7.4	Tax Burdens of Employed Persons Living in SMSAs over 250,000, by Population Size, Household Status, Race, and Gender	178
7.5	General Tax Efficiency (All Services) for Employed Persons Living in SMSAs over 250,000, by Region, Population Size, Household Status, Race, and Gender	180
7.6	Tax Efficiency (Poverty-Related Services) for Employed Persons Living in SMSAs over 250,000, by Household Status, Race, and Gender	182
8.1	Change in Revenue Level and Reliance of 340 Suburbs, by Revenue Source, 1962-72	189
8.2	Change in Revenue Level and Reliance of 340 Suburbs, by Revenue Source and Region, 1962-72	190
8.3	Change in Revenue Level and Reliance of 340 Suburbs, by Revenue Source and Population Size, 1962-72	190
8.4	Change in Revenue Level and Reliance of 340 Suburbs, by Revenue Source and Economic Base, 1962-72	191
8.5	Change in Revenue Level and Reliance of 340 Suburbs, by Revenue Source and Governmental Character, 1962-72	192

Table		Page
8.6	Change in Revenue Level and Reliance of 340 Suburbs, by Revenue Source and Functional Responsibility, 1962–72	193
8.7	Relationships between Changes in Demographic, Socioeconomic, and Governmental Characteristics and Changes in Revenue Levels of 340 U.S. Suburbs	203
8.8	Relationships between Changes in Demographic, Socioeconomic, and Governmental Characteristics and Changes in Revenue Reliance of 340 U.S. Suburbs	204
8.9	Determinants of Changes in Federal Intergovernmental Revenue Levels of 340 Suburbs, 1962–72	206
8.10	Determinants of Changes in State Intergovernmental Revenue Levels of 340 Suburbs, 1962–72	206
8.11	Determinants of Changes in Property Tax Levels of 340 Suburbs, 1962–72	207
8.12	Determinants of Changes in Nonproperty Tax Levels of 340 Suburbs, 1962–72	208
8.13	Determinants of Changes in Nontax Revenue Levels of 340 Suburbs, 1962–72	209
8.14	Determinants of Changes in Federal Intergovernmental Revenue Reliance Patterns of 340 Suburbs, 1962–72	211
8.15	Determinants of Changes in State Intergovernmental Revenue Reliance Patterns of 340 Suburbs, 1962–72	212
8.16	Determinants of Changes in Property Tax Reliance Patterns of 340 Suburbs, 1962–72	213
8.17	Determinants of Changes in Nonproperty Tax Reliance Patterns of 340 Suburbs, 1962–72	214
8.18	Determinants of Changes in Nontax Revenue Reliance Patterns of 340 Suburbs, 1962–72	215

Part I

Examining Current
Revenue Patterns

Chapter 1

Comparing Revenue Patterns:
Problems and Practical Solutions

Recent financial catastrophes in several major U.S. cities, particularly New York City, have demonstrated the costs of ignoring the revenue side of municipal budgets. Politicians and practitioners alike have suddenly become aware of the necessity of analyzing the revenue structures of their cities, no matter how large or small their populations, in order to avoid financial fates similar to those of New York City, Detroit, and others.

Unfortunately, very little research has been done on the revenue structures of U.S. municipalities that is of use to politicians and practitioners so desperately in need of such information. The literature to date on local government finances has tended to focus primarily on the expenditure side of the budgetary ledger. One plausible explanation for this expenditure concentration might be that it is far easier to conceptualize expenditures in terms of outputs than it is to view revenues in this way. However, revenues are equally to be regarded as outputs of the governmental system. It has been said that what the government gives, it must first take away. The point is also that it is far easier for municipalities to spend money than it is to obtain money in the first place. Fiscal irresponsibility occurs when governments spend money or authorize programs for which monies must be expended without properly analyzing the wheres and whens of revenue accumulation.

This study, recognizing the problems and limitations of municipal revenue data, will describe and explain variations in revenue structures among and between 243 central cities and 340 suburban municipalities located within the Standard Metropolitan Statistical Areas (SMSAs) existing in 1970. The study examines the relationships between various demographic, socioeconomic, and governmental

3

characteristics, and the revenue structures of these cities and suburbs in 1962, 1967, and 1972.*

Included in this intensive examination are all three major categories of municipal revenue: intergovernmental (federal and state); tax (property and nonproperty); and nontax (charges and miscellaneous general revenues). Specific revenue-related measures used to compare revenue usage by cities and suburbs include revenue level, revenue reliance, tax burden, effective property tax rate, and tax efficiency. Overall, the study is a revenue policy determinant study that, it is hoped, will provide politicians, administrators, practitioners, and students of municipal finance with an understanding of the revenue structures of both cities and suburbs throughout the United States.

TYPES OF MUNICIPAL REVENUES

There are three basic categories of municipal revenue: intergovernmental, tax, and nontax. Revenues labeled intergovernmental are viewed as external sources of municipal revenue whereas tax and nontax revenues are generally referred to as locally raised or internal sources of revenue.

Intergovernmental Revenues

Intergovernmental revenues are of two types: federal and state. In general, intergovernmental revenues help local governments pay for more of the costly, collectively consumed services, and in this sense are viewed as having a more redistributive effect than any of the revenues collected from a local government's own sources. Of the two types, certainly federal revenues are the more redistributive, or more equitably designed. "With the major exception of public education, state aid distribution formulas generally fail to recognize variations in local fiscal capacity to support public services."[1]

---

*It should be noted that this study analyzes revenue patterns of cities and suburbs from 1962 to 1972. Thus, the time frame of the study is prerevenue-sharing and preconsolidated-block-grant. It is vitally important that such a study be done so that the significance of the impacts of revenue sharing and block grants on local government revenues can be better discerned by a follow-up study. The follow-up study will not be possible until the results of the 1977 Census of Governments become available, which will probably not be until almost 1980.

Federal aid, since the 1930s and the advent of grants-in-aid, has been distributed on the basis of need with the goal being that of re-distribution and equalization. Consequently, the formulas allocating such monies have been constructed inversely to a governmental unit's ability to pay—an equity choice rather than an efficiency choice. Most grants have three characteristics: they are voluntary; they are on some sort of a matching basis; and they come with strings and guide-lines attached.

Most federal grants are categorical* rather than block;[†] they are very specifically designed and give the local government very lit-tle discretion in the expenditure decisions. There are two basic means of allocating or dispersing grant monies: by project or by for-mula. Project grants are competitive grants. A limited amount of

---

*Prior to 1972 over 90 percent of the federal grants were categori-cal, as opposed to block grants. Prior to 1972 only two block grants existed: Partnership for Health, enacted in 1966, and the Omnibus Crime Control and Safe Streets Act, enacted in 1968. However, both of these programs were small in relation to the total federal monies expended in the health and crime control areas. In 1972, general rev-enue sharing was enacted in the State and Local Fiscal Assistance Act. In 1973 and 1974 three large block grants were created by the Com-prehensive Employment and Training Act of 1973, the Housing and Community Development Act of 1974, and the 1974 amendments (Title XX) to the Social Security Act of 1935, for social services. According to the Advisory Commission on Intergovernmental Relations, by fiscal year 1976, categorical grants still composed the greatest proportion of federal aid. However, the "categorical portion of the $59.8 billion federal aid pie had decreased from 98 percent a decade earlier to 79 percent, while the block grant share was nine percent and revenue sharing and general support aid accounted for 12 percent."[2]

[†]There are several common characteristics of a block grant. Federal aid is authorized for a wide range of activities within a broadly defined functional area; recipients have substantial discretion in identi-fying problems, designing programs to deal with them, and allocating resources; administrative, fiscal reporting, planning, and other fed-erally imposed requirements are kept to the minimum amount neces-sary to ensure that national goals are being accomplished; federal aid is distributed on the basis of a statutory formula, which has the effect of narrowing federal administrators' discretion and providing a sense of fiscal certainty to recipients; and eligibility provisions are statutor-ily specified and favor general purpose governmental units as recipi-ents, and elected officials and administrative generalists as decision makers.[3]

funds for a specific project are appropriated by Congress and interested governments must apply and compete for these funds. In other words, not all the applicants receive grant monies. It is the decision of the federal officials in the appropriate agencies to decide who gets the money. Thus, the need for grantsmanship activities arises when governments apply for grants of a project nature—a phenomenon that smaller municipalities claim is biased against them since they cannot afford such expertise.

The second type of allocation procedure is by formula. The funds are appropriated by Congress, governments apply if they so choose, and all applicant governments meeting the eligibility requirements established by Congress or the authorizing agency receive monies on the basis of the formula. Thus, the need for competition is reduced considerably, the only competition being in the initial establishment of the formula. However, from the beginning of the federal grants programs, the overwhelming number of grants have been of a project nature rather than of a formula nature.

State aid is generally of two types: grants-in-aid and shared taxes. Grants monies can either be appropriations made directly by the state legislature or they can be federal funds that are "passed through" the state government, leaving the distribution decisions (how much goes to each local government) to the state legislature or to the state agency responsible for dispensing the funds. Most state grants, either because of federal regulations or because of state officials' distrust of local officials' ability to spend money wisely, are very categorical in nature, most of the funds being, in fact, earmarked for specific types of activities such as education, highways, or welfare.

Shared taxes allow the municipal government that receives them more discretion in deciding how to spend them. Shared taxes are monies collected by the state and returned to local government. Examples are an extra penny local government sales tax (sometimes known as a piggyback tax), or a portion of the state gasoline tax, cigarette tax, or alcoholic beverage tax. The amount received by a municipal government does not depend on an annual appropriation by the legislature but on the amount of monies actually collected. There are two basic ways of distributing these shared taxes: on the basis of origin or on the basis of need. If shared taxes are returned on the basis of origin, they are returned in direct proportion to the monies collected in the municipality for the state. If they are returned on the basis of need, a local government might get back more or less than it collected, depending on its financial need. Certainly shared taxes returned on the basis of need are redistributive in nature and are more equitable than those returned on the basis of origin.

Tax Revenues

Tax revenues are of two types: property and nonproperty. Property taxes at the municipal level apply to both real property (land and improvements, including structures thereon) and personal property (tangible and intangible). Property taxes are the only major tax source utilized specifically by the local level of government, and are the only major taxes allowed by all states for use by local governments.

Real property is usually broken down into several categories, often paralleling the zoning classification scheme of the municipality. For example, real property might be classified as residential (single-family or multifamily), industrial, commercial, or agricultural. Often the property tax rate will differ among these classifications even within the same municipality.

Personal property is either tangible or intangible. Tangible property has substance and worth; it can be touched. Examples of tangible property include machinery, furniture, cars, boats, animals, furs, jewelry, clothes, and equipment. Intangible personal property is property that is of value but does not have physical substance; it is representative of value. Examples of intangible property are stocks, bonds, notes, mortgages, savings accounts, money, and so on.

Besides property, there are only three bases on which taxes can be levied: sales, income, and privileges. Nonproperty taxes include taxes on income (individual and corporate), on sales (general and selective), and on motor vehicle registration, operators' licenses, and on business and occupational licenses, the latter group all being privilege taxes. It has been said that "the shift to nonproperty taxes accompanies a basic shift in our economy from a rural to an urban economy and from an economy characterized by individual family ownership of small manufacturing plants to a system of national corporations."[4]

Nontax Revenues

Nontax revenues are generally classified by the Census Bureau under the groupings of current charges and miscellaneous general revenues. Current charges, as defined by the Bureau of the Census, are amounts received from the public for performance of specific services benefiting the person charged, and from sales of commodities and services. The following are the specific categories of current charges: education; hospitals; sanitation (activities connected with the collection and disposal of garbage and other waste); sewerage (provision of sanitary and storm sewers and sewage disposal facilities and services); local parks and recreation (museums, art galleries, swimming pools, golf courses, municipal parks, and special facilities for recreation, such as auditoriums, stadiums, harbors); natural resources (concessions in parklands and bird sanctuaries); housing and urban renewal (city housing rents and payments made by private developers); and others, such as airport charges, charges for operation of canals, docks, wharfs, and related facilities, monies received from sale of services to other local governments through contractual arrangements, and parking facilities, including meter collections and charges for the public use of municipally operated garages. [5]

Miscellaneous general revenues include three types of locally generated revenues: [6] interest earnings (earnings on deposits and securities other than the earnings of insurance trust funds or employee retirement systems); sale of property (receipts from the sale of real property and improvements thereon, excluding receipts from the disposition of commodities, equipment and other personal property, and from the sale of securities[7]); and special assessments (compulsory contributions collected from the owners of property benefited by specific public improvements to defray the costs of such improvements, and apportioned according to the assumed benefits to the property affected). Specific public improvements that are typically financed by special assessments are paving of streets, curbs, and sidewalks, construction of drainage or irrigation facilities, and installation of street lights.

COMMON MEASURES OF REVENUE USAGE

There are five measures that are commonly used to compare municipal revenue use patterns. The two most extensively used measures are revenue level and revenue reliance. The three less extensively used are all tax-revenue-related measures: tax burden, effective property tax rate, and tax efficiency. The latter three measures are all relatively new measures either to be reported by the Census Bureau or to be calculable from such data.

Revenue Level

Revenue level is defined as the per capita dollar amount from a particular revenue source. It is calculated by dividing a city's revenue from each source (intergovernmental, tax, nontax) by the city's total population. Level thus measures intensity of use of a particular reve-

nue source. It tells how much dollar intake per person there is from
each source of revenue used by a municipality. This is extremely
valuable information for two reasons. First, internally, such information enables city budgetary personnel to better estimate the expected
revenue for the coming year. It permits budgetary personnel to ap-
proximate the dollar amount per city resident that will come from each
source. It does not imply that an equal dollar amount comes from each
city resident nor does it imply that all revenue comes from city residents. It is merely a base figure from which to work.

Revenue level is also an important measure from a comparative
perspective. Comparing revenue levels of cities and suburbs can tell
one much about the relative financial status of each. For example, a
greater intensity of usage of the property tax (that is, higher property
tax levels) as opposed to a lesser intensity of usage is often an indicator of the relative financial status of the two municipalities compared.

Revenue Reliance

Revenue reliance is defined as the proportion of the total general
revenue collected by a city that it receives from each revenue source.
Revenue reliance is calculated by dividing the amount received from
each revenue source by the total general revenue received. It is expressed in percentages. Reliance is a measure of the scope of usage
of each type of revenue (as opposed to intensity of usage). This, too,
is an important measure for both internal budgetary purposes and for
external, comparative purposes. By analyzing reliance figures, one
can compare the relative dependence of cities and suburbs on each
type of revenue.

Tax Burden

Tax burden (property and nonproperty) is defined in terms of the
relationship between per capita tax revenue and per capita personal
income. It is calculated by dividing per capita tax revenue by per
capita personal income. It is expressed in percentages. Tax burden
thus expresses the relationship between the average per capita personal
income of all city residents and the average per capita tax revenue
collected from both city and noncity residents. This figure cannot,
and should not, be interpreted to mean that each person in the city
pays an equal percentage of his or her income in the form of municipal taxes. In fact, it cannot even be interpreted to mean that only city
residents pay taxes. Rather, it is merely a measure that enables a
relative comparison of the "bite" of taxes collected locally in relation

to the income of the residents of that city. Tax burdens are important comparative measures because they are fairly good predictors of both the level and type of municipal service distribution and, in addition, they are good indicators of the potential for expansion of services. They are also good measures of fiscal strain, in that higher tax burdens are closely related to greater use of other sources of revenue, particularly intergovernmental revenue, which is often one of the first signs of fiscal stress.

Effective Property Tax Rate

Effective property tax rate is defined as the relationship between the total tax bill on a piece of property and the sales price of that piece of property. It is calculated by dividing the tax bill of a piece of property by the sales price of that, or a similar, piece of property. This measure thus enables a comparison of the property tax rate across communities that was impossible to do, and highly inaccurate when done, using nominal (statutory) tax rates. The census people warn that:

> One cannot use the nominal property tax rate because the wide variation in assessment ratios across communities implies that the actual rate at which communities tax property is not likely to bear a systematic relationship to the nominal rates. . . . Effective rates usually lie substantially below nominal rates because market values which condition effective rates usually are substantially above assessed values.[8]

Tax Efficiency

Tax efficiency is generally referred to as the "service-tax burden ratio." It is defined in terms of the relationship between the benefits an individual or household receives from the expenditures of the government and the tax burden he or she bears as a result of the government's taxation policies.[9] It is an important comparative measure in that it is a significant factor in citizen locational decisions. "The individual household, when deciding on a place to live [or move to] will weigh the income which can be earned against the services which will be supplied, and the tax bill which must be paid in a particular location. As income opportunities and services rise, or as the tax bill falls, a location will become relatively more attractive."[10] To calculate general tax efficiency, service level (expenditures per capita) is divided by tax burden. Again, caution must be used not to interpret tax efficiency figures as meaning that all persons in a city receive the same proportion of services in relation to taxes paid. The importance of this measure is that it is a comparative that is an approximation of citizen perceptions of the relationship between taxes paid and services received. Regardless of the fact that many services are likely to be heavily subsidized by intergovernmental revenues from the federal or state government, or by nontax revenues, the average person does not see or understand the scope of such revenues. Rather, the average person (by subjective personal perception) considers the relationship between his or her tax bill (property and nonproperty) and the services provided by the municipal government to be a significant factor only in making locational decisions. Thus, tax efficiency is a useful comparative measure that is closely related to population mobility and growth, which are themselves often measures of a growing economy as opposed to a declining one.

LIMITATIONS OF EXISTING MUNICIPAL REVENUE DATA

The two basic sources of municipal revenue data are both publications of the U.S. Bureau of the Census: the Census of Governments, published every five years (1962, 1967, 1972, and so on); and City Finances, published annually. Unfortunately, the latter publication does not include individual data for cities under 50,000 population. Thus, one of the most obvious limitations, reflected in the existing literature on municipal revenues, is a size bias. Studies have focused on the revenues of the largest cities[11] at the expense of smaller municipalities, particularly those under 50,000 population. To compare extensively the revenues of cities and suburbs, the researcher must wait every five years for new, comparable data to be published.

Another consequence of the failure of the Census Bureau to publish comparable data on a regular basis has been that researchers have resorted to using a surrogate, or substitute, measure for suburbs. Because of the attention given to SMSAs, the Census Bureau annually reports data for the central city and for areas outside the central city (OCC) of each SMSA. These OCC figures represent an aggregation of the finances of all local governments outside the central city but still located within the boundaries of an SMSA.[12] There are, however, severe consequences of defining suburbs in this manner.

Lumping all the governmental units outside the central city into a broad category, suburbs, represents a failure to recognize that there are different types of suburbs; suburbs are not homogeneous in their demographic, socioeconomic, or governmental characteristics.

More erroneously, defining suburbs in this manner ignores the critical fact that suburban municipalities are governmental units with taxing, borrowing, and spending powers; they are separate policy-making units.

Several studies have correctly defined suburbs. However, it seems that in the studies in which suburbs are correctly defined, there is the problem of limited scope, again totally attributable to the unavailability of comparable data on a nationwide basis. These studies merely contrast suburbs within a single metropolitan area.[13] In other words, these studies are of a descriptive (case study) nature rather than of a comparative nature. Consequently, the results of these studies are not generalizable.

An additional consequence of the irregular collection of comparable data for smaller cities is that many studies have been restricted to narrow time frames. They have been designed as cross-sectional (static) analyses, often restricted to a single point in time, rather than as longitudinal (dynamic) analyses.

There are other data limitations in addition to the time frame and scope of collection that are particularly frustrating to the researcher who is interested in collecting the same type of data for large and small cities across the entire universe of metropolitan areas.

The data on intergovernmental revenues has several limitations. First, the data on federal aid cannot be dissected so as to tell how much comes from categorical grants and how much comes from block grants. This was not as severe a problem prior to 1972 as it is for those studying data since the inception of extensive use of block grants in 1972. Similarly, there is no way of determining how much of the federal money is allocated through project (competitive) grants and how much is allocated by formula grants (noncompetitive).

Another, more theoretical, problem is the question of how federal aid impacts on local government revenue. There are various opinions as to whether such federal (external) monies act to stimulate or to substitute for locally raised revenues. This controversy evolved as an outgrowth of the state-local expenditure determinant studies. The results thus far are very inconclusive. There are those who have found that federal aid stimulates local taxation and expenditure efforts; there are those who have found just the opposite—that federal aid substitutes for local taxation and expenditure efforts.[14] This type of question, stimulation versus substitution, cannot be resolved through a comparison of a large number of cities and suburbs with the data that currently exists.

Second, state aid monies cannot be dissected so that one can compare how much is in the form of a grant and how much is in the form of a shared tax. Another shortcoming of the reported data is

that it does not enable one to determine the amounts of the state grant
monies going to a municipality that are, in effect, federal grant monies
being passed through the state. Thus, in most cases, state aid figures
are somewhat inflated in comparison with federal aid figures. However,
the state aid figures for a few cities are likely to be deflated (in comparison with state aid figures for other cities). These few cities are
those who have primary financial responsibility for education and welfare, services that are most often provided by either special district
or county governments. Therefore, monies spent in these functional
areas are not included in the total state aid figures reported by the Census Bureau.

In summary, these limitations all add up to mean that an extensive comparative analysis of the use of intergovernmental revenues by
cities and suburbs must be restricted to a comparison of the broad
categories of aid, federal and state.

There are also several limitations of tax revenue data that reduce the extent to which a comparative study of tax revenue patterns
of cities and suburbs can be conducted. First, it must be recognized
that most states have legal restrictions on local government taxing
powers. State governments generally regulate the levels of property
taxes, the kinds of property subject to taxation, and the amount of
monies that municipalities can borrow using that tax base. In fact,
only 12 states do not place such limitations on municipal use of the
property tax.[15] To further complicate the situation, state restrictions
may vary within a given state. Suburban and smaller municipalities
tend to be even more restricted in their usage of the property tax than
are the larger cities of the state. Similarly, state tax restrictions
within a state often differ by type of property (residential, commercial,
industrial, agricultural, and so on). Unfortunately, until recently,[16]
such information has not been published. Another problem with the
tax revenue data is that there can be no distinction between real and
personal (tangible or intangible) property tax revenues collected by
a municipality.

States tend to be even more restrictive of municipal use of nonproperty taxes than of property taxes. Again, the restrictions may
vary within the same state, primarily by size of city, which makes a
true comparison even more difficult. At the time of this study, only
nine states allow their municipalities to collect and assess local income taxes.[17] To further complicate the situation, all the municipalities in those nine states have not chosen to assess local income taxes.
General sales taxes, another type of nonproperty tax, are allowed in
only 21 of the 50 states.[18] Selective sales taxes at the local level are
allowable in 24 of the states.[19] In addition, the data on nonproperty
taxes does not include the various categories of selective sales taxes,
thus making an extensive, detailed analysis of the nonproperty tax

revenues collected from the various sources difficult. These limitations necessitate that an extensive comparison of the tax revenues of cities and suburbs be confined to a comparison of the broad categories of property and nonproperty taxes.

There are also data limitations with regard to several of the tax-revenue-related comparative measures, specifically the measures of tax burden, effective property tax rate, and tax efficiency. First, the existence of externalities (spillovers)[20] in metropolitan areas makes the comparison of tax burdens of city residents somewhat limited. Externalities or spillovers occur when the services provided by one governmental unit for use by its own citizens end up simultaneously benefiting or costing other governmental units in close proximity. Likewise, it is difficult to measure how much of a city's tax revenue is collected from its own residents and how much is collected from nearby residents, out-of-town business persons, and tourists. Relatedly, it is impossible to gather data for municipalities under 50,000 that tell how much of the taxable property is residential, commercial, industrial, and so on in nature. This limits the assessment of the true tax burden borne by city residents. If a city is largely residential, then the assumption can be made that the tax burden is a much more accurate measure than it would be for a city that obtains a great proportion of its property tax revenue from commercial or industrial property—a tax that is likely to be passed on to consumers throughout the market area of the business establishment or industry. Thus, the lack of such information about the characteristics of the property of a city prevents accurate comparison of municipalities with similar land use characteristics.

Another problem exists in the comparison of the tax burdens of residents—the overlapping taxing jurisdictions within a metropolitan area. Certain services may be provided by one city, whereas in another city they may be provided by the special district or county governments.

There is also a time problem with the tax-burden measure, a problem that mandates cross-sectional analysis of tax burdens. The Census of Population did not report per capita personal income figures by municipality until 1970. Thus, any longitudinal analysis of tax burdens is nearly impossible on a large scale. This same problem exists with longitudinal analyses of tax-efficiency measures since such measures have, as one of their components, tax burden. All of these problems with the tax-burden measure are problems that, unfortunately, at this moment in time must be explained away by stating that it is the best measure that currently exists for comparison.

Effective property tax rate data is also limited from both a size and a time perspective. The effective property tax rate was first reported in the 1962 Census of Governments but was reported only for cities with populations of at least 300,000. The 1972 Census of Govern-ments reported effective property tax rates for all cities over 50,000, but this still excludes a large proportion of suburban municipalities.

Tax-efficiency measures are perhaps the most limited of all the tax-revenue-related measures. Such measures are, at best, crude because at present there are no standardized measures of the quantity (or quality) of services received by each city resident. To date, the best available measures of the benefits an individual receives from the expenditures of a government are the per capita expenditures of that government (for all services and for specific service areas). Relatedly, no comparative data exist that enable a researcher to de-termine whether the services go to those who need them most; there are no data that measure the equitability of service distribution. In summary, tax-efficiency measures, while extremely limited, are still the best approximation of the service/tax-burden ratio, an im-portant factor in personal locational decisions.

Many of the limitations that exist for tax revenue comparisons also exist for comparison of nontax revenue. Charges and miscella-neous general revenues are lumped together, particularly in the figures provided in the Census of Governments for smaller municipalities. It is only for the 48 largest cities that detailed nontax revenue data are provided annually (in the City Finances publication). Again, this is merely another piece of evidence explaining why existing research on municipal revenues is primarily limited to comparisons of the reve-nues of large cities.

OTHER SHORTCOMINGS OF PREVIOUS REVENUE RESEARCH

It has already been shown that much of the prior research on municipal revenues has been rather narrow in time frame and re-stricted to analyses of the revenue patterns of the very largest Ameri-can cities, primarily due to the limited nature of reported data. There are, in addition, research design problems with some of the earlier studies.

First, there have been relatively few revenue-determinant stud-ies. Instead, revenue variables have almost exclusively been used as independent variables in equations seeking to explain governmental expenditures. This relates to the fact that it is easier to conceptualize expenditures as outputs of the governmental system than it is to see revenues in the same light—a major shortcoming of revenue research.

Second, those revenue-determinant studies that have been com-pleted have almost exclusively focused primary attention on tax reve-nues, particularly property tax revenues.[21] Thus, the literature dealing with intergovernmental variables is inadequate; in fact, it is characterized by use of intergovernmental aid variables as independent, rather than dependent, variables.[22] The literature on determinants of nontax revenue usage among American municipalities is even more limited; it is practically nonexistent.

SUMMARY

The preceding discussions of the limitations of existing municipal revenue data and the shortcomings of the designs of some of the previous revenue studies are meant to inform the reader of the difficulties likely to be encountered in any attempt to conduct an extensive investigation of the revenue patterns of a large number of U.S. municipalities, particularly those with populations of less than 50,000. Likewise, they are meant to show that the author is all too aware of these problems and of the general criticisms of comparative revenue studies that are commonly expressed by those who have not undertaken such research and thus have not personally experienced the frustrations of dealing with limited data and limited revenue-related measures.

THE DESIGN OF THIS STUDY

Within a systems analytic framework, an examination will be made of the linkages between demographic, socioeconomic, and governmental characteristics (inputs) and revenues (outputs) of 243 central cities and 340 suburban municipalities located within the SMSAs existing in 1970. The 340 suburban municipalities were chosen by a random sample of the incorporated municipalities with populations of more than 10,000 (excluding central cities) located in the SMSAs.

The Data

Independent (Policy Input) Variables

Demographic and socioeconomic data were collected for 1960 and 1970 from the U.S. Census of the Population, the U.S. Census of Housing, FBI Uniform Crime Reports, and Vital Statistics of the U.S. Demographic variables included are measures of regional location, population size, density, mobility, and land use characteristics. (See Table 1.1 for a complete list of the demographic variables.) Socioeconomic variables include measures of age, education, class (economic status), race, ethnicity, and social pathology. (See Table

TABLE 1.1: Demographic Independent Variables

Variable	Definition
Regional location	Northeast; South; North Central; West
Population size	Total population
Density	
Land area density	Population per square mile
Residential crowding	Average number of persons per housing unit
Room crowding	Percent of homes with 1.01 or more persons per room
Mobility	
Moving to a different house	Percent of population living in different house five years before the census
Population growth rate	Percent change in population over a ten-year period between censuses
Land use characteristics	
Annexation rate	Percent of population annexed in ten-year period between censuses
Taxable real property	Percent of real property that is taxable; excludes exempt real property
Taxable personal property	Percent of personal property that is taxable; excludes exempt personal property
Taxable state property	Percent of state property located within a city's limits that is taxable
Economic base	Manufacturing; industrial; diversified manufacturing; diversified retailing; retailing; other (wholesaling; mining; transportation; resort; government; professional; hospital; education; service)

Source: Compiled by the author.

1.2 for a complete list of socioeconomic variables.) Governmental data were collected for 1962 and 1972 from The Municipal Yearbook, the Census of Governments, and City Finances. Governmental measures include measures of age of city, domination of central city, form of government, type of election ballot, plan of council member selection, governmental character (reformism), functional responsibility, and state legal constraints on property taxation. (See Table

TABLE 1.2: Socioeconomic Independent Variables

Variable	Definition
Age	
Median age of the population	
Aged population	Percent of population over 65 years of age
Youth population	Percent of population below 18 years of age
Education	
Median school years completed	By persons 25 years of age and over
College graduates	Percent of persons 25 years of age and over who completed four years of college or more
Class (economic status)	
Median family income	In dollars
Per capita personal income	In dollars
Affluence	Percent of families with incomes over $15,000
Homeownership	Percent of owner-occupied housing units
Housing value	Mean value of owner-occupied housing units, in dollars
White-collar employment	Percent of all employed persons 16 years and over in professional, managerial, sales, and clerical jobs
Government employment	Percent of persons employed in government
Manufacturing employment	Percent of persons employed in manufacturing
Females in the labor force	Percent of females 16 years and over in the labor force
Race	
Nonwhite population	Percent of population that is nonwhite
Ethnicity	
Foreign-born population	Percent of population that is foreign born
Social pathology	
Mortality ratio	Death rate per 1,000 population
Public assistance rate	Percent of families receiving public assistance
Poverty	Percent of families with incomes under $3,000
Crime rate	Number of serious crimes per 100,000 population, cities; per 10,000 population, suburbs
Fertility ratio	Number of children under five years of age per 1,000 women 15 to 49 years of age
Female-headed households	Percent female-headed households
Income inequality	Index of income concentration
Run-down housing	Percent of housing lacking plumbing facilities
Housing antiquity	Percent of population living in housing built before 1950
Residential segregation	Taueber index

Source: Compiled by the author.

TABLE 1.3: Governmental Independent Variables

Variable	Definition
Age of central city	Number of decades since city reached 50,000 population
Domination of central city	Percent of total SMSA population residing in central city
Structural variables	
Form of government	Mayor-council; council-manager; commission; town meeting; representative town meeting
Type of election ballot	Partisan; nonpartisan
Council-member selection plan	Single-member district; mixed; at large
Governmental character	Unreformed; mixed; reformed
Functional responsibility	
Total functional responsibility	Total number of services for which city has primary financial responsibility
Least common functions responsibility	City has financial responsibility for providing welfare, education, and/or hospitals
State legal constraints on local taxing power	
Legal level of assessment	Percent of full value of property that is to be assessed for tax purposes
Rate limit	Mills per dollar of assessed valuation
Type of limitation	Constitutional; statutory; both; none
Scope of limitation	All taxing units; some taxing units; none
Coverage of rate limitation	All purposes; for specific purposes only
Flexibility to exceed general limitations	By referendum; other method; none

Source: Compiled by the author.

1.3 for a complete list of governmental variables.) All of these variables were selected for inclusion in this study on the basis of previous research on municipal finances.

TABLE 1.4: Dependent (Policy Output) Variables: Revenue Measures

Revenue Measures	Categories
Revenue levels (per capita)	
Intergovernmental	Federal; state
Tax	Property; nonproperty
Nontax	
Revenue reliance (percent)	
Intergovernmental	Federal; state
Tax	Property; nonproperty
Nontax	
Tax burden (percent)	Property; nonproperty
Effective property tax rate	
All types of real property	
All residential real property	
Fully taxable single-family	First quartile; median; third quartile
Tax efficiency (service/tax burden ratio)	General; each service area (police, fire, and so on)

Source: Compiled by the author.

Dependent (Policy Output) Data

Revenue data were collected for three time points (1962, 1967, 1972) from the Census of Governments and City Finances publications of those years. The types of revenues included are intergovernmental (federal and state), tax (property and nonproperty), and nontax. Revenue-related measures employed include level, reliance, tax burden, effective property tax rate, and tax efficiency. (See Table 1.4 for a complete list of the dependent, revenue variables.)

Methodological Techniques

Methodological techniques employed in this study are descriptive analysis (comparison of means) as well as correlational and multiple regressional analysis of the demographic, socioeconomic, and governmental determinants of revenue usage of cities and suburbs.

The comparison of means analysis utilizes five control groups, each hypothesized to be related to fiscal policy differences of municipalities, in order more fully to delineate variations in revenue structures among and between central cities and suburbs. These control groups are region,[23] population size,[24] economic base,[25] governmental character (reformism),[26] and functional responsibility.[27]

Correlational analysis is used to help determine which demographic, socioeconomic, and governmental variables are most strongly and significantly associated with use of the various types of revenues.

Multiple regressional analysis, based on the results of the correlational analysis, is employed to determine which of the significant demographic, socioeconomic, and governmental indicators are the best predictors of city and suburban revenue use patterns. Particularly of interest is whether these variables impact differently on cities and suburbs.

The analysis is performed within diverse time frames: cross-sectional (three time points—1962, 1967, 1972); lagged (1960 independent variables regressed on 1967 and 1972 dependent variables); and dynamic (change in independent variables, 1960-70, regressed on change in dependent, revenue variables, 1962-72).

NOTES

1. L. L. Moak and A. M. Hillhouse, Concepts and Practices in Local Government Finance (Chicago: Municipal Finance Officers Association, 1975), p. 166.

2. Advisory Commission on Intergovernmental Relations (ACIR), Intergovernmental Perspective 3 (1977): 8.

3. Ibid., p. 9.

4. Moak and Hillhouse, Concepts and Practices, p. 139.

5. Ibid., p. 162.

6. Ibid.

7. Ibid.

8. U.S. Bureau of the Census, Census of Governments: 1972, vol. 2, Taxable Property Values and Assessment-Sales Price Ratios and Tax Rates (Washington, D.C.: Government Printing Office, 1973), p. 16.

9. Werner Z. Hirsch, The Economics of State and Local Government (New York: McGraw-Hill, 1970).

10. Stephen M. Miller and William K. Tabb, "A New Look at a Pure Theory of Local Expenditures," National Tax Journal 26 (June 1973): 163.

11. See, for example, Glenn W. Fisher, "Revenue and Expenditure Patterns in Five Large Cities," Quarterly Review of Economics 3 (Autumn 1963): 61-72; S. R. Johnson and Paul E. Junk, "Sources of Tax Revenues and Expenditures in Large U.S. Cities," Quarterly Re-

view of Economics and Business 10 (Winter 1970): 7-15; Mordecai
Feinberg, "The Implications of Core-City Decline for the Fiscal
Structure of the Core City," National Tax Journal 17 (September 1964):
213-31; Gerald W. Sazama, "Equalization of Property Taxes for the
Nation's Largest Central Cities," National Tax Journal 18 (June 1965):
151-61; and John W. Jack and Paul C. Reuss, "Financing Municipal
Government: Fiscal Challenge of the Seventies," Municipal Finance
(February 1971): 141-48.

12. Examples of studies that have defined suburbs as all the
area outside the central city but within the SMSA include: Alan K.
Campbell and Seymour Sacks, Metropolitan America: Fiscal Patterns
and Governmental Systems (New York: The Free Press, 1967); Seymour Sacks and John Callahan, "Central City-Suburban Fiscal Disparity," in Advisory Commission on Intergovernmental Relations,
City Financial Emergencies (Washington, D.C.: Government Printing
Office, 1973), pp. 91-152; Robert B. Pettengill and Jogindar S. Uppal,
Can Cities Survive? The Fiscal Plight of American Cities (New York:
St. Martin's Press, 1974); Woo Sik Kee, "City-Suburban Differentials
in Local Government Fiscal Effort," National Tax Journal 21 (June
1968): 183-89; and Dick Netzer, The Economics of the Property Tax
(Washington, D.C.: The Brookings Institution, 1966).

13. See Oliver P. Williams et al., Suburban Differences and
Metropolitan Policies: A Philadelphia Story (Philadelphia: University
of Pennsylvania Press, 1965); Julius Margolis, "Municipal Fiscal
Structure in a Metropolitan Area," Journal of Political Economy 65
(June 1957): 225-36; Jesse Burkhead, "Uniformity in Governmental
Expenditures and Resources in a Metropolitan Area: Cuyahoga County,"
National Tax Journal 14 (December 1961): 337-48; Donald J. Curran,
Metropolitan Financing: The Milwaukee Experience, 1920-1970 (Madi-
son: University of Wisconsin Press, 1973); Mark A. Haskell and
Stephen Leshinski, "Fiscal Influences on Residential Choice: A Study
of the New York Region," Quarterly Review of Economics and Business 9 (Winter 1969): 47-56; George E. Peterson and Arthur P. Solomon, "Property Taxes and Populist Reform," The Public Interest 30
(Winter 1973), pp. 60-75; Oliver Oldman and Henry Aaron, "Assessment-Sales Ratios under the Boston Property Tax," National Tax Journal 18 (March 1965): 36-49; Morris Beck, "Determinants of the Property Tax Level: A Case Study of Northeastern New Jersey," National
Tax Journal 18 (March 1965): 74-77; Wallace E. Oates, "The Effects
of Property Taxes and Local Public Spending on Property Values:
An Empirical Study of Tax Capitalization and the Tiebout Hypothesis,"
Journal of Political Economy 77 (December 1969): 957-71; and Henry
O. Pollakowski, "The Effects of Property Taxes and Local Public
Spending on Property Values: A Comment and Further Results," Jour-
nal of Political Economy 81 (July/August 1973): 994-1003.

14. See Jack Osman, "The Dual Impact of Federal Aid on State and Local Government Expenditures," National Tax Journal 19 (December 1966): 362–72; Elliott R. Morss, "Some Thoughts on the Determinants of State and Local Expenditures," National Tax Journal 19 (March 1966): 95–103; Thomas F. Pogue and L. G. Sgontz, "The Effects of Grants-in-Aid on State-Local Spending," National Tax Journal 21 (June 1968): 190–99; Wallace E. Oates, "The Dual Impact of Federal Aid on State and Local Government Expenditures: A Comment," National Tax Journal 21 (June 1968): 220–23; Edward M. Gramlich, "Alternative Federal Policies for Stimulating State and Local Expenditures: A Comparison of Their Effects," National Tax Journal 21 (June 1968): 119–29; James A. Wilde, "The Expenditure Effects of Grant-in-Aid Programs," National Tax Journal 21 (September 1968): 340–47; James A. Wilde, "Grants-in-Aid: The Analysis of Design and Response," National Tax Journal 24 (June 1971): 143–55; Charles Waldauer, "Grant Structures and Their Effects on Aided Government Expenditures: An Indifference Curve Analysis," Public Finance 28 (1973): 212–25; Thomas O'Brien, "Grants-in-Aid: Some Further Answers," National Tax Journal 24 (March 1971): 65–77; David L. Smith, "The Response of State and Local Governments to Federal Grants," National Tax Journal 21 (September 1968): 349–57; and David L. Smith, "Federal Grant Elasticity and Distortion: A Reply," National Tax Journal 22 (December 1969): 552–53.

15. Connecticut, Delaware, Hawaii, Maine, Maryland, Massachusetts, New Hampshire, New Jersey, Rhode Island, Tennessee, Vermont, and Virginia. Advisory Commission on Intergovernmental Relations, Federal-State-Local Finances: Significant Features of Fiscal Federalism (Washington, D.C.: Government Printing Office, 1974), pp. 219–35.

16. Ibid.

17. Alabama, Delaware, Kentucky, Maryland, Michigan, New York, Missouri, Ohio, and Pennsylvania. Ibid., p. 291.

18. Alabama, Alaska, Arkansas, Arizona, California, Colorado, Georgia, Illinois, Kansas, Louisiana, Minnesota, Missouri, Nebraska, New York, Oklahoma, South Dakota, Tennessee, Texas, Utah, Virginia, and Washington. Ibid., pp. 252–53.

19. Alabama, Alaska, Arizona, Arkansas, California, Colorado, Georgia, Illinois, Kansas, Louisiana, Minnesota, Missouri, Nebraska, Nevada, New Mexico, New York, North Carolina, Ohio, Oklahoma, South Dakota, Texas, Utah, Virginia, and Washington. Ibid., pp. 257–58.

20. Spillovers or externalities are discussed in: John L. Mikesell, "Central Cities and Sales Tax Rate Differentials: The Border City Problem," National Tax Journal 23 (June 1970): 206–13; Jay Forrester, Urban Dynamics (Cambridge, Mass.: MIT Press, 1969);

James M. Buchanan and Charles J. Goetz, "Efficiency Limits of Fiscal Mobility: An Assessment of the Tiebout Model," Journal of Public Economics 1 (April 1972): 25-43; W. E. Oates, E. P. Howrey, and W. J. Baumol, "The Analysis of Public Policy in Dynamic Urban Models," Journal of Political Economy 79 (January/February 1971), pp. 142-53; and Kenneth V. Greene and Claudia D. Scott, "Suburban-Central City Spillovers of Tax Burdens and Expenditure Benefits," Northeast Regional Science Review 3 (1973).

21. See, for example, Netzer, op. cit.; Sazama, op. cit.; Peterson and Solomon, op. cit.; R. B. Andrews and Jerome J. Dasso, "The Influence of Annexation on Property Tax Burdens," National Tax Journal 14 (March 1961): 88-97; Oldman and Aaron, op. cit.; Beck, op. cit.; and David E. Black, "The Nature and Extent of Effective Property Tax Variation within the City of Boston," National Tax Journal 25 (June 1972): 203-10.

22. See Seymour Sacks and Robert Harris, "The Determinants of State and Local Government Expenditures and Intergovernmental Flows of Funds," National Tax Journal 17 (March 1964): 75-85; Harvey Brazer, City Expenditures in the United States (New York: National Bureau of Economic Research, 1959); Roy W. Bahl, Jr. and Robert J. Saunders, "Determinants of Changes in State and Local Government Expenditures," National Tax Journal 18 (March 1965): 50-57; Mark A. Haskell, "Federal Grants-in-Aid: Their Influence on State and Local Expenditures," The Canadian Journal of Economics and Political Science 30 (November 1964): 585-90; Campbell and Sacks, op. cit.; Kee, op. cit.; Smith, op. cit.; Pogue and Sgontz, op. cit.; Osman, op. cit.; and Jack Osman, "On the Use of Intergovernmental Aid as an Expenditure Determinant," National Tax Journal 21 (December 1968): 437-47.

23. Examples of studies using a regional classification include Otis Dudley Duncan et al., Metropolis and Region (Baltimore, Md.: The Johns Hopkins Press, 1960); and Brian J. L. Berry and Frank E. Horton, eds., Geographic Perspectives on Urban Systems (Englewood Cliffs, N.J.: Prentice-Hall, 1970).

24. Examples of studies using population size classifications of cities and suburbs include: Colin Clark, "The Economic Functions of a City in Relation to Its Size," Econometrica 13 (April 1945): 97-113; Otis Dudley Duncan, "Community Size and the Rural-Urban Continuum," in Cities and Society, ed. Paul K. Hatt and Albert J. Reiss (Glencoe, Ill.: The Free Press, 1957), pp. 35-45; Frank D. Bean et al., "Size, Functional Specialization, and the Classification of Cities," Social Science Quarterly 53 (June 1972): 20-32; Leo F. Schnore, "The Social and Economic Characteristics of American Suburbs," in Bryan T. Downes, ed., Cities and Suburbs (Belmont, Calif.: Wadsworth, 1971), pp. 49-59.

25. Economic base classifications are also referred to by many researchers as functional classifications (not to be confused with functional responsibility classifications). Early articles in The Municipal Yearbook prompted many researchers to include economic base classifications in their studies: Grace Kneedler Olson, "Economic Classification of Cities," The Municipal Yearbook 1945 (Chicago: International City Managers Association [ICMA], 1945), pp. 30-38; Victor Jones, Richard L. Forstall, and Andrew Collver, "Economic and Social Classification of Metropolitan Areas," The Municipal Yearbook 1963 (Chicago: ICMA, 1963), pp. 37-115; Richard L. Forstall, "A New Social and Economic Grouping of Cities," The Municipal Yearbook 1970 (Chicago: ICMA, 1970), pp. 102-59; Nels Anderson, The Industrial Urban Community (New York: Appleton-Century-Crofts, 1971); and Robert C. Atchley, "A Size-Function Typology of Cities," Demography 4 (1967): 721-33.

26. For examples of studies using governmental structural classifications, see Leo F. Schnore and Robert Alford, "Forms of Government and Socioeconomic Characteristics of Suburbs," Administrative Science Quarterly 8 (June 1963): 1-17; Oliver P. Williams, "A Typology for Comparative Local Government," The Midwest Journal of Political Science 5 (May 1961): 150-64; Hal H. Winsborough, "City Growth and City Structure," Journal of Regional Science 4 (Winter 1962): 35-49; John H. Kessel, "Governmental Structure and Political Environment," American Political Science Review 56 (September 1962): 615-20; Bernard H. Booms, "City Governmental Form and Public Expenditure Levels," National Tax Journal 19 (June 1966): 187-99; John Weicher, "Aid, Expenditures, and Local Government Structure," National Tax Journal 25 (December 1972): 473-584; and Heywood T. Sanders, "Policies, Populations, and Governmental Structures," The Municipal Yearbook 1972 (Chicago: ICMA, 1973), pp. 160-64.

27. Studies that emphasize grouping cities by similar functional responsibilities include George J. Stigler, "Tenable Range of Functions of Local Government," U.S. Congress, Joint Economic Committee, Subcommittee on Fiscal Policy, Federal Expenditure Policy for Economic Growth and Stability (Washington, D.C.: Government Printing Office, 1957), pp. 213-19; Robert O. Warren, "A Municipal Services Market Model of Metropolitan Organization," Journal of the American Institute of Planners 30 (August 1964): 193-204; William Baumol, "Urban Services: Interactions of Public and Private Decisions," in Public Expenditure Decisions in the Urban Community, ed. Howard Schaller (Washington, D.C.: Resources for the Future, Inc., 1965), pp. 1-18; John D. Kasarda, "The Impact of Suburban Population Growth on Central City Service Functions," American Journal of Sociology 77 (May 1972): 1111-24; Roland J. Liebert, "Municipal Functions, Structure, and Expenditures: A Reanalysis of Recent Research,"

Social Science Quarterly 54 (March 1974): 765-83; and Robert L. Lineberry and Robert C. Welch, "Who Gets What: Measuring and Distribution of Urban Public Services," Social Science Quarterly 54 (March 1974): 700-12.

Chapter 2

Revenue Levels: How Much Dollar Intake per Person?

Revenue level is the per capita dollar amount from a particular revenue source. It is calculated by dividing a city's revenue from each source (intergovernmental, tax, nontax) by a city's total population. It measures the intensity of usage of a particular revenue source. Comparing revenue levels of cities and suburbs can tell one a great deal about the relative financial status of each.

In what regions of the country are municipal revenue levels highest? Are suburban revenue levels highest in the same region that central city revenue levels are highest? Are revenue levels highest among both large cities and large suburbs? Are revenue levels highest among cities and suburbs with more diverse economic bases? Are suburbs and central cities with the same type of economic base characterized by similar revenue levels? Are governments with unreformed characters characterized by higher revenue levels than municipalities with reformed characters? Do cities and suburbs differ in their revenue level patterns by governmental character? Do municipalities that have primary financial responsibility for some of the less common, more expensive, services have higher revenue levels than municipalities without such responsibilities? Do differences in functional responsibilities affect city and suburban revenue levels in the same manner? These are all questions that can be answered using regional, size, economic base, governmental character, and functional responsibility classification schemes to compare central city and suburban revenue levels.

The value of comparing revenue levels of cities and suburbs in such a manner is that: (1) it allows data exploration; it is a method by which to determine convenient, meaningful ways of summarizing information and by which to find new and potentially useful hypotheses; (2) it permits hypothesis-testing and model fitting; and (3) it enables the development of modes of prediction, using subgroups rather than an entire population. Such classifications are extremely useful in highlighting differences and similarities, particularly when one has a large volume of data.[1] The first part of the chapter will focus on this comparison.

The second part of the chapter will compare the impact of various demographic, socioeconomic, and governmental conditions on the level of usage of each type of revenue. Are the same kinds of conditions the best predictors of intergovernmental, tax, and nontax revenue levels in both cities and suburbs? Or are there significantly different predictors of revenue levels in cities as compared with suburbs? These are questions that can be answered using correlational and multiple regressional analytic techniques.

PREVIOUS REVENUE LEVEL STUDIES

The results of previous studies of revenue levels, while not identical in scope and design with this study, can still provide valuable insights into the relationships existing between various environmental conditions and revenue levels; that is, they provide testable hypotheses.

One of the earliest empirical studies of revenue patterns of local governments (counties) was conducted by Stephens and Schmandt in 1962.[2] They used three variables to explain wide variances in per capita revenue levels: population size, density, and median family income. They found that total general revenue levels were curvilinearly related to population size. The lowest revenues per capita were characteristic of medium-sized counties. They also concluded that wealth (median family income) and state fiscal policies were more important determinants of revenue patterns than were demographic characteristics (population size or density).

Another early study that focused on the revenue patterns of five large central cities found that revenue patterns are "clearly affected by the relationship of the city government to other governments and to the state government."[3] Important factors were the number of functions assigned to a city government, the taxing powers delegated to the city, and the type and amount of intergovernmental revenue provided by the state. Relatedly, a study of Johnson and Junk found that revenue level differences in 43 large cities could be explained by three variables: income, population, and grants.[4]

Several of the more recent general revenue studies have focused attention on the fiscal differences between central cities and their outlying suburbs. One such study, by Sacks and Callahan, examined central city and suburban fiscal disparities in 72 SMSAs.[5] (Unfortunately these authors, like many others, defined suburbs as the area outside the central city.) Through comparison-of-means analysis, they found that fiscal disparities were associated with environmental characteristics such as population growth, racial balance, age composition of the population, income distribution, and housing development. They also found that while tax levels were higher in the central cities, there was an increasing homogeneity between cities and suburbs. The disparity in per capita tax revenues collected had narrowed between 1957 and 1970.

Using a regional classification, Sacks and Callahan found that the greatest central city/suburban differentials in revenue levels existed among municipalities in the South and Midwest. They also found a regional bias in federal aid and state aid; both types of aid were greatest among municipalities located in the Northeast and West. The authors identified the greater responsiveness of state and federal aid to central cities as being one of the factors acting to hold down per capita tax collection disparity between cities and suburbs.

A study very similar to that of Callahan and Sacks was done by Pettengill and Uppal.[6] They performed a historical and cross-sectional review of the revenue problems of cities and suburbs in the United States, emphasizing differences in size, age, and region. Their study focused on the 37 largest SMSAs and included various time points between 1955 and 1972. Their findings were nearly identical to those of Callahan and Sacks, perhaps attributable to the marked similarity in research design.

The results of these earlier studies suggest that region, population growth, density, functional responsibility, state legal constraints, median family income, population growth, race, age, and housing antiquity are all important environmental factors affecting revenue levels of U.S. municipalities.

This study tests two hypotheses emerging from the results of these earlier studies. The first hypothesis is that environmental conditions do affect the revenue levels of cities and suburbs. The second hypothesis is that the same environmental conditions affect central cities and suburbs in an identical manner; the same conditions are predictors of revenue levels in both central cities and suburbs.

GENERAL REVENUE LEVELS

Revenue levels are considerably higher among central cities than among suburbs (see Table 2.1). Total general revenue per capita in central cities in 1972 was $203 compared to $171 in suburbs. Total general revenue per capita was 15.8 percent higher in the central cities than in the suburbs. Comparatively, levels of all types of revenue (intergovernmental, tax, and nontax) are higher in the cities ($54, $105, $44, respectively) than in the suburbs ($36, $102, $33, respectively). These findings are consistent with those of earlier studies and are largely attributable to the wider range of services that must be provided by central cities, particularly poverty-related services, and the consequent need to raise revenues to pay for those services.

Generally, both central cities and suburbs are characterized by relatively higher tax levels than intergovernmental or nontax levels. In fact, tax levels in both cities and suburbs are nearly twice as high as are intergovernmental or nontax revenue levels. This is largely explained by the fact that taxes have been the traditional source of revenue for all municipalities, regardless of size, since the inception of local governments. It is only in recent years that cities have come to depend on other sources of revenue to supplement tax sources.

Of the two lesser sources, intergovernmental revenue levels are slightly higher than nontax levels. For cities, intergovernmental revenue per capita is $54 and nontax revenue per capita is $44. For suburbs, intergovernmental revenue levels are $36 and nontax revenue levels are $33. However, as the figures in Table 2.1 show, the relative positions of intergovernmental and nontax revenue levels have reversed over the ten-year period (1962-72). In 1962, nontax revenue levels were slightly higher than intergovernmental revenue levels in both cities and suburbs. This finding shows that federal and state levels for both cities and suburbs have increased faster than nontax revenue levels.

The finding here is consistent with the findings of earlier studies: that both central cities and suburbs receive much greater per capita revenues from their own state governments than they do from the federal government. (Keep in mind that some of this state aid is federal aid passing through the state.) In 1972, cities received on the average $14 per capita from the federal government and $37 per capita from the state. Suburbs received $7 from the federal government and $29 from the state. Certainly the disparity between federal aid and state aid levels is greater in the suburbs. Suburban governments received four times more revenue per capita from the state than from the federal government, whereas cities received only twice as much revenue per capita from the state than from the federal government.

There are several plausible explanations for this central city/ suburban differential in federal and state aid levels. One explanation is that state governments are more responsive to suburban governments than to central cities. This explanation would more logically apply to differentials in the days preceding the reapportionment of state legislatures on the basis of one person/one vote. Another more likely explanation involves the nature of the distributional formulas of federal and state aid. As was pointed out in Chapter 1, federal aid

TABLE 2.1: Revenue Levels (per Capita): All Central Cities and Suburbs
(dollars)

Revenue Type	Central Cities			Suburbs		
	1962	1967	1972	1962	1967	1972
Total general	110	143	203	65	77	171
Intergovernmental	21	33	54	10	15	36
Federal	6	10	14	1	3	7
State	16	24	37	9	13	29
Tax	65	78	105	40	48	102
Property	52	60	77	32	38	75
Nonproperty	13	18	28	8	10	27
Nontax	24	32	44	14	14	33

Note: Revenue level is the per capita dollar amount received from a particular revenue source. It is calculated by dividing a city's revenue from each source by the city's total population.

Sources: U.S. Department of Commerce, Bureau of the Census, Census of Governments: 1962, 1967, 1972 (Washington, D.C.: Government Printing Office); City Finances (1962, 1967, 1972).

formulas are much more likely to include factors that are characteristic of central cities rather than suburbs: population size, poverty, race, and social pathology measures. This is related to the fact that the goal of most federal aid programs is redistribution, or equalization. Suburbs are not likely to qualify for many of these federal grants, particularly the categorical, project-funded grants. On the other hand, state aid formulas are less likely to be responsive to need factors. In fact, many states return shared tax monies, the largest proportion of state aid monies, to their municipalities on the basis of point of origin—that is, where they were collected. Consequently, suburbs may get back proportions of the state sales tax, cigarette taxes, and alcoholic beverage taxes equal to the proportion of the state taxes collected from each of these sources within their municipal limits. In summary, because of these distributional formula differences, suburbs are likely to receive proportionately more revenue per capita from the state than from the federal government.

Another possible explanation centers around the motives of suburbanites and their governmental officials. It is generally said that suburban governments prefer not to use federal monies so as to avoid the strings and guidelines attached to them. It is the feeling on the part of many suburbanites that the federal government already interferes with one's life too much. Thus, it could be that even though suburban governments may be eligible for federal money, they may make calculated decisions not to take these double-edged funds.

Finally, the central city/suburban disparity in levels of federal and state aid might be attributable to another aspect of federal policy. Recently there have been reported incidences of federal funds being deliberately kept out of certain "lily white" suburbs even though they may meet general eligibility requirements. This is an expression of the federal government's desire to force suburbs to desegregate residential housing patterns. At any rate, state aid levels in relation to federal aid levels are considerably higher in U.S. suburbs.

In contrast with intergovernmental revenue levels, there is not a great deal of central city/suburban disparity in tax revenue levels. Both cities and suburbs have much higher property tax levels than nonproperty tax levels. In 1972, central cities on the average received $77 per capita from property taxes and $28 per capita from nonproperty taxes. Suburbs received $75 per capita from property taxes and $27 per capita from nonproperty taxes. These figures show that there is relatively little difference in total per capita tax revenue received by cities and suburbs. This result is probably explainable by the fact that tax revenues have been the traditional source of local government revenue for governments of all sizes. Regardless of the fact that levels of assessment and tax millage rates may vary somewhat among municipalities within a state, they are generally relatively uniform across the state. This, then, helps account for the fact that tax levels are nearly equal among the 243 central cities and 340 suburban municipalities of this study.

All of the figures discussed thus far are averages for all 243 central cities and 340 suburbs. Revenue level differences among and between cities and suburbs are more observable when contrasted by region, population size, economic base, governmental character, and functional responsibility.

General Revenue Levels by Region

The regional classification used in this study is that commonly used by the U.S. Bureau of the Census: Northeast, South, North Central (or Midwest), and West. The results of the regional comparison of city and suburban revenue levels are shown in Table 2.2. The results generally indicate that, as was found in earlier studies, revenue levels are considerably higher among cities and suburbs located in the Northeast than among cities and suburbs located in other regions of

TABLE 2.2: Revenue Levels (per Capita) for Central Cities and Suburbs, by Region (dollars)

	Revenue Type														
	Intergovernmental						Tax								
	Federal			State			Property			Nonproperty			Nontax		
Region	1962	1967	1972	1962	1967	1972	1962	1967	1972	1962	1967	1972	1962	1967	1972
Central cities															
Northeast (53)	9	16	23	29	51	77	104	125	167	9	13	16	18	27	36
South (53)	5	7	9	10	14	22	33	39	48	8	19	30	24	33	45
North Central (62)	5	9	12	16	19	28	45	48	59	6	15	24	25	33	43
West (41)	4	7	15	11	15	28	34	40	52	20	24	41	27	34	52
Suburbs															
Northeast (96)	2	3	7	15	23	44	69	85	166	6	9	14	19	15	25
South (50)	1	4	9	4	7	11	15	18	38	7	12	28	9	15	40
North Central (109)	3	1	5	8	10	28	19	24	48	6	8	23	14	16	40
West (85)	2	2	7	7	8	23	18	14	31	14	12	44	13	12	29

Note: Revenue level is the per capita dollar amount received from a particular revenue source. It is calculated by dividing a city's revenue from each source by the city's total population. Figures in parentheses indicate the number of municipalities.

Sources: U.S. Department of Commerce, Bureau of the Census, Census of Governments: 1962, 1967, 1972 (Washington, D.C.: Government Printing Office); City Finances (1962, 1967, 1972).

the country. Much of this regional variation is probably explainable by the age of the city and the unique service responsibilities characteristic of northeastern municipalities.

Central City Differences by Region

Levels of all types of revenue (except nontax and nonproperty tax) are highest among northeastern central cities and lowest among southern cities (see Table 2.2). It has been suggested that southern and western central cities have been able to keep revenue levels low by using annexation or consolidation to capture a considerable amount of what would otherwise be suburban growth. [7]

A regional comparison shows that intergovernmental revenue levels are highest among central cities located in the Northeast (federal aid per capita, $23; state aid, $77) and lowest among southern cities (federal aid, $9; state aid, $22). Property tax levels are also markedly higher among central cities in the Northeast ($167) than cities in the South ($48). On the other hand, nonproperty tax levels are highest among cities in the West and South ($41 and $30 respectively) as are nontax revenue levels ($52 and $45 respectively).

Thus, it is primarily with regard to intergovernmental revenues (federal and state) and property tax revenues that northeastern central cities are characterized by the highest revenue levels. Nonproperty tax and nontax levels are highest among southern and western central cities. These cities have been able to supplement property taxes and thus keep property tax levels low by utilizing sales and privilege taxes and charges, fees, fines, and special assessments—all revenues of a direct assessment or user nature. They are not based on any sort of ability-to-pay principle. Northeastern central cities have not been able to receive the same levels of revenue from these sources, primarily because they are disproportionately inhabited by the poor, who are unable to pay such assessments.

Suburban Differences by Region

Generally, regional variations in revenue levels for all types of revenue are greater in suburbs than in central cities. There is also another difference in suburban and central city revenue levels when examined by region. Federal aid levels are higher in southern suburbs ($9) than in northeastern suburbs ($7) or midwestern suburbs ($5).

Generally, though, revenue level patterns by region are similar for both cities and suburbs. State aid and property tax levels are highest in suburbs in the Northeast ($44 and $166 respectively) and lowest in the South ($11 and $38). Nonproperty and nontax revenues tend to be highest in southern and western suburbs. In both cities and

suburbs, the greatest differences observable by regional comparison
are in state aid and property tax levels.

General Revenue Levels by Population Size

Next to region, population size is the most common way of
grouping municipalities. The standard U.S. Census Bureau population size categories for classifying central cities are 1,000,000 and
above, 500,000-999,999, 250,000-499,999, 100,000-249,999, and
50,000-99,999. Suburban size categories frequently used are 100,000
and above, 50,000-99,999, 25,000-49,999, and below 25,000. These
standard size categories have been adopted for this study.

By necessity, the size classification schemes must be different
for cities and suburbs. Thus, comparative analysis by population size
can tell one most about differences among cities and among suburbs
rather than between them. The city-suburb comparison by size categories is limited to a contrast of the largest cities and the largest
suburbs, the smallest cities and the smallest suburbs, and so on.
This analysis, while limited, does permit adequate delineation of the
relationship between population size and revenue levels.

The results of the comparison of central city and suburban revenue levels by population size are shown in Table 2.3. There is a very
close relationship between population size and revenue levels. Generally the larger the city, the higher the revenue levels.

Central City Differences by Population Size

Revenue levels in cities with populations over one million are
much higher than those of cities with populations under 100,000 (see
Table 2.3). Intergovernmental revenues in cities over one million
are 3.6 times higher than those in cities with populations under
100,000. Federal aid levels are 4.5 times higher in the largest central cities ($36) than in the smallest cities ($8). State aid levels are
3.6 times higher in the largest central cities ($93) than in the smallest
cities ($26). These differences in aid levels are mostly the products
of aid formulas (both federal and state), which generally include population size as one of the formula factors.

A strong relationship also exists between population size and
tax levels. Central cities with populations over one million on the
average have property tax levels of $102 and nonproperty tax levels of
$83. In contrast, cities with populations under 100,000 have property
tax levels of $64 and nonproperty tax levels of $19. It is thus obvious
that as central city size increases, so does the balance between property and nonproperty tax levels. Central cities of over one million

TABLE 2.3: Revenue Levels (per Capita) for Central Cities and Suburbs, by Population Size (dollars)

	Revenue Type														
	Intergovernmental						Tax								
	Federal			State			Property			Nonproperty			Nontax		
Population Size	1962	1967	1972	1962	1967	1972	1962	1967	1972	1962	1967	1972	1962	1967	1972
Central Cities															
Over 1,000,000 1970 (6) 1960 (5)	6	14	36	29	47	93	69	79	102	38	50	83	28	33	51
500,000–999,999 1970 (20) 1960 (16)	5	11	18	26	38	61	63	64	88	17	24	46	25	31	57
250,000–499,999 1970 (27) 1960 (26)	10	14	21	16	24	44	49	61	81	17	25	39	27	39	58
100,000–249,999 1970 (69) 1960 (64)	7	10	19	17	25	40	57	65	94	12	18	28	22	31	45
50,000–99,999 1970 (121) 1960 (132)	4	8	8	14	19	26	47	56	64	12	13	19	22	30	38
Suburbs															
Over 100,000 1970 (12) 1960 (6)	3	5	14	23	28	45	95	96	98	16	18	36	16	14	27
50,000–99,999 1970 (43) 1960 (27)	2	2	6	10	13	29	41	40	64	13	15	33	15	15	28
25,000–49,999 1970 (77) 1960 (58)	2	5	8	13	18	34	49	55	103	12	11	25	15	17	31
10,000–24,999 1970 (208) 1960 (249)	1	2	6	7	10	26	26	30	66	6	8	26	14	13	35

Note: Revenue level is the per capita dollar amount received from a particular revenue source. It is calculated by dividing a city's revenue from each source by the city's total population. Figures in parentheses indicate the number of municipalities.

Sources: U.S. Department of Commerce, U.S. Bureau of the Census, *Census of Governments: 1962, 1967, 1972* (Washington, D.C.: Government Printing Office); *City Finances* (1962, 1967, 1972).

have nearly equal property and nonproperty tax levels, whereas cities with populations of 50,000-99,999 have much higher property than non-property tax levels. This is attributable to two factors. First, the largest cities have, in many cases, reached their maximum legal millage rate and level of assessment and have had to increase non-property taxes to meet expenditure needs. Nonproperty taxes are also much easier to raise with regard to citizen acceptance than are property taxes. Second, larger cities are less likely to have prohibitions placed on their use of nonproperty tax sources than are smaller cities (see Chapter 1).

The relationship between nontax revenue levels and population size is the least distinctive. However, the larger cities do have higher nontax revenue levels ($51) than the smaller cities ($38).

Suburban Differences by Population Size

The relationship between population size and revenue levels is not as marked in suburban municipalities as it is in central cities, although the patterns are very similar. Revenue levels of all types (except nontax) are generally higher in the larger suburbs (those over 100,000 population).

Intergovernmental (federal and state) and property tax levels show the most variation by population size. The greatest disparity among size categories occurs in federal aid levels, which are 2.3 times higher in the largest suburbs ($14) than in the smaller ones ($6). Property tax levels are also higher in the largest suburbs ($98) than in the smaller ones ($66).

In summary, it can be said that population size has almost the same effect on suburban and city revenue levels, except on nontax revenue levels. Population size is positively related to higher inter-governmental (federal and state) and tax (property and nonproperty) levels but is negatively related to nontax revenue levels. This negative relationship is explainable by the fact that smaller suburbs are more likely to use direct-assessment-type revenue structures (nontax revenues), such as charges for garbage collection, special assessments for street lights, and so on, than are the larger suburbs.

General Revenue Levels by Economic Base

Since the 1950s, The Municipal Yearbook has periodically published data on the economic bases of cities. For this study, the five broadest categories have been adopted and the remaining seven have been collapsed into a category labeled "other." Consequently, the economic base categories used in this study are manufacturing, industrial, diversified manufacturing, diversified retailing, retailing, and other (wholesaling, mining, transportation, resort, government and armed forces, professional, hospital, education, or service). Basically, these categories can be ranked as moving from the broader, more complex economic bases (manufacturing) to the narrower, less complex, more specialized economic bases (retailing, other).

Classifying cities and suburbs by economic base is primarily done to avoid criticisms of treating all suburbs as "bedroom" suburbs. Frederick Wirt specifically attacked political analysis of suburbs that:

> has routinely treated all suburbs as though they were similar. They are thought to be residential and peopled only by middle-middle to upper-middle class or higher status; they contain only retail businesses, generally the hive-like shopping centers; the breadwinners leave en masse for the city in the morning and return to the split level and dry martini in the evening. [8]

An early study that suggested the importance of economic base on tax revenue levels was Robert Wood's 1400 Governments. Wood suggested that tax assessors in communities with large industrial or commercial economic bases have a particularly productive source of revenue. [9]

The results of the comparison of city and suburban revenue levels by economic base are shown in Table 2.4. Generally, revenue levels are highest in municipalities (both cities and suburbs) with manufacturing or diversified manufacturing economic bases.

Central City Differences by Economic Base

The relationship between revenue level and economic base is strongest with regard to intergovernmental (federal and state) and property tax levels. Generally, intergovernmental revenue levels are much higher in the more complex economic-based cities (manufacturing, industrial, and diversified manufacturing). These cities are more likely to have greater proportions of poor, low-skilled, and/or minority persons—factors that are often components of intergovernmental aid formulas.

Property tax levels are also highest in cities with complex economic bases, confirming Wood's hypothesis. Property taxes on manufacturing and industrial property are often "shifted forward" to the price of the product, thereby spreading such taxes throughout the market area rather than confining them within the city limits or close proximity thereof. These cities with more complex economic bases are also characterized by much higher property than nonproperty tax levels (again attributable to the ability to shift such taxes forward easily and without political consequences). Cities with less complex bases (retailing, diversified retailing, and other) are more balanced in their property and nonproperty tax levels, often choosing to keep property tax levels down so as to keep such retail business within the city limits.

There does not appear to be a close relationship between economic base and nonproperty or nontax revenue levels in central cities.

Suburban Differences by Economic Base

Suburban revenue levels are more strongly related to economic base than are revenue levels of central cities. However, the pattern is identical. Again, the greatest relationship is between economic base, and suburban intergovernmental (federal and state) and property tax levels. Likewise, there appears to be no relationship between economic base, nonproperty, and nontax revenue levels among these 340 suburban municipalities.

General Revenue Levels by Governmental Character (Reformism)

Municipalities have been classified by their governmental character—unreformed, mixed, or reformed. Unreformed governments are those with mayor-council governments, partisan elections, and single-member district council member selection plans. Mixed governments are those with at least one unreformed and one reformed governmental characteristic. Reformed governments are those with council-manager governments, nonpartisan elections, and at-large council member selection plans.

Reform theory is premised on efficiency, or "getting the most out of the government for the least amount of money." As Lineberry and Sharkansky state, "Much of the rhetorical thunder in support of municipal reform (manager governments, nonpartisan elections, and at-large constituencies) claims that lower taxes . . . will follow their adoption."[10]

The results of the comparison of city and suburban revenue levels by governmental character are shown in Table 2.5. The results show that there is a fairly strong relationship between governmental character and revenue levels in both central cities and suburbs. It has often been stated that it is really the differences in the environmental conditions surrounding governments that affect policy outputs, rather than differences in governmental structural arrangements. It

TABLE 2.4: Revenue Levels (per capita) for Central Cities and Suburbs, by Economic Base (dollars)

	Revenue Type														
	Intergovernmental						Tax						Nontax		
	Federal			State			Property			Nonproperty					
Economic Base*	1962	1967	1977	1962	1967	1977	1962	1967	1977	1962	1967	1977	1962	1967	1977
Central Cities															
Manufacturing	8	13	18	23	33	45	72	79	101	11	17	25	19	32	42
1963 (86)															
1957 (74)															
Industrial	2	8	15	24	47	39	57	80	88	9	8	1	25	23	29
1963 (3)															
1967 (9)															
Diversified manufacturing	8	11	13	20	28	54	53	58	83	19	20	32	24	34	50
1963 (60)															
1957 (52)															
Diversified retailing	4	8	13	8	15	22	39	50	62	13	16	27	23	28	42
1963 (50)															
1957 (57)															
Retailing	3	4	11	7	7	13	35	41	42	14	19	30	25	32	39
1963 (29)															
1957 (36)															
Other*	3	4	3	4	6	13	27	27	35	14	14	24	29	31	48
1963 (15)															
1957 (14)															

Manufacturing	2	5	11	15	22	39	57	63	104	10	15	26	25	22	33
1963 (87)															
1957 (75)															
Industrial	5	1	3	7	15	24	22	48	87	9	7	23	12	24	44
1963 (12)															
1957 (10)															
Diversified manufacturing	1	2	7	12	18	33	46	67	116	8	11	26	19	15	22
1963 (19)															
1957 (17)															
Diversified retailing	2	2	6	8	10	23	32	29	64	13	12	30	14	16	34
1963 (41)															
1957 (41)															
Retailing	2	2	4	9	11	21	37	32	53	13	13	31	22	16	26
1963 (61)															
1957 (59)															
Other*	2	4	5	10	16	35	39	47	87	13	13	28	18	18	38
1963 (24)															
1957 (19)															

*The first five economic-base types are the five basic economic types (collected on the basis of place of work). The "Other" category represents cities with very specialized economic bases: wholesaling, mining, transportation, resort, government and armed forces, professional, hospital, education, or service.

Note: Revenue level is the per capita dollar amount received from a particular revenue source. It is calculated by dividing a city's revenue from each source by the city's total population. Figures in parentheses indicate number of municipalities.

Sources: The Municipal Yearbook, 1963 and 1957 (Chicago: International City Managers Association, 1963 and 1957) (the classification scheme has not been reported since 1963); U.S. Department of Commerce, Bureau of the Census, Census of Governments: 1962, 1967, 1972 (Washington, D.C.: Government Printing Office); City Finances (1962, 1967, 1972).

TABLE 2.5: Revenue Levels (per Capita) for Central Cities and Suburbs, by Governmental Character (dollars)

| | Intergovernmental | | | | | | Tax | | | | | | Nontax | | |
| | Federal | | | State | | | Property | | | Nonproperty | | | | | |
Governmental Character	1962	1967	1972	1962	1967	1972	1962	1967	1972	1962	1967	1972	1962	1967	1972
Central Cities															
Unreformed[a] 1968 (20) 1958 (19)	7	14	21	19	35	80	82	111	169	10	9	15	20	25	37
Mixed[b] 1968 (126) 1958 (149)	6	10	13	16	24	36	52	60	75	12	17	27	22	30	44
Reformed[c] 1968 (76) 1958 (72)	5	7	14	14	19	27	43	48	58	15	19	30	28	36	46
Suburbs															
Unreformed[a] 1968 (11) 1958 (18)	5	1	2	7	14	37	48	58	97	11	14	28	38	14	30
Mixed[b] 1968 (213) 1958 (252)	1	3	7	8	14	32	30	42	85	7	9	22	12	13	29
Reformed[c] 1968 (116) 1958 (70)	2	2	7	10	11	23	33	28	56	14	11	33	15	18	41

[a]Unreformed cities are those with a mayor-council form of government, partisan elections, and a single-member district council member selection plan.

[b]Mixed cities are those having at least one reformed characteristic and one unreformed characteristic.

[c]Reformed cities are those with a council-manager form of government, nonpartisan elections, and an at-large council member selection plan.

Note: Revenue level is the per capita dollar amount received from a particular revenue source. It is calculated by dividing a city's revenue from each source by the city's total population. Figures in parentheses indicate number of municipalities.

Sources: The Municipal Yearbook, 1968 and 1958 (Chicago: International City Manager Association, 1968, 1958); U.S. Department of Commerce, Bureau of the Census, Census of Governments: 1962, 1967, 1972 (Washington, D.C.: Government Printing Office); City Finances (1962, 1967, 1972),

has been shown that governmental structural arrangements can, in fact, be fairly accurately predicted using such variables as population size, regional location, density, income, race, education, and so on.[11] Generally, intergovernmental (federal and state) and property tax levels are highest in unreformed municipalities and lowest in reformed cities. Conversely, nonproperty tax and nontax revenue levels are highest in reformed municipalities and lowest in unreformed municipalities. True to theory, revenue levels of mixed municipalities fall between those of reformed and unreformed cities.

Central City Differences by Governmental Character

The greatest variations in central city revenue levels, when contrasted by governmental character, occur in state aid and property tax revenue levels. State aid levels are nearly three times higher in unreformed cities ($80) than in reformed cities ($27). Likewise, property tax levels are very much higher in unreformed cities ($169) than in reformed cities ($58). This is largely due to the differences in functional responsibilities. Unreformed cities are more likely to be larger cities that provide more services, particularly poverty-related services. Reformed cities are likely to be the medium-sized or smaller cities, characterized by wealthier populations expecting less governmental provision of services, particularly poverty-related services such as welfare and hospitals.

With regard to the balance between property and nonproperty tax levels, it is obvious that reformed cities are by far the most balanced, raising $58 per capita from property taxes and $30 per capita from nonproperty taxes. Unreformed cities are characterized by markedly higher property tax levels ($169) than nonproperty tax levels ($15).

Finally, governmental character is not found to be very strongly related to central city nontax revenue levels, although nontax revenue levels are slightly higher in reformed cities ($46) than in unreformed cities ($37). This finding is congruent with the efficiency goals of reformed governments, since nontax revenues are direct assessment-type revenues based on use, not ability to pay, and are more likely to be used by medium-sized council-manager type governments.

Suburban Differences by Governmental Character

The relationships between revenue levels and governmental character in suburbs are very similar to those observed in cities, with one exception. Federal aid levels are higher in reformed and mixed suburbs ($7) than in unreformed suburbs ($2). Size may explain this finding. Unreformed governments are characteristic of the very largest and the very smallest cities. There are more small suburbs than large suburbs; thus many of these small suburbs would not qualify for federal funds nor would many of them want to qualify for federal funds because of a general aversion to federal aid.

Otherwise, state aid and property tax levels are highest in un-reformed suburbs, whereas nonproperty tax and nontax levels are highest in reformed suburbs—identical patterns to those observed in central cities.

General Revenue Levels by Functional Responsibility

Recent research efforts have studied municipalities by grouping them according to the functions they perform. The standard technique has been to group cities and analyze them on the basis of the four most commonly provided functions: police, fire, recreation, and sanitation. However, this common-functions approach does little to distinguish the differences among municipalities, particularly financial differences. The New York City incident has served to demonstrate that it is the performance of the least common functions that puts the most severe financial strains on municipalities. Better to analyze the impact of financial responsibility for the performance of such services, municipalities in this study have been grouped by least-common/no-least-common functional responsibility. (Table 2.6 shows the functional responsibility distribution for cities and suburbs in 1972.) Specifically, municipalities have been grouped according to whether they have primary financial responsibility for education, welfare, hospitals, or housing and urban renewal (suburbs only), or for all of these least common functions.

The precedent for such analysis was set by Woo Sik Kee in his article on state and local fiscal systems. Kee divided cities into mutually exclusive classes by the presence or absence of the responsibility of providing education and/or public welfare.[12] He also suggested that hospitals should be studied in this way. Similarly, Thomas Stinson excluded cities with city-financed schools and public welfare from his study of the impact of population changes on local government finance.[13] As far back as 1962, Stephens and Schmandt found that there is a wide diversity in the role that local government plays in the various regions of the country. According to these authors, the major portion of the variation can be explained by differences in the amount and level of services that local governments furnish their customers.[14]

The results of the comparison of revenue levels by functional responsibility are shown in Table 2.7. Across all functional categories, cities and suburbs with responsibility for the least common functions are characterized by higher revenue levels than municipalities with-

TABLE 2.6: Functional Distribution for Central Cities and Suburbs (from Most Common to Least Common)

Central Cities		Suburbs	
Functions	Total	Functions	Total
Police	242	Highways	255
Fire	242	Police	254
Highways	242	Fire	237
Parks and recreation	241	Parks and recreation	234
Sanitation	237	Sanitation	223
Sewerage	229	Sewerage	212
Water	208	Libraries	186
Libraries	175	Water	180
Health	171	Health	172
Housing and urban re-		Welfare	89
newal	143	Education	49
Welfare	80	Hospitals	45
Hospitals	78	Housing and urban re-	
Education	76	newal	43

Note: A city is regarded as having functional responsibility for a service if it has primary financial responsibility for provision of that service.

Source: U.S. Department of Commerce, Bureau of the Census, Census of Governments: 1972 (Washington, D.C.: Government Printing Office, 1972).

out such functional responsibilities. The least common function that is found to be the most strongly related to higher revenue levels, particularly state aid and property tax levels, is education.

Central City Differences by Functional Responsibility

Of all the classificatory schemes utilized in this study of revenue levels, classification by functional responsibility is superior. The most dramatic differences in revenue levels appear when cities with responsibility for performing and paying for all three least common functions (education, welfare, hospitals) are contrasted with cities providing none of these functions.

While levels of all types of revenue were highest in cities providing education, welfare, and/or hospitals, the greatest differentials

TABLE 2.7: Revenue Levels (per Capita) for Central Cities and Suburbs, by Functional Responsibility (dollars)

| | Intergovernmental | | | | | | Tax | | | | | | | | |
| | Federal | | | State | | | Property | | | Nonproperty | | | Nontax | | |
Functional Responsibility	1962	1967	1972	1962	1967	1972	1962	1967	1972	1962	1967	1972	1962	1967	1972
Central cities															
Education (76)	10	17	21	34	55	81	93	113	159	15	22	20	24	35	48
No education (167)	4	6	11	8	9	16	33	36	45	12	16	26	23	30	42
Hospitals (78)	8	6	17	23	37	56	66	79	102	15	22	32	30	41	58
No hospitals (165)	4	8	13	13	17	27	45	52	66	12	15	25	20	27	37
Welfare (80)	9	15	20	28	46	70	85	102	136	15	22	33	23	33	47
No welfare (163)	4	7	11	10	13	20	35	40	48	12	15	26	24	31	42
All three least common functions (33)	12	18	24	40	68	105	107	127	170	18	27	34	28	41	57
None of the three least common functions (116)	4	6	11	8	9	16	33	36	45	13	15	24	20	27	36
Suburbs															
Education (49)	3	7	13	29	48	77	112	142	261	6	8	17	15	23	36
No education (291)	1	2	6	5	7	21	19	20	44	8	10	28	14	13	33

Hospitals (45)	3	4	11	20	32	49	89	109	196	9	13	22	30	28	50
No hospitals (295)	1	2	6	7	10	26	24	27	57	7	9	27	12	12	31
Welfare (89)	2	5	9	18	29	51	76	94	173	8	11	21	20	20	32
No welfare (251)	5	2	6	1	7	21	17	18	41	8	9	29	12	13	33
Housing and urban renewal (43)	5	5	14	13	21	40	65	69	111	12	14	30	15	19	33
No housing and urban renewal (297)	1	2	6	8	11	27	28	33	70	7	10	26	14	14	33
All four least common functions (4)	8	6	29	29	55	90	131	147	273	9	11	13	11	19	30
None of the least common functions (218)	1	2	5	4	6	21	14	14	38	7	8	25	11	10	31

Note: Revenue level is the per capita dollar amount received from a particular revenue source. It is calculated by dividing a city's revenue from each source by the city's total population. A city is regarded as having functional responsibility for a service if it has primary financial responsibility for provision of the service. If it does not have primary financial responsibility, it is regarded as not having functional responsibility for that service. The service areas analyzed in this table are all services that are among those for which municipalities least often have primary financial responsibility. Figures in parentheses indicate number of municipalities.

Sources: U.S. Department of Commerce, Bureau of the Census, Census of Governments: 1962, 1967, 1972 (Washington, D.C.: Government Printing Office); City Finances (1962, 1967, 1972).

between those with such functional responsibilities and those without are in state aid and property tax levels. State aid levels are 6.5 times higher in cities with responsibility for all three least common functions ($105) than in those cities without such responsibility ($16). Similarly, property tax levels are nearly four times higher in cities providing all three services ($170) than in those not providing any of these services ($45). The latter findings seem to lend credence to complaints by property owners that they are bearing an unfair proportion of the burden of educating and taking care of the community's populace. This pattern is further confirmed when the balance between property and nonproperty tax levels is examined. Cities with all three least common functional responsibilities have property tax levels ($170) that are five times greater than their nonproperty tax levels ($34).

The least disparity among cities' revenue levels, when compared by functional responsibility, is in their nonproperty and nontax revenues, which are not as likely to be tied in with the expenditures for any of the least common functions in the same way that property taxes are tied in (either by formulas or as backing for general obligation bonds).

Suburban Differences by Functional Responsibility

With patterns similar to those observed in central cities, suburbs with financial responsibility for the least common suburban functions (education, welfare, hospitals, and housing and urban renewal) are characterized by much higher revenue levels (except nontax levels) than suburbs without such responsibilities. Likewise, suburbs with least common functional responsibilities differ most from those without such responsibilities in their property tax and state aid levels. Property tax levels ($273) are seven times higher among suburbs providing all four least common suburban functions than in those providing none of these services ($38). This appears to confirm the belief that property taxes in suburbs largely support the costs of education. State aid levels are four times higher among suburbs providing all four functions ($90) than in suburbs providing none of them ($21). Since the greatest differential is between suburbs providing education and those not providing education, it appears that state aid to suburbs is largely in the form of categorical grants for education.

For reasons similar to those previously discussed, suburban nonproperty and nontax revenue levels, like those of central cities, do not vary markedly by functional responsibility.

DETERMINANTS OF REVENUE LEVELS

Having gained a better understanding of the actual revenues per capita obtained by cities and suburbs located in different regions of

the country, of differing sizes, economic bases, governmental characters, and functional responsibilities, the remainder of the chapter will
focus on the impact of demographic, socioeconomic, and governmental conditions on city and suburban revenue levels. This is known as
policy determinant research. Specifically of interest is whether the
same kinds of conditions are significant determinants of intergovernmental, tax, and nontax levels in both cities and suburbs, or whether
the significant determinants of revenue levels differ for cities and
suburbs.

Methodology

The statistical method used to identify the environmental determinants of revenue levels in the 243 central cities and 340 suburban
municipalities is stepwise multiple regression. With a large number
of independent variables, it is the most appropriate procedure for
selecting the independent variables that go into a multiple regression
analysis from a large set of variables.[15] It has also been characterized as "a powerful variation of multiple regression which will provide
the best prediction possible with the fewest independent variables."[16]
In addition to the simple correlation coefficient (r), the other
statistics reported in the tables are the R^2 (the ratio of explained to
total variation, or simply the proportion of explained variance) and
the Beta weight (β), the standardized regression coefficient. It is important to note that explained variance may or may not refer to a good
substantive explanation. As Tufte warns, a large R^2 means only that
x is relatively successful in predicting the value of y—not necessarily
that x causes y or even that x is a meaningful explanation of y. He
also states that "whether or not there really is a causal relationship
between y_1 and x_1, x_2, ... , x_k depends on having a theory consistent with the data that links the variables."[17] The selection of variables for inclusion in this study is theoretically based; thus the results
are likely to provide meaningful explanations of variation in municipal
revenue levels.

Results

As was stated in Chapter 1, several types of regressional analysis were performed on the data: lagged (1960 environmental variables
used to predict 1962, 1967, and 1972 revenue levels); and cross-sectional (1960 environmental variables used to predict 1962 revenue levels, 1970 environmental variables used to predict 1972 revenue levels).
The results indicate that lagging seven and ten years does not improve

prediction of revenue levels of either cities or suburbs. Lagged analysis indicates that the best explanatory models are constructed by using variables close in time to the revenue intake. Thus, the remainder of the chapter concentrates on examining the 1970 environmental determinants of 1972 revenue levels.

Intergovernmental Revenue Level Determinants

Most studies of intergovernmental revenues have treated both federal and state aid as independent variables in multivariate equations explaining variance in levels of state and local expenditures. Usually the purpose of such studies has been to determine whether intergovernmental revenues have stimulative or substitutive effects on state and local government expenditures. This type of investigation is not, however, the purpose of this study.

Intergovernmental revenues have become an integral part of local government budgets as well as the budgets of the donor governments. Thus, the focus of this study is on determining which demographic, socioeconomic, and governmental variables are the best predictors of the level of this external aid, admitting that decisions to administer aid come from both directions, particularly since most aid is in the form of matching grants.

Transfers of funds from higher to lower levels of government can be seen as being mutually beneficial. The funds are a source of additional revenue for the lower-level government and are also a method of accomplishing policy objectives of a higher level of government (usually redistribution or equalization of income and/or services). In fact, it has been stated that "under fiscal and political federalism, it is not clear which level of government is the prime decision-maker."[18]

Federal Aid Revenue Level Determinants

It has often been said that the federal government is more responsive to municipal governments that are their own state governments, especially in providing monies for poverty-related services. Most federal aid is redistributive and directed at the socioeconomically underprivileged. On the basis of this fact, it is hypothesized that measures of poverty, race, ethnicity, social pathology, education, age distribution, and economic status will be significant determinants of federal aid to municipalities.

Determinants of Federal Aid Levels in Central Cities. The results shown in Table 2.8 indicate that levels of federal aid are determined by a city's poverty, racial, ethnic, age, and income distributions and

TABLE 2.8: Determinants of Federal Aid Revenue Levels: Central Cities

Variable	r	β	R^2
Age of city	.42	-.09	.18
Ethnicity	.26	-.20	.19
Youth	-.18	-.96	.20
Median age	.04	-1.13	.22
Mobility (different house)	-.15	-.23	.23
Per capita personal income	-.12	-.32	.24
Condition of housing	-.06	-.42	.26
Middle-aged persons	.02	-.91	.27
Age of housing	.25	-.23	.28
Female-headed households	.09	.38	.29
Crime rate	.21	.42	.31
Domination of central city	-.12	.40	.33
Residential crowding	-.14	.42	.34
Housing value	.05	-.07	.35
Public assistance rate	.27	-.07	.36
Median family income	.02	1.66	.36
Poverty	-.02	.93	.38
Homeownership	-.26	-.52	.40
Affluence	-.03	-.57	.41
Mortality rate	.17	-.29	.43
Aged persons	.22	1.15	.43

Source: Compiled by the author.

by incidences of social pathology. In fact, these variables can explain 43 percent of the variation in federal aid levels among these 243 central cities.

Older cities, more dominating of the SMSA population, characterized by greater proportions of poor, low-skilled, aged, minority persons, living in crowded, old, run-down housing structures, and characterized by high crime and welfare rates, are likely to be the recipients of greater federal aid per capita than cities with healthier and wealthier populations. Federal aid, then, is much more responsive to the socioeconomic conditions of a city than to its demographic or governmental conditions.

Determinants of Federal Aid Levels in Suburbs. The results shown in Table 2.9 reveal that the determinants of suburban federal aid lev-

TABLE 2.9: Determinants of Federal Aid Revenue Levels: Suburbs

Variable	r	β	R^2
Taxable real property	-.52	-.88	.27
Index of income concentration	.43	.28	.35
Domination of central city	-.05	-.66	.44
Taxable state property	-.08	-.61	.66

Source: Compiled by the author.

els are significantly different from those observable in central cities. One reason is that suburbs are much more homogeneous in their social and economic characteristics than central cities. A second reason is that suburban governments, because of lesser poverty-related functional responsibilities and a general dislike for federal funds for such services, are likely to apply for different types of federal monies than central cities. Suburbs are likely to apply for developmental-type grants for major capital outlay projects such as sewers, sanitation systems, airports, recreational facilities, and so on. It is no surprise that socioeconomic characteristics do not turn out to be significant determinants of suburban federal aid levels.

The results show that as taxable property decreases, suburbs turn to the federal government for assistance (primarily for construction-type monies). The results also show that the smaller the size of the central city in the SMSA, the better the chance of the suburb's receiving federal monies. About the only sign of the federal government's goal of redistribution in its aid to suburbs is that as income becomes more concentrated, federal aid levels increase.

State Aid Revenue Level Determinants

It has been pointed out in Chapter 1 that state aid is of a different nature than federal aid. Federal aid is much more redistributive and responsive to the financial needs of municipalities. State aid is of two types—grants-in-aid and shared taxes—neither of which is as redistributive as federal aid. Shared taxes make up the largest proportion of state aid to municipalities and are allocated either on the basis of origin (where collected) or on the basis of financial need. Both types of allocation formulas include population size as one of the components. Thus it is likely that state aid will be more responsive to demographic and governmental conditions than to socioeconomic conditions.

Determinants of State Aid Levels in Central Cities. The results shown in Table 2.10 indicate that, as predicted, the most significant determinants of state aid levels among central cities are demographic and governmental variables: density, population size, age of city, regional location, and total functional responsibilities. But, the results show that these variables are negatively related to state aid, which is interpretable as meaning that most state aid is allocated on the basis of origin, not need, and is not as positively responsive to socioeconomic conditions as is federal aid.

Determinants of State Aid Levels in Suburbs. Significant determinants of suburban state aid levels also include demographic and governmental variables: regional location, taxable property, and total functional responsibilities (see Table 2.11). State aid to suburbs increases as one moves west. This is explainable by the existence of a large number of suburbs, fairly homogeneous in size and socioeconomic make-up, in the western states. These are often new developments being aided by the state to stimulate economic growth of the entire state.

The most significant determinants of suburban aid levels are the proportions of taxable personal and real property located in the

TABLE 2.10: Determinants of State Aid Revenue Levels: Central Cities

Variable	r	β	R^2
Total functional responsibility	.53	-.81	.28
Density	.53	-.69	.42
Housing value	.25	-.00	.44
Room crowding	-.09	2.84	.45
Fertility ratio	-.13	-3.99	.45
Region	.25	-.58	.46
Age of city	.45	-.55	.46
Condition of housing	-.12	-.88	.47
Taxable personal property	-.13	-.93	.47
Index of income concentration	-.11	-.22	.47
Population size	.33	-.22	.47
Mortality rate	.11	-1.54	.48
Aged persons	.20	7.11	.48
Median age	.08	-7.04	.50
Crime rate	.22	1.20	.55
Birthrate	-.16	-.85	.68

Source: Compiled by the author.

TABLE 2.11: Determinants of State Aid Revenue Levels: Suburbs

Variable	r	β	R^2
Total functional responsibility	.52	2.73	.27
Residential crowding	.12	3.29	.33
Taxable personal property	.22	15.88	.35
Region	-.18	3.08	.36
Crime rate	-.08	-2.78	.38
Mortality rate	.06	2.24	.39
Taxable real property	-.14	-16.99	.43
Ethnicity	.09	1.68	.71

Source: Compiled by the author.

suburbs. As they decline, state aid per capita increases. This seems to indicate that state governments are more responsive to the needs of the suburbs that have the least amount of taxable property. However, it is more a function of size than of the intent of the state. These suburbs are usually the larger suburbs which are more likely to have a considerable amount of nontaxable property devoted to schools, churches, hospitals, recreational facilities, sewerage, sanitation, water plants, and so on.

Tax Revenue Level Determinants

Taxes, particularly property taxes, are the most visible of all government resources. The general hostility most Americans feel toward taxes is largely the result of having to pay a rather large lump sum of money annually. Once or twice a year, they see on paper (bill) exactly how much the services they take for granted daily (such as police and fire protection, garbage collection, water, and so on) are costing them. But unlike the competitive market system, they have no alternative source from which to purchase these public goods, which are in reality natural monopolies.

Recent tax research has been of the determinant type. A study by Baird and Landon used eight independent variables (log of the number of competing governmental units in the county, Gini coefficient, income extremes, per capita income, population density, land area in square miles, population per governmental unit and intergovernmental unit, and intergovernmental revenue from the state) to explain 68 percent of the variance in tax revenues of counties.[19]

Another general tax determinant study was done by Campbell and Sacks who examined the determinants of tax level variations in 212 central cities.[20] Using three variables (per capita differences in income, per capita differences in state aid, and central city proportion of the total SMSA population), the authors were able to explain 40 percent of the per capita tax differences of central cities. Similarly, Lineberry and Fowler examined the linkage between environmental characteristics and revenue (tax) policies of 200 American cities.[21] They selected 12 independent variables (population, growth rate, race, ethnicity, median income, poverty, affluence, median school years completed by adult population, percent high school graduates, percent white-collar, percent elementary schoolchildren in private schools, and percent owner-occupied dwelling units) to explain 52 percent of the variance in taxes among these 200 cities.

On the basis of prior research, it is predicted that the significant determinants of variation in tax levels will be demographic measures of population size, growth rate, density, taxable property, and central city domination of the SMSA population; socioeconomic measures of race, ethnicity, age distribution, economic status, education, and social pathology; and governmental measures of functional responsibility, governmental character, and state legal constraints on municipal property taxing powers.

Determinants of Property Tax Revenue Levels: Central Cities

The results shown in Table 2.12 reveal that, as predicted, variations (86 percent) in central city property tax levels can be explained by measures of population size, regional location, proportion of taxable property, ethnicity, housing conditions, age distribution, economic status, social pathology, age of city, and total functional responsibilities.

More specifically, older cities, located in the Northeast, with more functional responsibilities and greater proportions of ethnics, minorities, poor persons, youth and elderly, crowded housing conditions, and incidences of poverty, tend to have the highest property tax levels.

It is important to note that state legal constraints on local government fiscal powers are conspicuously absent from the list of significant determinants of central city property tax levels. Instead, the results show that legal constraints are not very good predictors of municipal variation in taxation policies.

There are several possible explanations for the failure of these legal constraint measures to explain variations in municipal taxing policies. First, "in spite of the states' legal power to act separately in devising patterns of government and financing arrangements, they

TABLE 2.12: Determinants of Property Tax Revenue Levels: Central Cities

Variable	r	β	R^2
Ethnicity	.55	.17	.30
Total functional responsibility	.55	.00	.44
Housing value	.47	-.08	.51
Region	-.41	-.36	.59
Poverty	-.28	.37	.61
Age of city	.36	-.13	.62
Population size	.18	-.11	.63
Taxable personal property	.02	-.14	.64
Median age	.08	-2.51	.64
Aged persons	.20	2.62	.67
Cumulative fertility ratio	-.15	-1.49	.69
Room crowding	-.06	.67	.75
Mortality rate	.04	-.59	.79
Median family income	.32	1.04	.86

Source: Compiled by the author.

have actually done a good deal of copying from one another."[22] Recent years have seen an increase in the passage of constitutional and statutory home rule provisions which ultimately has meant less state intervention in local government fiscal decisions. Second, the Bureau of the Census regularly develops statistics on state and local finances within a framework that groups various items according to certain standard definitions, rather than according to their diverse handling by the governments themselves in their reporting schemes.[23]

Determinants of Property Tax Revenue Levels: Suburbs

The determinants of suburban property tax levels are primarily measures of economic status (wealth), rather than measures of race, ethnicity, age distribution, or social pathology as among central cities. (See Table 2.13.)

Suburbs characterized by more functional responsibilities, greater concentrations of wealth, greater incidences of homeownership and housing of above-standard quality, receive more taxes per capita than suburbs not so characterized. In these suburban communities, property taxes appear to be almost progressive—based on ability to pay (certainly not the case among central cities).

TABLE 2.13: Determinants of Property Tax Revenue Levels: Suburbs

Variable	r	β	R^2
Total functional responsibility	.61	+.37	.37
Region	-.50	-.23	.43
Affluence	.14	-.05	.47
Public assistance rate	-.00	+.43	.48
Homeownership	.02	+.67	.50
Condition of housing	-.01	-.54	.51
Taxable state property	-.24	-.40	.53
Index of income concentration	.27	+.56	.60

Source: Compiled by the author.

Nontax Revenue Level Determinants

Nontax revenues refer to the category of revenues labeled "current charges and miscellaneous revenues" by the U.S. Bureau of the Census. The Census Bureau defines these revenues as "amounts received from the public for performance of specific services benefiting the person charged, and from sales of commodities and services."[24] Nontax revenues, then, differ from other revenue types primarily in that they involve a direct exchange between the government and the individual citizen.

Nontax revenues are at the opposite end of the fiscal spectrum from intergovernmental revenues. The purpose of intergovernmental (external) aid sent from a higher level of government down to a municipality is the redistribution of goods and services, that is, an equitable purpose. On the other hand, the purpose of nontax revenues collected by the local government itself is the direct allocation of services or goods in proportion to payment for these goods and services, that is, an efficiency purpose.

There have been no previous studies that have examined the determinants of nontax revenues among U.S. municipalities. Thus, the only basis for hypothesizing about which variables are likely to be significant determinants of nontax revenue is the knowledge that they are more efficiency-related than equity-related revenues. On this basis, one might predict that measures of economic status will be the best predictors of municipal nontax revenue levels.

Determinants of Nontax Revenue Levels: Central Cities

The results shown in Table 2.14 indicate that central city non-tax revenue levels are mainly determined by measures of economic status (particularly housing), age distribution, and functional responsibilities of the government.

Cities characterized by proportionately more persons employed in white-collar jobs, new housing, more middle-aged residents, and fewer functional responsibilities (none of which is likely to be a least common function) have higher nontax revenue levels than cities not so characterized. It is politically and economically more pragmatic for cities having these characteristics to take in higher levels of money from user-related (efficient) revenue sources than it would be for cities with poorer, needier populations, unable to pay on a direct basis for many of these services, to do so.

TABLE 2.14: Determinants of Nontax Revenue Levels: Central Cities

Variable	r	β	R^2
White-collar occupations	.28	.03	.08
Total functional responsibility	.21	-.24	.14
Mortality rate	.07	-.11	.17
Age of housing	-.11	-.23	.19
Median age	-.08	-3.38	.21
Aged persons	.06	3.86	.26
Cumulative fertility ratio	-.05	-1.90	.40
Residential crowding	-.12	.94	.47
Crime rate	.17	.93	.60

Source: Compiled by the author.

Determinants of Nontax Revenue Levels: Suburbs

The determinants of suburban nontax revenue levels are quite different from those observed in central cities (see Table 2.15).

Suburban nontax revenue levels are most affected by measures of population mobility, income, housing conditions, and functional responsibilities of the government.

The results suggest that the older transitional suburbs, characterized by population movement (probably in-migration of upwardly mobile, yet low- to middle-income central city residents), higher mor-

TABLE 2.15: Determinants of Nontax Revenue Levels: Suburbs

Variable	r	β	R^2
Mobility	.19	.42	.04
Mortality rate	.14	.64	.07
Index of income concentration	-.09	-1.12	.14
Total functional responsibility	.17	.38	.19
Condition of housing	.09	.65	.22
Housing value	-.05	.69	.37

Source: Compiled by the author.

tality rates, less concentrated income, poorer housing, and more functional responsibilities than other suburbs, are likely to receive more nontax revenues per capita than newer, wealthier suburbs. This is primarily explainable by the fact that newer suburbs are more likely to have many of these charge-type services delivered by special districts or counties, rather than by the suburban government.

SIGNIFICANCE OF THE FINDINGS

This chapter has highlighted the differences in city and suburban revenue levels (intergovernmental, tax, and nontax). It has also discussed the various demographic, socioeconomic, and governmental characteristics that help account for these differences. The results show that cities and suburbs do differ in their revenue levels, and that the determinants of central city and suburban revenue levels are significantly different.

To gain a better perspective of what these findings mean for the future financial status of cities and suburbs, it is important to conclude by noting that the average increase (1962-72) in total general revenue levels in suburbs was $106, compared with an average increase of $94 in central cities. It appears that suburbs are maturing and becoming more resemblant of central cities, both in environmental characteristics and in financial characteristics (that is, revenue levels). Suburban governments should take heed of the causes and consequences of increased revenue levels in central cities.

NOTES

1. Brian J. L. Berry, ed., City Classification Handbook: Methods and Applications (New York: Wiley, 1972).

2. G. Ross Stephens and Henry J. Schmandt, "Revenue Patterns of Local Governments," National Tax Journal 15 (December 1962): 432-37.

3. Glenn W. Fisher, "Revenue and Expenditure Patterns in Five Large Cities," Quarterly Review of Economics and Business 3 (Autumn 1963): 61-72.

4. S. R. Johnson and Paul E. Junk, "Sources of Tax Revenue and Expenditures in Large U.S. Cities," Quarterly Review of Economics and Business 10 (Winter 1970): 7-15.

5. Seymour Sacks and John Callahan, "Central City-Suburban Fiscal Disparity," in Advisory Commission on Intergovernmental Relations, City Financial Emergencies: The Intergovernmental Dimension (Washington, D.C.: ACIR, 1973), pp. 91-152.

6. Robert B. Pettengill and Jogindar S. Uppal, Can Cities Survive? The Fiscal Plight of American Cities (New York: St. Martin's Press, 1974).

7. Sacks and Callahan, op. cit., p. 134.

8. Frederick M. Wirt, "The Political Sociology of American Suburbia: A Reinterpretation," in H. R. Mahood and Edward L. Angus, eds., Urban Politics and Problems (New York: Scribner's 1969), p. 183.

9. Robert C. Wood, 1400 Governments (Cambridge, Mass.: Harvard University Press, 1961).

10. Robert L. Lineberry and Ira Sharkansky, Urban Politics and Public Policy, 2nd ed. (New York: Harper & Row, 1974).

11. See Thomas R. Dye and Susan A. MacManus, "Predicting City Government Structure," American Journal of Political Science, 20 (May 1976), pp. 257-71.

12. Woo Sik Kee, "State and Local Fiscal Systems and Municipal Expenditures," Public Administration Review 27 (March 1967), pp. 39-41.

13. Thomas R. Stinson, "Population Changes and Shifts in Local Government Finance," Municipal Finance 42 (August 1969), pp. 134-39.

14. Stephens and Schmandt, op. cit.

15. Gudmund R. Iverson, Applied Statistics (Ann Arbor, Mich.: Inter-University Consortium for Political Research, 1971), p. 74.

16. Norman H. Nie, Dale H. Brent, and C. Hadali Hull, SPSS: Statistical Package for the Social Sciences (New York: McGraw-Hill, 1970), p. 180.

17. Edward R. Tufte, Data Analysis for Politics and Policy (Englewood Cliffs, N.J.: Prentice-Hall, 1974), p. 139.

18. Werner Z. Hirsch, The Economics of State and Local Government (New York: McGraw-Hill, 1970), p. 112.

19. Robert N. Baird and John H. Landon, "Political Fragmentation, Income Distribution, and the Demand for Government Services," Nebraska Journal of Economics and Business 11 (Autumn 1972): 171-84.

20. Alan K. Campbell and Seymour Sacks, <u>Metropolitan America: Fiscal Patterns and Governmental Systems</u> (New York: The Free Press, 1967).

21. Robert L. Lineberry and Edmund P. Fowler, "Reformism and Public Policies in American Cities," in <u>City Politics and Public Policy</u>, ed. James Q. Wilson (New York: Wiley, 1968), pp. 97-123.

22. Advisory Commission on Intergovernmental Relations, <u>Measuring the Fiscal Capacity and Effort of State and Local Areas</u> (Washington, D.C.: Government Printing Office, 1971), p. 2.

23. Ibid., p. 2.

24. U.S. Bureau of the Census, <u>City Government Finances in 1971-72</u> (Washington, D.C.: Government Printing Office, 1973), p. 1.

Chapter 3

Revenue Reliance:
What Proportion Comes
from Each Revenue Source?

INTRODUCTION

Revenue reliance is the proportion of the total general revenues collected by a city that it receives from each revenue source. It is calculated by dividing the amount received from each source (intergovernmental, tax, nontax) by the total general revenue received from all sources. By analyzing reliance figures, one can compare the relative dependence of cities and suburbs on each type of revenue.

Reliance and level, while related, are not identical measures. Two cities may have identical property tax levels ($125) but may differ markedly in their reliance patterns. For example, one city may rely heavily on the property tax (75 percent of its revenue comes from the property tax), whereas the other city may rely only moderately on the property tax for its general revenue (45 percent). As was stated in Chapter 2, revenue level is a measure of the intensity of usage of a particular type of revenue. Reliance, however, measures the scope of usage of each type of revenue. Whereas level figures are most useful in internal budgeting calculations and in comparing the "spreading out" of the revenue intake, using a per person figure as a reference point, reliance figures are perhaps more useful as indicators of stress on a city's fiscal resources.

A greater reliance on intergovernmental or externally obtained revenues (federal and state aid) often indicates that a city's own capacity to raise revenues is somewhat limited. Relatedly, increases in reliance on nonproperty taxes, coupled with constant or decreasing reliance on property taxes, suggests that the property tax structure in that city is no longer capable of expanding (whether for economic or political reasons). Thus, reliance patterns can serve as warning signals of possible fiscal imbalances in the future.

While it is generally known that use of the property tax is diminishing among all types of cities, very little is known about whether reliance patterns are similar in all types of cities and suburbs throughout the United States or about the environmental conditions that affect cities' reliance patterns.

The first part of this chapter focuses on the patterns of reliance upon intergovernmental (federal and state), tax (property and nonproperty), and nontax revenues among and between 243 central cities and 340 suburban municipalities. Of specific interest is whether cities (and suburbs) differ among themselves in their proportional use of certain types of revenues depending on the region of the country in which they are located, their population size, economic base, governmental character, and functional responsibilities. A second point of interest is whether there is a difference between cities and suburbs in their reliance patterns, although they may be located in the same region, be of a similar size, economic base, and governmental character, and have similar functional responsibilities.

The second part of the chapter focuses on the analysis of the demographic, socioeconomic, and governmental conditions affecting the reliance patterns of cities and suburbs. The key question to be answered, using multiple regressional analytic techniques, is whether these environmental conditions impact similarly on the revenue use patterns of both cities and suburbs, or, whether the impacts of these conditions are significantly different, both in strength and in direction (positive or negative), on city and suburban reliance patterns.

PREVIOUS REVENUE RELIANCE STUDIES

In the past, examinations of municipal revenue reliance patterns have almost exclusively been in the context of broader studies of municipal growth patterns. Several studies have examined the effect of population growth (change) on revenue use patterns. Feinberg (1964) looked at the relationship between growth rate and changes in reliance patterns among the ten largest central cities during the 1950s.[1] He found that growth is related to change in tax revenue reliance, but not to changes in reliance upon intergovernmental or nontax revenues.

A similar study by Stinson analyzed the shifts that occurred in local government revenues following major population change (1952–62), but did so for cities with 1950 populations of 25,000–50,000 located outside SMSAs.[2] Stinson found that growing cities relied much more heavily on the property tax than nongrowth cities. However, he found that all cities decreased their reliance on taxes during the study period. The study also observed, in contrast with the Feinberg study, that growth is related to increased reliance on charges and miscellaneous (nontax) revenues. Similar to the results of the Feinberg study, Stinson found that intergovernmental revenues as a proportion of the total revenues remained fairly constant, regardless of the growth rate of a municipality.

A more recent study by Jack and Reuss examined changing revenue patterns in 39 large cities (populations over 250,000) between 1950-69.[3] They found that the greatest change in this 20-year period was in the role of intergovernmental revenues. "Higher levels of government with access to flexible, progressive taxes have assumed a greater responsibility for provision of public wants via grants to localities, thus partially redressing existing fiscal disparities."[4] They also observed that within the category of revenues from own sources, the relationship of taxes and nontaxes shifted drastically, so that by 1969 taxes had declined to about 42 percent of all revenues, while nontax revenues had increased to 12 percent.

Several studies have contrasted reliance patterns of cities and suburbs, although these studies suffer from previously mentioned limitations, that is, inaccurate definitions of suburbs as all the area outside the central city but within an SMSA, instead of as independent governmental units. A study done for ACIR by Sacks and Callahan (1973) examined city-suburban fiscal disparities within 72 SMSAs.[5] They found that cities and suburbs are becoming more similar in their tax reliance patterns (although they did not distinguish between property taxes and nonproperty taxes). The greatest difference they observed was in reliance upon intergovernmental revenues. In fact, they identified the greater responsiveness of state and federal aid to central cities as one factor holding down per capita tax collection disparities between central cities and suburbs. Sacks and Callahan observed that while central cities received much higher levels of intergovernmental aid than suburbs, suburbs relied more on intergovernmental aid, particularly state aid, than did central cities. They pointed out that the type of aid is important in distinguishing between cities and suburbs, since suburbs received much greater proportions of state aid and cities received greater proportions of federal aid.

John Pazour performed the same type of analysis as Sacks and Callahan but, rather than limiting his analysis to central cities and suburbs within the larger SMSAs, he included a broader group of cities and suburbs.[6] He examined city revenues by population size, city type, and geographic region for three time periods (1962-63; 1964-65; and 1968-69). He found that suburban reliance on property taxes increased during this time period, whereas central city property tax reliance declined. However, both cities and suburbs increased their reliance on nonproperty taxes. With regard to intergovernmental revenue reliance, both cities and suburbs were found to receive more state aid than federal aid. Pazour concluded that all differences in revenue reliance could be attributed to the relationship between legal constraints and local government revenues. "The availability of these sources depends largely upon state constitutional and statutory limits."[7]

It is obvious that the results of these earlier studies are inconclusive and somewhat contradictory. Besides the fact that all of these studies have erroneously and incorrectly defined suburbs, they have tended to focus their analyses on two of the three broad categories of revenue (intergovernmental and tax) to the exclusion of nontax revenues. An additional shortcoming is that they have not adequately contrasted city and suburban reliance patterns with regard to the specific types of intergovernmental revenue (federal, state) or tax revenue (property, nonproperty).

It is hoped that the following discussion will help clarify knowledge of the reliance patterns among and between cities and suburbs throughout the 243 SMSAs of the United States.

GENERAL REVENUE RELIANCE PATTERNS

Cities and suburbs are characterized by different revenue reliance patterns. The figures shown in Table 3.1 reveal that while both cities and suburbs rely most heavily on tax revenues (48 percent and 60.2 percent, respectively), they differ in their relative dependence upon intergovernmental and nontax revenues. Central cities, somewhat surprisingly to the casual observer, tend to rely more heavily on nontax revenues (31.5 percent) than on intergovernmental revenues (20.5 percent), whereas the reverse is typical of suburban governments (17.4 percent from nontax revenues, 22.4 percent from intergovernmental revenues).

The differences in reliance upon nontax revenues are tied in with the differences in expenditures of cities and suburbs. As Feinberg pointed out, nontax revenues are directly tied in with expenditures (since they are by definition charges issued for specific services rendered).[8] Thus, since suburbs have comparatively lesser total general expenditures than central cities, it follows that suburban reliance on nontax revenues is proportionately lesser than that of central cities.

The differences in city and suburban reliance on intergovernmental revenues are also easily explainable. Sacks and Callahan attribute this phenomenon to suburban specialization in education-related expenditures—a function that receives a large proportion of state aid. Since state aid is by far the largest source of intergovernmental revenue for both cities and suburbs, this explains overall central city and suburban differences in reliance upon intergovernmental revenues. They suggest, however, that "as suburbs began to experience more

TABLE 3.1: Revenue Reliance: All Central Cities and Suburbs (percent)

	Central Cities			Suburbs		
Revenue Type	1962	1967	1972	1962	1967	1972
Intergovernmental	16.6	18.6	20.5	10.9	12.5	22.4
Federal	4.8	6.1	7.7	1.6	1.4	5.9
State	11.8	12.6	12.8	9.3	11.1	16.5
Tax	58.7	54.7	48.0	43.0	43.0	60.2
Property	44.8	40.4	32.4	31.5	31.4	36.7
Nonproperty	13.9	14.7	15.2	11.5	11.6	23.5
Nontax	24.7	26.6	31.5	46.1	44.2	17.4

Note: Revenue reliance is the proportion of a city's total general revenue received from a particular source. Figures do not add to 100 percent due to rounding.

Sources: U.S. Department of Commerce, Bureau of the Census, Census of Governments: 1962, 1967, 1972 (Washington, D.C.: Government Printing Office); City Finances (1962, 1967, 1972).

demands in the non-educational functions, their proportion of aid (in relation to the central cities) may decrease."[9] At any rate, it appears to be the greater proportion of suburban expenditures devoted to education that accounts for central city/suburban differences in intergovernmental revenue reliance patterns.

Cities and suburbs also differ in their dependence on property and nonproperty tax revenues. Both rely most heavily on the property tax (32.4 percent and 36.7 percent, respectively), primarily because it is the sole major revenue source reserved for use by local governments in the United States. However, they do differ in their relative dependence on property and nonproperty taxes. Cities rely much more heavily on property taxes (32.4 percent) than on nonproperty taxes (15.2 percent). Suburbs, on the other hand, are more balanced in their dependence, generally receiving 36.7 percent of their total revenues from property taxes and 23.5 percent from nonproperty taxes. Perhaps this is explainable by the age of suburban municipalities in relation to the age of central cities. Suburbs, being newer and more aware of the causes and consequences of heavy reliance on property taxes, have made more calculated decisions to balance reliance upon property and nonproperty taxes, whereas it is far too late for such a decision on the part of central cities.

Revenue Reliance Patterns by Region

Revenue reliance patterns show marked regional variations. As the figures shown in Table 3.2 indicate, reliance patterns differ both among and between central cities and suburbs when analyzed by region. *

Central City Differences by Region

Generally, reliance upon intergovernmental revenues (both federal and state) and property tax revenues is greatest in northeastern cities and lowest in southern cities. On the other hand, reliance upon nonproperty tax and nontax revenues is greatest in southern cities and lowest in northeastern cities.

The finding that northeastern cities rely more on intergovernmental revenues (26.8 percent) than cities in other regions of the country confirms Sacks' and Callahan's finding that intergovernmental aid "showed the greatest responsiveness to central city needs in the Northeast, the West, and Midwest."[10] It is significant that northeastern cities rely more on both federal and state, or external, resources than cities located elsewhere and that these cities are also characterized by the heaviest reliance upon property taxes (44.8 percent).

Pettengill and Uppal suggest that cities differ in their reliance on property taxes for two reasons: variation in functional responsibilities and tradition. "Older cities like Boston stay with the property tax while younger ones like Los Angeles and Seattle rely more heavily on nonproperty taxes."[11] This explanation seems plausible here, especially when the property tax reliance of southern and western cities, the younger cities, is compared with that of northeastern cities. Southern and western cities rely much less (29.1 percent and 27.1 percent, respectively) on the property tax than do northeastern central cities (44.8 percent).

Table 3.2 also indicates that southern and western cities rely more on nonproperty taxes (18.2 percent and 17.0 percent) than cities located in the Northeast (6.2 percent) or the Midwest (14.1 percent). This finding can also be explained in terms of the age of the city. Newer cities have made conscientious choices to maintain more balance in their reliance on property and nonproperty taxes, learning from the experiences of older cities' almost exclusive reliance upon property taxes.

---

*The regional classifications are the same as those used in the analysis of revenue levels. See Chapter 2 for an explanation of the classification scheme.

TABLE 3.2: Revenue Reliance for Central Cities and Suburbs, by Region (percent)

	Revenue Type														
	Intergovernmental						Tax						Nontax		
	Federal			State			Property			Nonproperty					
Region	1962	1967	1972	1962	1967	1972	1962	1967	1972	1962	1967	1972	1962	1967	1972
Central cities															
Northeast (53)	6.4	7.4	6.9	15.4	18.5	18.6	59.9	52.2	44.8	6.6	7.6	6.2	11.6	14.3	22.2
South (53)	4.7	5.7	5.1	7.7	7.8	7.8	40.3	37.2	29.1	16.9	17.1	18.2	30.4	32.2	37.6
North Central (62)	3.9	6.1	6.3	15.4	14.9	14.4	45.1	40.0	31.5	10.0	11.9	14.1	25.6	27.1	32.4
West (41)	4.0	5.0	6.6	10.5	11.5	13.5	34.7	32.4	27.1	22.3	20.7	17.0	28.5	30.5	29.0
Suburbs															
Northeast (96)	2.3	1.8	2.8	8.9	11.9	15.5	49.2	53.5	58.8	8.3	10.1	9.5	31.3	22.7	13.5
South (50)	1.8	2.2	5.7	5.1	5.8	6.7	26.1	23.4	30.8	9.8	12.3	22.3	57.2	56.4	34.5
North Central (109)	0.1	1.3	2.7	12.5	13.4	18.8	27.9	30.3	32.5	10.2	11.6	19.9	48.8	43.3	26.1
West (85)	2.4	2.4	5.3	9.4	10.7	18.5	22.9	15.3	23.1	18.8	15.7	29.7	46.5	56.0	23.4

Note: Revenue reliance is the proportion of a city's total general revenue received from a particular source. Figures in parentheses indicate number of municipalities.

Sources: U.S. Department of Commerce, Bureau of the Census, Census of Governments: 1962, 1967, 1972 (Washington, D.C.: Government Printing Office); City Finances (1962, 1967, 1972).

Suburban Differences by Region

Suburban reliance patterns differ slightly from those of central cities when examined by region. Suburban reliance upon intergovernmental revenues is much greater in western suburbs (23.8 percent) than in northeastern suburbs, as was characteristic of central cities. Federal aid reliance is greatest in southern suburbs (5.7 percent) and lowest in northeastern and midwestern suburbs (2.8 percent and 2.7 percent). This finding might be more easily explainable if census figures enabled one to tell what type of aid comes into a suburb. It is highly likely that the rapidly growing suburbs turn to the federal government for financial aid for capital improvements (building projects), whereas the somewhat more stable suburbs still prefer not to take federal funds for the typical reasons suggested earlier—a general distaste for federal money with strings and guidelines attached, and for involvement of the federal government in local affairs.

Suburbs in all regions other than the South rely more heavily on state aid than federal aid. This is largely explainable by the fact that suburbs in other regions of the country are likely to have their own municipally financed school systems, whereas in the South, education is generally a county or a special district function.

Suburban tax reliance patterns are similar to those observed in central cities. Property tax reliance is much greater (58.8 percent) in northeastern suburbs than in western (23.1 percent) or southern (30.8 percent) suburbs. Again, age of the suburb is a likely explanation for this finding. The greatest growth and greatest number of newly incorporated suburban municipalities is characteristic of the West and the South. These newly developing communities are aware of the political and economic dangers in relying too heavily on the property tax.

Suburban nonproperty and nontax revenue reliance patterns are also identical to those observed in central cities. Both types of reliance are greatest in southern and western suburbs. These newer, more prosperous suburbs can focus on these efficiency, direct-user-type revenue sources much more easily than can the older, more socio-economically heterogeneous suburbs located in the Northeast and Midwest.

Revenue Reliance Patterns by Population Size*

At first glance, it appears that revenue reliance variations are unrelated to population differences in both cities and suburbs (see Ta-

---

*The population size classifications are the same as those used in the analysis of revenue levels. See Chapter 2 for an explanation of the classification scheme.

TABLE 3.3: Revenue Reliance for Central Cities and Suburbs, by Population Size (percent)

	Revenue Type														
	Intergovernmental						Tax								
	Federal			State			Property			Nonproperty			Nontax		
Population Size	1962	1967	1972	1962	1967	1972	1962	1967	1972	1962	1967	1972	1962	1967	1972
Central Cities															
Over 1,000,000	4.6	7.2	10.6	14.5	13.3	15.1	40.6	39.0	30.9	22.9	22.8	25.4	17.5	17.7	16.8
1970 (6)															
1960 (5)															
500,000-999,999	3.4	6.4	6.9	13.7	15.7	16.0	43.7	34.7	28.5	13.2	16.4	19.9	26.0	26.8	26.6
1970 (20)															
1960 (16)															
250,000-499,999	7.5	7.7	8.1	12.4	11.5	13.6	39.4	37.0	31.1	14.7	16.1	19.1	26.0	27.8	25.6
1970 (27)															
1960 (26)															
100,000-249,999	5.6	6.0	7.2	12.1	12.9	14.2	46.8	41.5	37.4	13.2	14.8	15.6	22.3	24.9	23.5
1970 (69)															
1960 (64)															
50,000-99,999	4.0	5.6	4.6	11.2	12.1	11.2	45.3	41.5	31.4	13.6	12.8	12.9	25.9	40.8	38.8
1970 (121)															
1960 (132)															
Suburbs															
Over 100,000	2.4	3.7	5.3	13.7	17.9	19.4	57.0	35.3	36.0	14.7	14.6	24.1	12.2	28.6	15.1
1970 (12)															
1960 (6)															
50,000-99,999	1.8	2.1	3.9	13.0	15.4	18.1	46.3	37.9	34.5	20.1	21.2	24.3	18.8	23.4	19.1
1970 (43)															
1960 (27)															
25,000-49,999	2.7	3.2	4.1	14.4	13.5	17.2	41.6	37.2	40.4	17.2	12.9	17.8	24.0	32.4	20.8
1970 (77)															
1960 (58)															
10,000-24,999	1.4	1.2	3.6	8.0	9.0	15.0	28.1	28.8	36.9	9.6	9.8	19.4	52.9	51.1	25.2
1970 (208)															
1960 (249)															

Note: Revenue reliance is the proportion of a city's total general revenue received from a particular source. Figures in parentheses indicate number of municipalities.

Sources: U.S. Department of Commerce, Bureau of the Census, Census of Governments: 1962, 1967, 1972 (Washington, D.C.: Government Printing Office); City Finances (1962, 1967, 1972).

ble 3.3). However, a closer analysis indicates that revenue reliance is related to population size, particularly intergovernmental (federal and state), nonproperty tax, and nontax revenue reliance. Property tax reliance patterns appear to be the least related to population size.

Central City Differences by Population Size

Table 3.3 shows that size is directly related to intergovernmental revenue reliance. The largest central cities, with populations over one million, rely on intergovernmental revenues for 26.9 percent of their total general revenue, whereas smaller cities with populations under 100,000 rely on intergovernmental revenues for only 16.9 percent of their revenues. This confirms an earlier finding by Pettengill and Uppal that "intergovernmental revenues were more important for big cities than for smaller ones."[12] The relationship between population size and intergovernmental revenue reliance is most marked for federal aid. The largest cities rely on federal aid nearly twice as heavily (10.6 percent) as do the smaller cities (4.6 percent). Much of this variation is attributable to the fact that most federal aid formulas have population size as one of their components. The relationship between population size and reliance on state aid, while not as strong, does exist. The largest cities receive 15.1 percent of their total revenues from state aid whereas the smallest cities receive only 11.2 percent.

Central city property tax reliance patterns are less related to population size than nonproperty tax reliance patterns. As size increases, so does reliance on nonproperty taxes. Pettengill and Uppal also observed this relationship between city size and the use of nonproperty taxes. They stated that "almost all large and medium-sized cities in the past 30 years have moved strongly in the direction of nonproperty taxes."[13]

The balance in central city reliance on property and nonproperty taxes is closely related to size; as size increases, so does the balance. For example, in the largest cities (over one million), 55 percent of their total tax revenue comes from the property tax and 45 percent comes from nonproperty taxes. This is quite different from the pattern observed among the smaller cities (below 100,000) which obtain 71 percent of their total tax revenue from property taxes and only 29.7 percent from nonproperty tax sources.

Finally, central city reliance on nontax revenues (charges and miscellaneous general revenues) is strongly related to population size. The smaller the city, the greater the reliance on nontax (efficiency-related) revenues.

Suburban Differences by Population Size

Suburban revenue reliance patterns, when analyzed using population size classifications, are similar to those observed among central cities. Larger suburbs, like larger cities, rely more on intergovernmental revenues (24.8 percent) than smaller suburbs (18.5 percent). In fact, the largest suburbs (over 100,000) rely more on both federal (5.3 percent) and state (19.4 percent) aid than the smallest suburbs (3.5 percent federal aid, 15.0 percent state aid). Again, this is attributable to the inclusion of population size factors in both state and federal aid formulas.

Suburban tax reliance patterns are also similar to central city tax reliance patterns. First, there is very little relationship between property tax reliance and population size. Second, there is a strong relationship between both nonproperty tax reliance and the balance between property and nonproperty tax reliance. The larger suburbs rely more on nonproperty taxes (24.1 percent) than the smaller ones (19.4 percent) and are also more balanced in their reliance on property taxes (36.0 percent) and nonproperty taxes (24.1 percent). The smaller suburbs, on the other hand, generally rely twice as heavily on property as on nonproperty taxes. Part of the explanation for this fact may be state constraints on the use of nonproperty taxes, which are generally much more restrictive for smaller municipalities than for larger ones.

Finally, smaller suburbs, like smaller central cities, rely much more heavily on nontax revenues (25.2 percent) than do the larger suburbs (15.1 percent). Smaller suburbs are more likely to have greater proportions of services financed by charges and special assessments than are the larger suburbs.

Revenue Reliance Patterns by Economic Base*

Revenue reliance patterns do not vary as markedly using economic base classifications as they do using regional or population size classifications. However, there are some general patterns that can be observed (see Table 3.4). The more diverse or complex the economic base, the greater the reliance upon intergovernmental (federal and state) and property tax revenues, in both cities and suburbs. On the other hand, differences in economic base do not appear to be re-

---

*The economic base classifications are the same as those used in the analysis of revenue levels. See Chapter 2 for an explanation of the classification scheme.

lated to differences in nonproperty tax or nontax revenue reliance patterns.

Central City Differences by Economic Base

Economic base is closely related to federal aid, state aid, and property tax reliance patterns in these 243 central cities. The more diverse the economic base of the city, the greater the reliance upon intergovernmental and property tax revenues. For example, cities with complex manufacturing economic bases rely on intergovernmental revenues twice as heavily (23.5 percent) as do cities with very specialized economic bases, whether retailing (14.5 percent) or other (11.7 percent). This pattern holds true both for reliance on federal aid and on state aid. Likewise, manufacturing cities, complex economic-based cities, rely on property taxes for 34.8 percent of their total revenues, whereas cities with very specialized economic bases rely on property taxes for only 25.8 percent of their total revenue.

There is one rather interesting pattern that can be observed from the figures shown in Table 3.4. The specialized economic-based cities are more balanced in their reliance on property and nonproperty taxes than are the complex economic-based cities. The property tax is the most important revenue source in manufacturing and industrial cities, since the tax is a politically and economically acceptable tax because it can easily be passed on to consumers without having negative impacts on the locational decisions of these industries. In other words, there is less need for these types of cities to rely on nonproperty taxes than there is for retailing or other cities that must make very conscious and obvious efforts to keep businesses within their city limits to begin with; and this can be done most expediently by keeping property tax reliance (and rates) relatively low.

Suburban Differences by Economic Base

There is a much weaker relationship between economic base and revenue reliance patterns in suburbs than in central cities. Generally, the more complex, more diversified, economic-based suburbs (manufacturing, industrial, and diversified manufacturing) rely more on intergovernmental revenues than on nontax revenues, whereas the opposite is true of the more specialized economic-based suburbs (diversified retailing, retailing, and other). Likewise, these more complex economic-based cities rely much more on property taxes than on nonproperty taxes than do the specialized economic-based suburbs. Again, this finding is consistent with earlier findings that manufacturing and commercial properties provide excellent tax sources for local governments.

TABLE 3.4: Revenue Reliance for Central Cities and Suburbs, by Economic Base (percent)

	Revenue Type														
	Intergovernmental						Tax								
	Federal			State			Property			Nonproperty			Nontax		
Economic Base	1962	1967	1972	1962	1967	1972	1962	1967	1972	1962	1967	1972	1962	1967	1972
Central Cities															
Manufacturing	5.8	6.8	7.0	15.5	16.5	15.4	51.3	43.0	34.8	8.9	12.6	12.7	18.5	21.1	29.0
1963 (86)															
1957 (74)															
Industrial	1.9	4.4	7.8	16.6	23.8	12.8	48.8	47.3	30.6	9.8	9.5	9.6	22.9	15.0	45.6
1963 (3)															
1957 (9)															
Diversified manufacturing	6.0	6.8	5.5	13.2	12.9	15.8	41.1	37.1	32.1	17.3	14.9	16.0	22.4	28.3	27.6
1963 (60)															
1957 (52)															
Diversified retailing	3.8	6.0	6.3	9.0	9.6	8.8	43.9	43.3	33.7	15.3	14.2	16.2	28.0	26.9	33.5
1963 (50)															
1957 (57)															
Retailing	3.4	4.0	5.6	8.1	7.0	8.0	42.1	38.5	30.7	16.2	17.1	20.3	30.1	33.5	34.5
1963 (27)															
1957 (36)															
Other	3.2	3.1	2.3	4.6	7.0	8.3	32.6	31.1	25.8	18.5	17.6	16.3	41.1	41.3	46.2
1963 (15)															
1957 (14)															

Suburbs															
Manufacturing 1963 (87) / 1957 (75)	1.6	3.1	5.1	12.9	15.5	18.1	47.5	43.9	41.2	12.8	16.1	18.0	25.2	20.7	17.6
Industrial 1963 (12) / 1957 (10)	9.2	1.5	2.0	10.1	11.7	13.5	21.0	42.9	40.5	17.5	12.8	21.8	32.2	31.1	22.1
Diversified manufacturing 1963 (19) / 1967 (17)	1.9	1.4	3.0	11.5	12.7	14.0	40.3	51.6	50.2	11.0	13.2	18.7	35.3	21.0	14.1
Diversified retailing 1963 (41) / 1957 (41)	2.8	2.4	4.0	10.7	12.1	15.4	43.3	35.9	34.5	23.5	17.7	23.0	19.7	31.2	23.1
Retailing 1963 (61) / 1957 (59)	1.5	1.6	2.7	10.5	12.6	15.1	42.9	37.6	34.8	17.3	17.8	24.4	27.7	30.4	23.0
Other 1963 (24) / 1957 (19)	2.2	3.3	3.0	15.5	14.2	17.2	43.1	41.0	39.7	16.7	12.6	18.1	17.9	28.9	22.0

Note: Revenue reliance is the proportion of a city's total general revenue received from a particular source. The first five economic-base types are the five basic economic types (collected on the basis of place of work). The "other" category represents cities with very specialized economic bases: wholesaling; mining; transportation; resort; government and armed forces; professional; hospital; education; or service. The classification scheme has not been reported since 1963; therefore it is assumed that cities have not changed economic bases drastically. (Suburbs do not add to total due to missing data.) Figures in parentheses indicate number of municipalities.

Sources: U.S. Department of Commerce, Bureau of the Census, Census of Governments: 1962, 1967, 1972 (Washington, D.C.: Government Printing Office); City Finances (1962, 1967, 1972); and The Municipal Yearbook 1963 and 1957 (Chicago: International City Managers Association, 1963 and 1957).

In contrast, the more specialized economic-based suburbs rely more on nontax revenues than do the complex economic-based suburbs. Specifically, other-based suburbs rely on nontax (efficiency-related) revenues for 22.0 percent of their total revenues, whereas manufacturing-based suburbs rely on them for only 17.6 percent of their total revenue. Perhaps this finding is more explainable by population size than by economic base, since manufacturing-based suburbs are generally larger than other or retail-based suburbs.

Revenue Reliance Patterns by
Governmental Character*

The literature on reformism suggests that reformed governments are more efficient governments; they have lower tax revenue levels. Yet virtually no studies have looked at the revenue reliance patterns of cities and suburbs grouped by governmental character.

The results of such an analysis, reported in Table 3.5, show that revenue reliance patterns do differ significantly among central cities and suburbs as their governmental characters (unreformed, mixed, or reformed) vary. Revenue reliance patterns also differ significantly in cities and suburbs with identical governmental characters.

Central City Differences by Governmental Character

As the figures in Table 3.5 indicate, unreformed central cities, as might be expected, rely more on intergovernmental revenues (27.0 percent) than reformed cities (18.2 percent). However, the results of comparing federal aid and state aid reliance patterns by governmental character are somewhat surprising. Reformed cities rely more on federal aid (6.5 percent) than unreformed cities (5.3 percent) but less on state aid (10.6 percent) than unreformed cities (20.8 percent). Thus, it is apparent that unreformed cities rely much more heavily on state aid than federal aid (whereas reformed cities are much more balanced in their reliance upon the two external sources of revenue). It is likely that this is not so much a function of governmental character as it is of variations in functional responsibility. The greatest proportion of unreformed cities are located in the Northeast, a region characterized by less common and more costly municipal functional

---

*The governmental character classifications are the same as those used in the analysis of revenue levels. See Chapter 2 for an explanation of the classification scheme.

TABLE 3.5: Revenue Reliance for Central Cities and Suburbs, by Governmental Character (percent)

	Revenue Type														
	Intergovernmental						Tax								
	Federal			State			Property			Nonproperty			Nontax		
Governmental Character	1962	1967	1972	1962	1967	1972	1962	1967	1972	1962	1967	1972	1962	1967	1972
Central Cities															
Unreformed[a]	5.17	7.6	5.3	11.5	15.2	20.8	58.7	53.1	47.9	7.8	6.8	8.8	17.0	17.2	16.3
1968 (20)															
1958 (19)															
Mixed[b]	4.9	6.4	5.9	12.4	13.1	12.9	45.0	39.9	33.1	13.9	15.0	15.6	23.8	25.6	30.5
1968 (126)															
1958 (149)															
Reformed[c]	4.5	5.0	6.5	10.5	10.8	10.6	40.9	38.0	28.3	15.2	14.8	16.2	28.9	31.3	37.3
1968 (76)															
1958 (72)															
Suburbs															
Unreformed[a]	0.0	1.0	1.1	9.5	11.5	17.8	49.0	42.8	46.9	17.0	13.2	15.1	23.8	31.6	19.0
1968 (11)															
1958 (18)															
Mixed[b]	1.6	1.8	3.7	9.2	11.3	16.2	29.7	34.2	39.6	9.9	11.5	18.8	49.6	41.1	21.6
1968 (213)															
1958 (252)															
Reformed[c]	2.2	1.9	4.2	11.4	10.9	15.6	37.7	27.7	32.3	17.4	13.1	21.8	31.3	46.4	26.1
1968 (116)															
1958 (70)															

[a]Unreformed cities are those with a mayor–council form of government, partisan elections, and a single member district council member selection plan.

[b]Mixed cities are those having at least one "reformed" characteristic and one "unreformed" characteristic.

[c]Reformed cities are those with a council–manager form of government, nonpartisan elections, and an at-large council member selection plan.

Note: Revenue reliance is the proportion of a city's total general revenue received from a particular source. Figures in parentheses indicate number of municipalities.

Sources: The Municipal Yearbook, 1968 and 1958 (Chicago: International City Management Association, 1958, 1968); U.S. Department of Commerce, Bureau of the Census, Census of Governments: 1962, 1967, 1972 (Washington, D. C.: Government Printing Office); City Finances (1962, 1967, 1972).

responsibilities (welfare, education, hospitals)—functions that are heavily subsidized by state governments in that region.

Tax reliance patterns, by governmental character, are much more predictable in terms of reform theory. Unreformed cities rely much more heavily on property tax revenues (47.9 percent) than do reformed cities (28.3 percent), but less heavily on nonproperty taxes (8.8 percent) than reformed cities (16.2 percent). Reformed cities, usually the newer, smaller cities located in the South or West, are also more balanced in their tax reliance patterns. Unreformed cities rely on property taxes 5.4 times more than they rely on nonproperty taxes (compared to 1.8 times among reformed cities).

Another pattern consistent with the efficiency aspect of reform theory is the reliance on nontax revenues. Reformed cities rely twice as heavily on nontax revenue (37.3 percent) as do unreformed cities (16.3 percent).

Suburban Differences by Governmental Character

Suburban reliance patterns, when analyzed by governmental character, differ only slightly from those observed in central cities. There is actually very little difference in reliance on intergovernmental revenues among suburbs characterized by unreformed (19.0 percent), mixed (19.9 percent), or reformed (19.7 percent) characters. It is obvious that among these 340 suburbs, reformed and mixed governments (rather than unreformed suburbs) rely more, though admittedly only slightly more, on intergovernmental revenues. However, much of this may be attributable to population size as opposed to governmental character. Unreformed suburbs are the smallest suburbs (as contrasted with cities where unreformed governments are found in the largest cities). These small, unreformed suburbs cannot afford to hire professionally trained, full-time city managers to prepare applications for federal or state grants, nor, with population size being one of the formula components, can they expect to get a lot from external revenue sources.

When the two types of intergovernmental revenue are examined individually, it is apparent that the patterns are identical to those of cities: reformed suburbs rely more on federal aid (4.2 percent) than unreformed suburbs (1.1 percent), whereas unreformed suburbs rely slightly more on state aid (17.8 percent), probably shared-tax state aid, than reformed suburbs (15.6 percent). Again, the differences in relative reliance on federal aid are more likely to be explainable by population size than by the mere structural arrangements of a municipality.

Suburban tax (property and nonproperty) and nontax reliance patterns are also identical to those of central cities. Unreformed suburbs rely more on property taxes (46.9 percent) than reformed suburbs (32.3 percent, but less on nonproperty tax (15.1 percent) or nontax revenue (19.0 percent) than reformed suburbs (21.8 percent nonproperty tax, 26.1 percent nontax). Similarly, the unreformed suburbs depend much more on property than on nonproperty taxes, whereas the reformed suburbs are more balanced in their relative reliance on the two types of tax revenue, probably attributable to the state constraints on use of nonproperty taxes by smaller municipalities.

Finally, the figures in Table 3.5 show that cities and suburbs with the same governmental character differ in their reliance patterns. For example, reformed cities rely more on intergovernmental and nontax revenues but less on state aid, property taxes, and nonproperty taxes than do reformed suburbs. Similarly, unreformed cities have heavier reliance on federal and state aid but lesser reliance on property, nonproperty tax, or nontax revenues than unreformed suburbs. These findings reaffirm earlier findings that governmental structural arrangements do not have independent effects on governmental fiscal policy, but are themselves the products of variations in demographic and socioeconomic conditions.[14]

Revenue Reliance Patterns by
Functional Responsibility*

Generally, as the figures in Table 3.6 indicate, cities and suburbs with primary fiscal responsibility for the least common municipal functions (education, welfare, hospitals, and housing and urban renewal) rely proportionately more on intergovernmental, particularly state aid, and property tax, but less on nonproperty tax and nontax revenue sources than those municipalities without such fiscal responsibilities.

Central City Differences by Functional Responsibility

Today, central cities having fiscal responsibilities for the least common, but most costly, municipal services are among the cities experiencing the greatest fiscal crises. Thus, it is particularly interesting to compare the revenue reliance patterns of cities with such responsibilities and those without.

The figures shown in Table 3.6 reveal that cities with responsibilities for education, welfare, and hospitals rely on intergovernmen-

---

*The functional responsibility classifications are the same as those used in the analysis of revenue levels. See Chapter 2 for an explanation of the classification scheme.

TABLE 3.6: Revenue Reliance for Central Cities and Suburbs, by Functional Responsibility (percent)

	Revenue Type														
	Intergovernmental						Tax								
	Federal			State			Property			Nonproperty			Nontax		
Functional Responsibility	1962	1967	1972	1962	1967	1972	1962	1967	1972	1962	1967	1972	1962	1967	1972
Central cities															
Education (76)	5.8	6.8	5.2	18.0	20.4	19.7	50.4	44.3	38.1	10.4	11.1	10.5	15.4	17.4	24.1
No education (167)	4.3	5.7	6.4	9.0	9.0	9.7	42.3	38.6	30.4	15.4	15.8	17.4	29.1	31.0	34.9
Hospitals (78)	5.9	6.1	5.5	12.6	14.5	14.6	43.2	38.4	32.9	13.1	13.4	14.0	25.2	27.5	31.0
No hospitals (165)	4.2	6.0	6.3	11.4	11.6	12.0	45.6	41.3	32.8	14.2	14.7	15.8	24.6	25.3	31.7
Welfare (80)	5.3	6.3	5.9	14.9	16.7	17.1	50.5	45.3	39.1	12.3	12.5	12.9	17.0	19.2	23.2
No welfare (163)	4.5	5.9	6.1	10.3	10.5	10.7	42.1	38.1	29.7	14.5	15.1	16.4	28.6	30.4	35.6
All three least common functions (33)	7.0	6.4	5.6	18.5	22.1	22.2	50.6	43.2	38.8	10.2	10.5	8.4	13.7	17.8	22.7
None of the least common functions (116)	4.4	6.0	6.5	9.9	9.8	10.6	43.5	39.6	30.6	15.3	15.4	16.3	27.0	29.2	34.8
Suburbs															
Education (49)	1.9	2.0	3.5	15.5	21.0	19.5	58.9	61.2	62.5	4.5	5.0	5.4	19.2	9.8	9.1
No education (291)	1.6	1.6	3.8	8.6	9.5	15.4	27.9	27.2	33.1	13.0	13.5	22.2	48.8	48.1	25.4

Hospitals (45)	2.5	2.4	3.5	12.2	15.6	15.0	52.6	54.1	52.3	8.2	10.4	10.5	24.6	17.5	18.7
No hospitals (295)	1.6	1.8	3.8	9.2	10.5	16.2	29.3	28.7	35.1	12.3	12.6	21.1	47.6	46.4	23.8
Welfare (89)	2.0	2.6	3.1	11.4	15.4	17.4	52.5	55.6	52.9	9.7	10.4	11.4	24.4	16.1	14.2
No welfare (251)	1.5	1.6	4.1	9.0	9.7	15.5	25.3	23.8	31.5	12.5	12.9	22.7	51.7	52.0	26.2
Housing and Urban renewal (43)	5.2	3.6	6.9	10.9	14.4	16.9	51.1	44.5	42.7	11.7	12.7	17.1	21.1	24.8	16.3
No housing and urban renewal (297)	1.2	1.6	3.3	9.4	10.7	15.9	29.7	30.3	36.6	11.8	12.5	20.1	47.9	45.2	24.1
All four least common functions (4)	5.8	2.9	5.5	15.0	23.2	23.8	68.9	62.4	61.1	4.9	4.7	3.2	5.4	6.8	6.4
None of the least common functions (218)	1.0	1.5	3.6	8.5	9.2	15.9	23.1	22.0	31.5	12.2	12.3	22.8	55.2	55.1	25.1

Note: Revenue reliance is the proportion of a city's total general revenue received from a particular source. A city is regarded as having functional responsibility for a service if it has primary financial responsibility for provision of the service. If it does not have primary financial responsibility, it is regarded as not having functional responsibility for that service. The service areas analyzed in this table are all services that are among those for which municipalities least often have primary financial responsibility. Figures in parentheses indicate number of municipalities.

Sources: U.S. Department of Commerce, Bureau of the Census, Census of Governments: 1962, 1967, 1972 (Washington, D.C.: Government Printing Office); City Finances (1962, 1967, 1972).

tal revenues almost twice as heavily (30.1 percent) as those without (18.3 percent). A closer analysis indicates that most of this difference is attributable to proportionately greater reliance on state aid (22.2 percent) by cities with least common responsibilities than by those without (10.6 percent). State subsidization of education, welfare, and hospitals is seen in the results shown in Table 3.6, not only by the individual reliance figures but by the balance figures as well. Cities without such subsidization get almost the same proportion of their total revenue from federal and state sources. There is not much difference in reliance upon federal aid by cities, regardless of functional responsibilities, although those without tend to rely slightly more on federal aid than those having fiscal responsibilities.

Tax reliance patterns of cities with least common functional responsibilities and those without are quite different. Cities with least common functional responsibilities rely on property taxes for 38.8 percent of their total revenues; cities without rely on property taxes for only 30.6 percent of their total revenues. The reverse is true of nonproperty tax reliance, which is twice as heavy among cities with these responsibilities (16.3 percent) as among those without (8.4 percent). On the basis of these findings, property owner complaints that they are supporting the costs of education and welfare appear to be well justified (among cities that provide these services). This claim is even more justifiable in light of the balance figures. Cities paying for these three least common functions rely on property taxes for 80 percent of their total tax revenue, whereas cities not having the responsibility of paying for any of these costly functions rely on property taxes for 65 percent of their total tax revenue.

Finally, reliance upon nontax revenues is proportionately greater among cities not having responsibilities for education or welfare. This is due to the fact that these cities provide and finance a greater proportion of their services on a direct-user assessment basis.

Suburban Differences by Functional Responsibility

Suburban reliance patterns are nearly identical to those observed in central cities. Suburbs with primary fiscal responsibility for education, hospitals, welfare, and housing and urban renewal (the least common suburban functions) rely more on intergovernmental revenues (29.3 percent) than those without (19.6 percent). Likewise, suburbs with least common functional responsibilities tend to rely less on federal aid but more on state aid than those without. It should be noted, however, that differences in suburban reliance on state aid by functional responsibility are not as marked as in central cities.

Suburban reliance on tax revenues (both property and nonproperty), on the other hand, differs tremendously between suburbs pay-

ing for the least common functions, especially education, and those
not doing so. For example, a look at the figures reveals that suburbs
paying for education rely twice as heavily on property taxes (62.5) percent) than suburbs not saddled with education as a primary fiscal responsibility (33.1 percent). Again, it appears that suburban property
owners, even more than central city property owners, can claim that
they are supporting education in their respective municipalities. Relatedly, these suburbs with least common functional responsibilities
depend much more on the property tax as a revenue source than on
the nonproperty tax.

The suburbs without responsibility for provision of education,
welfare, hospitals, or housing and urban renewal, rely on nontax
revenues four times more (26.1 percent) than those having such responsibilities (6.4 percent). As was observed in the discussion of
cities, this finding is explainable by the fact that suburbs without a
great number of social service responsibilities are more likely to provide services that can be financed by direct user assessments (or
charges).

DETERMINANTS OF REVENUE
RELIANCE PATTERNS

The format of the following analysis is identical to that used in
the analysis of the determinants of revenue levels (see Chapter 2).
Having gained a better understanding of the revenue reliance patterns
of cities and suburbs located in different regions of the country, of
differing sizes, economic bases, governmental characters, and functional responsibilities, the remainder of the chapter will focus on the
impact of demographic, socioeconomic, and governmental conditions
on city and suburban revenue reliance patterns. Specifically of interest is whether the same kinds of conditions are significant determinants
of intergovernmental, tax, and nontax levels in both cities and suburbs
or whether the significant determinants of revenue reliance differ between cities and suburbs.

Determinants of Intergovernmental Revenue
Reliance Patterns

The results of the comparison of means analysis showed that
central cities that rely most heavily on intergovernmental revenues
are those in the Northeast, which have larger populations, more complex (diverse) economic bases, unreformed governmental characters,
and responsibility for the least common functions of local government
(education, welfare, or hospitals).

Suburbs that rely most heavily on intergovernmental revenues to fulfill their budgetary needs are those located in the western and midwestern regions of the country. These suburbs tend to have populations over 100,000, complex economic bases (manufacturing or industrial), reformed or mixed governmental characters, and responsibility for the least commonly financed suburban functions (education, welfare, hospitals, or housing and urban renewal).

As stated previously, it is important to analyze separately the two types of intergovernmental revenue (federal aid and state aid). The results of the analysis of the determinants of intergovernmental revenue levels revealed that determinants of federal aid tend to be socioeconomic variables, whereas the determinants of state aid tend to be demographic (land use and population size) and economic status (housing-related) variables. It was also found that different variables emerged as significant predictors of city (as contrasted with suburban) intergovernmental revenue levels. It will be interesting to observe whether these distinctions also characterize determinants of intergovernmental revenue reliance patterns.

Determinants of Reliance on Federal Aid

On the basis of the general characteristics of federal aid and of the earlier findings, it is hypothesized that measures of population size, regional location, age of the city, economic status, social pathology, and functional responsibility will be among the most significant determinants of a city's reliance on federal aid. In contrast, among suburbs, which generally apply for a different type of federal aid (less for social services than for construction, or capital outlay, projects), it is hypothesized that population size, mobility (growth rate), and land use characteristics, plus functional responsibilities, will be the best determinants of reliance upon federal aid.

Determinants of Central City Reliance on Federal Aid. The results shown in Table 3.7 reveal that the hypotheses regarding determinants of reliance on federal aid among these 243 central cities are correct. Reliance upon federal aid is related to the age of the city, its functional responsibilities, its poverty and income levels, and its social pathologies. Larger, older cities, with less-mobile populations, less taxable property, whose residents are poorer, less likely to own their own homes and to live in crowded housing conditions, and with higher crime rates, more females in the labor force, and more functional responsibilities, tend to rely more on federal aid than cities not so characterized. These findings suggest that the worse off cities become, the more they must rely on federal aid to secure revenues needed to provide the services demanded by their populations. The

TABLE 3.7: Determinants of Federal Aid Revenue Reliance: Central Cities

Variable	r	β	R^2
Age of city	.28	-.27	.08
Per capita personal income	-.17	-.30	.10
Density	.08	-.12	.12
Birthrate	.10	-.10	.14
Race (nonwhite)	-.06	-.01	.15
Taxable personal property	.06	-.12	.18
Poverty	.12	1.10	.19
Population size	.21	.31	.20
Mobility (different house)	-.14	-.14	.21
Index of income concentration	-.00	-.27	.21
Youth	-.03	-2.54	.22
Residential crowding	.00	.55	.22
Female-headed households	-.01	-1.15	.25
Crime rate	.12	.43	.26
Median family income	-.12	.78	.30
Condition of housing	.06	-.47	.31
Domination of central city	-.02	-.44	.33
Total functional responsibility	.04	.36	.36
Females in labor force	-.07	.18	.37
Mortality rate	.08	-.31	.39
Homeownership	-.01	-.25	.41

Source: Compiled by the author.

findings also suggest that federal aid is responsive to city socioeconomic conditions and is generally redistributive in nature.

Determinants of Suburban Reliance on Federal Aid. Somewhat unexpectedly, only two variables (both land use variables) emerge as significant predictors of suburban reliance on federal aid (see Table 3.8).

TABLE 3.8: Determinants of Federal Aid Revenue Reliance: Suburbs

Variable	r	β	R^2
Taxable real property	-.60	-2.46	.36
Taxable personal property	.48	-1.91	.56

Source: Compiled by the author.

As the proportion of taxable property (both real and personal) declines, suburban reliance on federal aid increases. This can be interpreted in several ways. First, it can be interpreted as meaning that comparatively these suburbs (like their central city counterparts) are the more crisis-ridden suburbs. On the other hand, it is possible that these suburbs are the larger ones, with faster growth rates, which have less taxable property because they contain greater proportions of governmental, educational, cultural, and recreational (tax-exempt) property than the very smallest suburbs. At any rate, these two land use variables can explain over half of the variance (56 percent) in suburban reliance upon federal aid.

Determinants of Reliance on State Aid

Earlier findings of this study indicate that both central cities and suburbs rely more on state aid than on federal aid. It has also been pointed out that state aid is of two types (grants-in-aid and shared taxes), neither of which is as redistributive as federal aid. State grants-in-aid money is often earmarked for specific functions such as education, highways, or welfare. Thus, it is easy to hypothesize that reliance on state aid will be determined more by demographic (particularly population) and governmental (functional responsibility) variables than by socioeconomic variables (with the exception of income variables).

Determinants of Central City Reliance on State Aid. As the figures shown in Table 3.9 indicate, reliance upon state aid is largely determined by demographic (regional location, land use, density) and governmental (functional responsibility) measures rather than by socioeconomic measures (with the exception of housing-related measures).

Cities located in the West and Midwest, of lower population densities, with fewer functional responsibilities, less concentrated income distributions, and characterized by greater proportions of taxable property, valuable homes, and age disparity (youth and aged), rely more on state aid than other cities.

State aid, particularly the shared-tax type, does not tend to be allocated on a redistributive basis. Rather, it is most often returned on the basis of origin, or point of collection. Thus, cities that are relatively well off can count on substantial returns of shared-tax monies, such as sales tax monies, and can afford to rely more on state aid than the worse-off cities.

Determinants of Suburban Reliance on State Aid. Table 3.10 shows that demographic measures are generally the best predictors of suburban reliance on state aid (as is the case among central cities). How-

TABLE 3.9: Determinants of State Aid Revenue Reliance: Central Cities

Variable	r	β	R^2
Total functional responsibility	.38	-.35	.15
Index of income concentration	-.28	-.58	.21
Density	.35	-.60	.25
Taxable state property	.12	1.33	.27
Taxable real property	.21	1.37	.30
Housing value	.21	.31	.33
Manufacturing employment	.31	.37	.35
Region	-.06	.58	.41
Median age	.01	-3.94	.43
Aged persons	.20	3.15	.48
Cumulative fertility ratio	-.01	-2.50	.55
Room crowding	-.20	1.25	.79

Source: Compiled by the author.

ever, the impact of these demographic variables differs markedly between central cities and suburbs. The larger suburbs, with lesser proportions of taxable property (real and state), located in the West or Midwest, less dominated by a central city but close to a larger central city, with lesser proportions of aged persons, nonwhites, and white-collar workers (that is, the more homogeneously populated

TABLE 3.10: Determinants of State Aid Revenue Reliance: Suburbs

Variable	r	β	R^2
Aged	-.27	-.53	.07
Population size	.17	.08	.11
Race (nonwhite)	-.17	-.42	.13
White-collar occupations	-.11	-.07	.16
Housing value	.04	.11	.17
Taxable state property	.06	-1.06	.18
Domination of central city	-.06	-.43	.19
Taxable real property	-.03	-1.14	.21
Region	.19	.69	.27
Size of central city	-.00	.62	.37

Source: Compiled by the author.

suburbs), rely more heavily on state aid than other suburbs. The explanation for this finding is again attributable to the allocation formulas attached to the shared-tax monies, which generally reward larger, yet fairly prosperous, municipalities.

Determinants of Tax Revenue Reliance

The property tax is the primary source of revenue for most central cities and suburbs. State governments have traditionally reserved this revenue source for use by their local governments. While the general pattern of state governments has been to establish maximum millage rates and levels of assessment, state governments are still much more restrictive of local governments' usage of nonproperty taxes than of property taxes, particularly for smaller municipalities. Thus, it is not surprising that reliance on the property tax is relatively heavy among both cities and suburbs. Yet the consequences of heavy reliance on property taxes (loss of residents and industry, and increasing proportions of needy persons and poverty-related service responsibilities) are well known to officials in the younger, newly developing cities, primarily located outside the Northeast. They have generally attempted to balance their reliance on property taxes with other sources of revenue, usually nonproperty taxes and nontax revenues.

On the basis of these facts, it is hypothesized that demographic (age of city, population size, regional location, land use) and socioeconomic (income-related) variables, as well as the number of functions for which the municipality has primary financial responsibility, will be significant determinants of reliance upon property tax revenue.

Determinants of Central City Property Tax Reliance

The results shown in Table 3.11 indicate that greater reliance on property taxes is associated with cities in the Northeast, which contain a large proportion of the population of the entire SMSA, have more functional responsibilities to perform and finance, and have greater proportions of working females, ethnic minorities, age extremes, crowded housing conditions, as well as greater proportions of taxable property. This heavy reliance on property taxes by the more desperate cities is likely to be very closely related with their very high tax rates, which have been increased regularly to meet rising expenditures, which, in turn, have increased because of rising tax rates—a phenomenon not dissimilar to the familiar wage-price spiral.

Determinants of Suburban Property Tax Reliance

The determinants of suburban property tax reliance, like those of central city property tax reliance, are primarily demographic variables (regional location, population size, mobility, land use characteristics) and economic status, socioeconomic variables (affluence, income concentration, and housing value) as well as total functional responsibilities performed (see Table 3.12).

TABLE 3.11: Determinants of Property Tax Revenue Reliance: Central Cities

Variable	r	β	R^2
Females in the labor force	.30	.02	.09
Ethnicity	.27	-.00	.16
Region	-.26	-.38	.20
Median school years completed	.02	-.02	.24
Cumulative fertility ratio	.05	-1.94	.27
Taxable personal property	.15	-.01	.29
Taxable real property	.21	.29	.32
Domination of central city	.16	.96	.33
Median family income	.26	.26	.35
Aged persons	.07	3.60	.37
Median age	-.06	-3.64	.43
Room crowding	.02	1.49	.54
Total functional responsibility	.20	-.86	.63
Condition of housing	-.05	.82	.82

Source: Compiled by the author.

The larger suburbs, usually the older ones located in the Northeast, characterized by less mobile populations, greater proportions of tax-exempt property, with lesser proportions of affluent residents and more functional responsibilities, usually including schools, rely more heavily on property tax revenues than newer, growing, suburbs located in the West or South, with more affluent residents and without financial responsibility for schools, which are provided by either county or special district governments.

Determinants of Reliance on Nontax Revenues

Extensive use of nontax revenues (charges and miscellaneous general revenues) as demonstrated by the comparison of means analy-

TABLE 3.12: Determinants of Property Tax Revenue Reliance: Suburbs

Variable	r	β	R^2
Region	-.59	-.89	.35
Affluence	.21	-1.59	.41
Total functional responsibility	.48	.16	.47
Taxable personal property	.10	-1.10	.49
Mobility (different house)	-.40	-.85	.51
Taxable state property	-.25	-.53	.54
Population size	.03	.34	.57
Housing value	.12	2.07	.60
Index of income concentration	.19	-.86	.73

Source: Compiled by the author.

sis, is associated with smaller cities (under 100,000 population), located in either the South or Midwest, with reformed governmental characters, and without primary fiscal responsibility for the least common municipal functions. These municipalities are generally better off and are characterized by philosophies of revenue collection and service distribution that maximize efficiency. As previously stated, these cities are more likely to provide fewer services of a poverty-related nature and are, in fact, much more likely to provide services and pay for these services on a direct-user assessment basis. For example, garbage collection is financed by assessing residents in relation to the amount of garbage they dispose of. The more garbage disposed of by an individual or household, the more must be paid for collection and disposal of that garbage. Obviously, cities characterized by poorer populations can less readily provide or pay for services using nontax revenue sources and must, instead, rely more on tax and intergovernmental revenue sources for major portions of their budgets.

On the basis of these facts, it is hypothesized that socioeconomic indicators, particularly economic status measures, will be the best predictors of reliance on nontax revenues.

Determinants of Central City Reliance on Nontax Revenues

Table 3.13 shows somewhat unexpectedly that age and familism measures are the best predictors of central city reliance on nontax revenues, rather than income measures. It appears that the newer cities, with lesser proportions of elderly residents, and characterized by more familistic life styles, contain residents who are more likely,

TABLE 3.13: Determinants of Nontax Revenue Reliance: Central Cities

Variable	r	β	R^2
Age of city	-.39	-.06	.15
Mortality rate	.05	1.09	.21
Aged persons	-.29	-2.78	.40
Median age	.06	2.42	.65
Cumulative fertility ratio	-.11	1.07	.93

Source: Compiled by the author.

politically and financially, to accept and even demand service provision through user charges rather than through increased reliance on property tax revenues.

Determinants of Suburban Reliance on Nontax Revenue

Much less of the variance in suburban reliance on nontax revenue can be accounted for (43 percent) than in central city reliance (93 percent). The results of the analysis are also very different (see Table 3.14).

The most significant determinants of suburban reliance on nontax revenues are measures of affluence, race, and age distribution of the population. Suburbs with more economically homogeneous populations, more valuable homes, and greater proportions of aged persons and racial minorities, rely more on charges, special assessments, and other kinds of nontax revenue than other suburbs. Again, these suburbanites are more capable financially and more in favor philosophically of providing and paying for a greater number of services through direct-user assessments. And, indeed, from the analysis of their socioeconomic characteristics, they can more easily af-

TABLE 3.14: Determinants of Nontax Revenue Reliance: Suburbs

Variable	r	β	R^2
Index of income concentration	-.24	-1.47	.06
Race (nonwhite)	.19	.91	.18
Aged persons	-.05	.88	.26
Housing value	-.09	.61	.43

Source: Compiled by the author.

ford to have efficiency-oriented governments than equity-oriented governments.

SIGNIFICANCE OF THE FINDINGS

This chapter has focused on the differences in revenue reliance patterns (intergovernmental, tax, and nontax) among and between central cities and suburbs by contrasting them by their regional location, population size, economic base, governmental character, and functional responsibility, and by comparing the impact of various demographic, socioeconomic, and governmental variables on their reliance patterns.

The results show that greater reliance on federal aid and property tax revenue sources (particularly when compared to nonproperty tax revenues) is most characteristic of the cities regarded to be in the worst financial shape today. These are the larger, older cities, located in the Northeast, and characterized by greater proportions of poor persons and greater financial responsibility for poverty-related services (welfare, hospitals, housing and urban renewal) and education.

It is fitting to conclude the chapter by contrasting the relative changes in the reliance patterns of cities and suburbs in order to ascertain if there is truth in the commonly held view that suburbs, while still better off financially, are going down the same path that central cities have gone down before them.

An analysis of the changes in revenue reliance patterns (1962-72) of central cities and suburbs shows that tax revenue reliance, in particular, has declined in central cities but has increased in suburbs. These figures, however, are somewhat misleading. Central cities have decreased reliance on property taxes while increasing reliance on nonproperty taxes. Suburbs, on the other hand, have increased reliance on both property tax and nonproperty tax revenue, but have tended to increase reliance on nonproperty taxes three times more than on property taxes. Thus, it appears that suburbs are trying to avoid the excessive reliance on property taxes that has characterized declining central cities.

There are also some rather interesting differences in the changes in reliance on intergovernmental revenues. The increase in intergovernmental revenue reliance was much greater among suburban governments than central city governments (four times greater). Again, however, it is important to distinguish between federal aid and state aid. In central cities, the increases in reliance on federal and state aid were nearly identical, although slightly greater increases occurred in federal aid reliance. In suburbs, reliance on federal aid declined, whereas reliance on state aid increased markedly. There are several plausible explanations for this finding. One may be a desire on the part of the suburban residents to resist federal monies that have strings and guidelines attached. Another possible explanation centers on the nature of federal aid; most of the direct federal aid to municipalities is in the form of categorical, matching type grants (prerevenue-sharing), and figures indicate that many of these categories are simply not attractive to suburban officials and citizens who must match the federal funds. A third possibility is linked to federal policy; federal policy decisions may have been made to keep federal funds out of "lily white" suburbs, that is, to deny federal funds for segregated neighborhoods.

Central cities and suburbs also differ in their changes in reliance on nontax revenues. Whereas suburbs still rely considerably more on nontax revenues than central cities, the change patterns indicate that suburbs decreased overall reliance, whereas central cities increased reliance on nontax revenues. This suburban decrease can generally be explained by the simultaneous increase in suburban reliance on tax revenues. It appears that as suburbs expand their boundaries, populations, and levels of service provision, their revenue structures must also expand to accommodate these service demands. When suburban growth and annexation rates (1950-70) are contrasted with similar figures for central cities, it becomes apparent that by necessity they have expanded reliance on tax revenues and decreased relative reliance on nontax revenues.

In summary, if these revenue reliance patterns continue, it appears that suburbs may be able to avoid going down the path of central cities, avoiding the markedly heavier reliance on external (particularly federal) and property tax revenue sources by trying to maintain more balanced revenue reliance patterns. However, if they cannot do so, for either economic or political reasons, the chances are fairly high that today's suburbs will be tomorrow's declining suburbs with fiscal conditions similar to those of their central city counterparts.

NOTES

1. Mordecai Feinberg, "The Implications of Core-City Decline for the Fiscal Structure of the Core City," National Tax Journal 17 (September 1964): 213-31.

2. Thomas F. Stinson, "Population Changes in Local Government Finance," Municipal Finance 42 (August 1969): 134-39.

3. John W. Jack and Paul C. Reuss, "Financing Municipal Government: Fiscal Challenge of the Seventies," Municipal Finance (February 1971): 141-48.

4. Ibid., p. 143.

5. Seymour Sacks and John Callahan, "Central City Suburban Fiscal Disparity," in Advisory Commission on Intergovernmental Relations, City Financial Emergencies (Washington, D.C.: Government Printing Office, 1973), pp. 91-152.

6. John Pazour, "Local Government Fiscal Conditions," in International City Management Association, The Municipal Yearbook 1972 (Chicago: ICMA, 1973), pp. 281-90.

7. Ibid., p. 282.

8. Feinberg, op. cit.

9. Jack and Reuss, op. cit.

10. Sacks and Callahan, op. cit., p. 126.

11. Robert B. Pettengill and Jogindar S. Uppal, Can Cities Survive? The Fiscal Plight of American Cities (New York: St. Martin's Press, 1974), p. 39.

12. Pettengill and Uppal, op. cit., p. 51.

13. Ibid., p. 41.

14. Thomas R. Dye and Susan A. MacManus, "Predicting City Government Structure," American Journal of Political Science 20 (May 1976): 257-71.

Chapter 4

Tax Burdens: How Much
Strain on the Personal
Incomes of Municipal Residents?

INTRODUCTION

Defining Tax Burden

Tax burden is defined in terms of the relationship between per capita tax revenue and per capita personal income. It is calculated by dividing per capita tax revenue by per capita personal income. Tax burden thus expresses the relationship between the average per capita personal income of all city residents and the average per capita tax revenue collected from both city and noncity residents.* It is a measure that enables a relative comparison of the "bite" of taxes collected locally in relation to the incomes of the residents of that city. It is also a good measure of fiscal strain in that higher tax burdens are closely related to greater use of other sources of revenue, particularly intergovernmental revenue, which is often one of the first signs of fiscal stress.

---

*This figure cannot, and should not, be interpreted to mean that each person in the city pays an equal percentage of his/her income in the form of municipal taxes. It also cannot be interpreted to mean that only city residents pay taxes. See Chapter 1 for an in-depth discussion of the limitations of tax burden as a comparative measure.

Why Compare Tax Burdens?

Besides being a valuable comparative measure to the researcher, tax burden data is of primary interest to politicians and citizens alike. First, tax burdens (efforts) are important components of the federal revenue sharing formulas[1] and, similarly, are often used in grant-in-aid distributional formulas as stimuli to local governments to adopt more progressive tax structures.

Second, a heavy tax burden at the local level serves to restrict levels of governmental service and/or hinder expansion of services. Candidates for public office in municipalities characterized by heavy tax burdens and minimum levels of service provision are often heard making conflicting campaign promises to increase services on the one hand but to hold the line on taxes on the other. This incongruity has the effect of frustrating both politicians trapped by the political necessity of such stances and the citizens who must bear the consequences of such promises.

From a different perspective, tax burdens are important criteria for making locational (residential) decisions. The Tiebout consumer-choice model of residential location indicates that when given the choice of moving, holding constant for occupational opportunities, a person will move to (or remain in) the community that offers the lowest tax burden.[2] This is particularly relevant to central cities whose representatives charge that the lighter tax burdens of the suburbs serve to encourage taxpayers capable of supporting the costs of central city operations to move to the suburbs. In other words, the central city/suburban tax burden differential stimulates the exodus of central city taxpayers and places a heavy financial strain on the central city budget. This exodus, in turn, necessitates higher taxes and further adds impetus to taxpayer exits from the already financially troubled central cities—a negative dynamic process.

For all of these reasons, the need for comparative studies of municipal tax burdens is great. In fact, Pettengill and Uppal in a recent study of the fiscal plight of American cities conclude that the "total amount per capita of the tax burden . . . is the crucial element in the fiscal distress of our cities."[3]

Framework of Analysis

The first part of the chapter describes and explains variations in the tax burdens (property and nonproperty) of central cities and suburbs, using regional, population size, economic base, governmental character, and functional responsibility classification schemes. By necessity the time frame within which the analysis is performed is a single time point—1972.*

The second half of the chapter examines the impact of various demographic, socioeconomic, and governmental conditions on central city and suburban tax burdens (property and nonproperty). The purpose of this analysis is to determine which of the demographic, socioeconomic, and governmental indicators are the best predictors of tax burden differentials among central cities and suburbs.

PREVIOUS RESEARCH

Weaknesses

To date there have been relatively few studies of a comparative nature analyzing variation in tax burdens of U.S. cities and suburbs. These studies have tended to suffer from one or more weaknesses.

First, attention has been focused exclusively on property tax burdens. However, recent studies of revenue trends in local government have indicated an increasing usage of nonproperty taxes to supplement the highly unpopular property tax as a source of revenue. [4] Local nonproperty taxes typically include local personal income taxes, local retail sales taxes, cigarette taxes, alcoholic beverage taxes, occupational license taxes, business taxes, and airport taxes.

A second weakness of previous tax burden research is related specifically to the definition of suburbs. The general tendency has been to define suburbs as all the area outside the central city but within the SMSA. This lumping together of all governmental units outside the central city and classifying them as suburbs represents a failure to recognize that there are differing types of suburbs; suburbs are not homogeneous in their demographic, socioeconomic, or governmental characteristics. Similarly, defining suburbs in this manner ignores the critical fact that suburban municipalities are governmental units with taxing, borrowing, and spending powers; they are separate policy-making units. In summary, to define suburbs in the traditional manner is to err in assuming that all suburbs within an SMSA are homogeneous units, all making fiscal decisions in an identical manner.

---

*The Census of the Population did not report per capita personal income figures by municipality until 1970. Thus, any longitudinal analysis of tax burdens is nearly impossible on a large scale.

A third weakness of the previous research on tax burdens is the general failure to compare central city and suburban tax burden differentials. The few studies that have compared cities and suburbs have analyzed such differentials within a single SMSA. This is a crucial weakness in view of the speculated importance of central city/ suburban tax burden differentials.

There are several plausible explanations for the lack of comparative research on this important fiscal policy area. Perhaps the greatest handicap thus far has been the failure to include per capita personal income figures by city in the U.S. Census data. (These figures were not reported until 1970.) This is especially critical in that per capita personal income figures are essential in the calculation of municipal tax burdens.

Part of the explanation for defining suburbs as all the area outside the central city within an SMSA again lies in the U.S. Census reported data. Data for smaller municipalities (under 50,000) is sparse, sporadic, and generally unobtainable on a large scale.

The general tendency to concentrate attention on the property tax segment of the total tax burden has several possible explanations. First, property taxes are the single most important source of local government revenue and, until recently, nonproperty taxes were utilized almost exclusively by larger cities. Second, and especially important in studies of city/suburban tax burden differentials within the framework of the Tiebout residential-choice model, attention has been focused on the property tax portion of the total tax burden because of the high probability that taxpayers contemplating leaving the central city will later become suburban homeowners.

Earlier Studies: Findings

Of the previous research conducted in the area of tax burdens, the most important study was by Woo Sik Kee.[5] Kee researched city/ suburban differentials in local government fiscal and tax effort. He was specifically interested in examining the great discrepancies between metropolitan central cities and their suburbs in the fiscal capacity to raise adequate revenue on the one hand and the need for public services on the other. His units of analysis were the 22 central cities and suburbs of the 1960 SMSAs with populations over one million. (Unfortunately, Kee defined suburbs as the entire SMSA outside the central city.) Kee found that city/suburban differences in local tax effort may be causally associated with four socioeconomic factors: per capita income, state grants-in-aid for noneducation purposes, employment/ resident ratios; and enrollment ratios. (It should also be noted here that Kee did not attempt to separate property from nonproperty tax effort.)

A study by Heywood Sanders added another dimension to the work of Kee by examining the linkage between governmental structural arrangements and tax effort as well as the linkage between socioeconomic characteristics and tax burdens.[6] Sanders linked governmental structural characteristics with local government revenue policies of 667 cities with populations over 25,000. His tax policy measure was tax effort, which he calculated by dividing the total tax revenue by aggregate personal income. His results indicated that tax effort in U.S. cities is higher in cities with a mayor-council form of government, partisan ballot, and a ward plan of council member selection. In his examination of the linkage between population (environmental) characteristics and tax policies, he found a positive relationship between ethnicity and social status. Then, controlling for ethnicity and social status, Sanders found that a relationship between governmental structure and tax effort still existed. (Sanders did not attempt to analyze city/suburban tax burden differentials.)

To summarize the results of previous municipal tax burden research, there has been relatively little comparative analysis of the tax burden structures of either cities or suburbs. Likewise, there have been virtually no analyses contrasting the tax burdens of cities and suburbs when suburbs are properly defined as distinctive individual governing units.

GENERAL TAX BURDEN PATTERNS

The image of the central city as a much heavier taxer than its surrounding suburban municipalities is confirmed as indicated by the figures in Table 4.1. In general, central city residents bear tax burdens that are nearly twice the tax burdens borne by their suburban neighbors. Central city residents pay 4.7 percent of their incomes to the city in the form of taxes, whereas suburban residents pay only 2.5 percent of their incomes to their suburban governments in the form of taxes. This two-to-one ratio applies to both property and nonproperty tax burdens, central city residents bearing both property and nonproperty tax burdens that are twice as heavy as those borne by suburban residents. Explanations commonly offered for the heavier tax burdens of central cities include: a wider range of service provision; greater expectations of and greater need for provision of poverty-related services (welfare, health, hospitals, housing and urban renewal); and emigration of capable central city taxpayers to the suburbs, resulting in a declining central city tax base and consequent higher tax burdens for remaining central city residents.

TABLE 4.1: Central City and Suburban Tax Burdens, 1972 (percent)

Tax Burden	Central City (n = 243)	Suburbs (n = 340)
Total	4.7	2.5
Property	3.5	1.8
Nonproperty	1.2	0.7

Note: Tax burden is the relationship between per capita tax revenue and per capita personal income. It is calculated by dividing per capita tax revenue (property, nonproperty) by per capita personal income.

Sources: U.S. Department of Commerce, Bureau of the Census, Census of the Population 1970; Census of Governments: 1972.

Tax Burden Patterns by Region

Central City Differences by Region

The results of a regional comparison of tax burdens (shown in Table 4.2) indicate that northeastern central cities have much heavier tax burdens (9.0 percent) than central cities located in any other region of the country. In fact, central cities located in the South, Midwest, and West do not differ dramatically in their total tax burdens, which range from 3.4 percent to 4.0 percent.

Several other interesting patterns emerge through this regional analysis of central city tax burdens. First, regional disparities in property tax burdens are greater than regional disparities in nonproperty tax burdens. However, the general regional pattern initially observed also applies to property tax burdens. Northeastern central cities are characterized by property tax burdens that are four times greater (8.1 percent) than those of central cities in other regions, property tax burdens being lightest among central cities located in the South (2.0 percent).

Second, central cities of the South, Midwest, and West not only have slightly greater nonproperty tax burdens than those of the Northeast, but, overall, they are more balanced in their tax burden structures. That is, cities outside the Northeast generally have more equal property and nonproperty tax burdens than northeastern central cities, which have much greater property tax burdens (8.1 percent) than nonproperty tax burdens (.9 percent).

TABLE 4.2: Tax Burdens for Central Cities and Suburbs, by Region, 1972
(percent)

Region	Total Tax Burden	Property Tax Burden	Tax Burden
Central cities			
Northeast (53)	9.0	8.1	0.9
South (87)	3.4	2.0	1.4
North Central (62)	3.4	2.4	1.0
West (41)	4.0	2.2	1.8
Suburbs			
Northeast (96)	4.8	4.4	0.4
South (50)	2.0	1.1	0.9
North central (109)	1.9	1.3	0.6
West (85)	2.0	1.0	1.0

Notes: Tax burden is the relationship between per capita tax revenue and per capita personal income. It is calculated by dividing per capita tax revenue (property, nonproperty) by per capita personal income. Figures in parentheses indicate number of municipalities.

Sources: U.S. Department of Commerce, Bureau of the Census, Census of the Population 1970; Census of Governments: 1972.

Suburban Differences by Region

Suburban tax burden patterns, when analyzed by region, are similar to those observed in central cities, although the regional disparity among suburbs is less. Northeastern suburbs have much heavier total tax burdens (4.8 percent) than suburbs located in other regions (ranging from 1.9 percent to 2.0 percent). Likewise, property tax burdens of northeastern suburbs are nearly four times heavier than property tax burdens of suburbs located in other regions. Suburbs of the northeastern and midwestern regions tend to be the least balanced in their tax burden structures; they are characterized by much heavier property than nonproperty tax burdens. Southern and western suburbs, on the other hand, have nearly equal property and nonproperty tax burdens. Possible explanations for this pattern relate to the more heterogeneous nature of suburbs located in the Northeast, a pattern that is strongly related to the age of the central cities they surround. Suburbs of the Northeast, then, strongly resemble central cities of the Northeast in their tax burden patterns.

Tax Burden Patterns by Population Size

Central City Differences by Population Size

As the figures in Table 4.3 indicate, tax burdens are positively related to population size. As the size of the city increases, tax burdens (both property and nonproperty) increase. The very largest cities (over one million) have total tax burdens (9.8 percent) that are nearly three times heavier than those of the smallest cities (3.6 percent). These figures indicate a pattern of an incremental relationship between population size and tax burdens of central cities.

When property and nonproperty tax burdens are examined independently by size categories, the results show a much greater relationship between size and nonproperty tax burdens than between size and property tax burdens. Nonproperty tax burdens of central cities over one million are five times greater than those of cities under 99,999. Property tax burdens, however, are only twice as heavy in the largest cities as in the smallest.

Another observable pattern that emerges when analyzing tax burdens by population size is that the largest cities, while having the heaviest total tax burdens, do have a greater balance in their tax burden structures, property and nonproperty tax burdens being nearly equal. Smaller cities, on the other hand, have property tax burdens that are nearly three times heavier than nonproperty tax burdens. Explanations for this difference in balance might include the fact that older, larger cities long characterized by the heaviest property tax burdens, have had to turn to nonproperty taxes for revenue more quickly and at a greater rate than have the smaller, younger cities, and have had more cooperative state legislatures that have enabled them to do so.

Suburban Differences by Population Size

The size/tax burden relationship observed in central cities is also evident in suburbs (see Table 4.3). Again, however, the differences among suburbs are not as marked as among central cities. The range of suburban total tax burdens is from 2.5 percent (below 25,000 population) to 3.5 percent (over 100,000 population), which is in sharp contrast to the range of total tax burdens among cities (3.6 percent in the smallest cities to 9.8 percent in the largest cities).

Aside from the general incremental relationship between size and tax burdens, suburban tax burden patterns when analyzed by population size, do differ from central city patterns. First, suburban municipalities differ most in property tax burdens and are more homogeneous in their nonproperty tax burdens (the reverse of the pat-

TABLE 4.3: Tax Burdens for Central Cities and Suburbs, by Population Size, 1972 (percent)

Population Size	Total Tax Burden	Property Tax Burden	Nonproperty Tax Burden
Central cities			
Over 1,000,000 (6)	9.8	5.2	4.6
500,000-999,999 (20)	5.6	3.7	1.9
250,000-499,999 (27)	5.5	3.8	1.7
100,000-249,999 (69)	5.6	4.5	1.1
50,000-99,999 (121)	3.6	2.7	0.9
Suburbs			
Over 100,000 (12)	3.5	2.6	0.9
50,000-99,999 (43)	2.5	1.7	0.8
25,000-49,999 (77)	3.4	2.8	0.6
Below 25,000 (208)	2.5	1.8	0.7

Notes: Tax burden is the relationship between per capita tax revenue and per capita personal income. It is calculated by dividing per capita tax revenue (property; nonproperty) by per capita personal income. Figures in parentheses indicate number of municipalities.

Sources: U.S. Department of Commerce, Bureau of the Census, Census of the Population 1970; Census of Governments: 1972.

tern observed in central cities). Second, suburban tax burden patterns differ from those of cities when an examination is made of the balance between property and nonproperty tax burdens. Whereas the largest-sized cities have nearly equal property and nonproperty tax burdens, the largest-sized suburbs are more imbalanced in their tax burdens, having nearly three times heavier property than nonproperty tax burdens. (Again, the absolute differential among suburbs is less than among central cities.) Possible explanations here might also be related to the age of the suburbs, but in the reverse direction of that observed for central cities. Larger, older suburbs traditionally have relied on property taxes as their major source of revenue, but when compared to central cities, they have not yet reached the point of major fiscal crisis and consequently have not had to rely as heavily on nonproperty taxes as central cities. Younger, smaller suburbs, being much more affected by the increasing unpopularity of the heavily regressive property tax, have turned to nonproperty tax sources much more quickly than have the older, larger suburbs.

TABLE 4.4: Tax Burdens for Central Cities and Suburbs, by Economic Base, 1972
(percent)

Economic Base	Total Tax Burden	Property Tax Burden	Nonproperty Tax Burden
Central cities			
Manufacturing (86)	5.9	4.7	1.2
Industrial (3)	3.0	2.9	0.1
Diversified manufacturing (60)	5.0	3.7	1.3
Diversified retailing (50)	3.9	2.7	1.2
Retailing (29)	3.3	2.0	1.3
Other (15)	2.2	1.3	0.9
Suburbs			
Manufacturing (87)	3.6	3.0	0.6
Industrial (12)	3.3	2.6	0.7
Diversified manufacturing (19)	3.6	2.9	0.7
Diversified retailing (41)	2.5	1.6	0.9
Retailing (61)	2.0	1.3	0.7
Other (24)	2.9	2.2	0.7

Notes: The first five economic-base types are the five basic economic types (collected on the basis of place of work). The Other category represents cities and suburbs with very specialized economic bases: wholesaling, mining, transportation, resort, government and armed forces, professional, hospital, education, or service. (Suburbs do not add to total due to missing data.) Tax burden is the relationship between per capita tax revenue and per capita personal income. It is calculated by dividing per capita tax revenue (property; nonproperty) by per capita personal income. Figures in parentheses indicate number of municipalities.

Sources: U.S. Department of Commerce, Bureau of the Census, Census of the Population 1970; Census of Governments: 1972.

Tax Burden Patterns by Economic Base

Central City Differences by Economic Base

Figures shown in Table 4.4 indicate that there is a relationship between the economic base of central cities and their total tax burdens.

Total tax burdens of the more complex economic-based cities are nearly three times heavier than tax burdens of the less complex economic-based cities. Residents of manufacturing-based cities bear total tax burdens of 5.9 percent, contrasted to the total tax burdens borne by residents of cities with the most specialized economic bases (2.2 percent).

Analysis of tax burdens by economic base highlights variations in property tax burdens but fails to do so for nonproperty tax burdens. In fact, there appears to be very little relationship between economic base and central city nonproperty tax burdens. One possible explanation for the relationship between economic base and property tax burden centers around the variation in assessment procedures and tax rates applied to different types of property within a city. As Robert Wood so accurately observed in his 1400 Governments, tax assessors in communities with a large industrial or commercial base (the more complex, less specialized bases) find this type of property to be a particularly productive source of revenue.[7] Relatedly, cities with a manufacturing or industrial base have proportionately less residential property, which means that the few residents must foot heavier proportions of the property tax burden.

Again, as in the regional and population size analyses of variation in central city tax burdens, there is a relationship between economic base and the tax burden balance of cities. The more complex economic-based cities have much heavier property than nonproperty tax burdens, whereas the less complex economic-based cities are characterized by nearly equal property and nonproperty tax burdens. This pattern might be explained by the tendency of less complex economic-based cities (cities that also tend to be the smaller, younger cities) to encourage industry to locate within their municipal boundaries by relying less on property taxes as sources of revenue and making up the difference by levying nonproperty taxes at rates nearly equal to property tax rates.

Suburban Differences by Economic Base

Analysis of suburban differences in tax burdens by economic base turns up identical patterns (though less marked) as those discovered in the examination of central city tax burdens. Manufacturing, industrial, and diversified manufacturing suburbs have heavier total tax burdens than do suburbs of other economic bases. Also, as in central cities, the relationship between economic base and property tax burdens is strong, but there appears to be virtually no relationship between economic base and nonproperty tax burdens. As Andrews and Dasso have hypothesized, "the evidence seems to show comparatively heavier tax burdens as the price that must be paid for continuing independence from the city of heavily developed suburban areas where property taxes are the main criterion of financial burden."[8]

The balance of property and nonproperty tax burdens is greater among the less complex, more specialized economic-based suburbs for the same reasons offered for a similar pattern in central cities.

Tax Burden Patterns by Governmental Character

Reform theory is premised on efficiency that is often translated in terms of tax burdens to mean light tax burdens. As Lineberry and Sharkansky state, "much of the rhetorical thunder in support of municipal reform (manager governments, nonpartisan elections, and at-large constituencies) claims that lower taxes . . . will follow their adoption."[9]

Central City Differences by Governmental Character

The results shown in Table 4.5 reveal that a clear relationship exists between governmental character and tax burdens of central cities. Unreformed cities have total tax burdens (7.8 percent) that are nearly twice as heavy as those of reformed cities (4.2 percent), with mixed cities falling between the two (4.6 percent). Interestingly, however, when property tax burdens are separated from nonproperty tax burdens, two different patterns emerge. First, property tax burdens are negatively associated with reformism. Second, nonproperty tax burdens are positively associated with reformism. This means that reformed cities characteristically have lighter property tax burdens but heavier nonproperty tax burdens than unreformed cities. This pattern is in keeping with the reform movement, a movement that has been interpreted as stressing the decreased reliance on property taxes for local governmental financing. This interpretation is further strengthened when the balance between property and nonproperty tax burdens is examined. Reformed cities are much more balanced (2.9 percent property tax burden, 1.3 percent nonproperty tax burden) than unreformed cities (7.1 percent property tax burden, 0.7 percent nonproperty tax burden).

Suburban Differences by Governmental Character

Suburban patterns of governmental character/tax burden relationships are nearly identical to those observed in central cities. The figures in Table 4.5 show that unreformed suburbs have heavier total tax burdens (3.6 percent) than reformed suburbs (2.4 percent), with mixed suburbs falling between the two types (2.9 percent). Similarly,

TABLE 4.5: Tax Burdens for Central Cities and Suburbs, by Governmental Character, 1972 (percent)

Governmental Character	Total Tax Burden	Property Tax Burden	Nonproperty Tax Burden
Central cities			
Unreformed (20)	7.8	7.1	0.7
Mixed (147)	4.6	3.3	1.3
Reformed (76)	4.2	2.9	1.3
Suburbs			
Unreformed (11)	3.6	2.7	0.9
Mixed (213)	2.9	2.3	0.6
Reformed (116)	2.4	1.4	1.0

Note: Reformed cities and suburbs are those with a council-manager form of government, nonpartisan elections, and at-large council member selection plans. Unreformed cities and suburbs are those with a mayor-council form of government, partisan elections, and a ward council member selection plan. Mixed cities and suburbs are those having at least one reformed characteristic and one unreformed characteristic. Tax burden is the relationship between per capita tax revenue and per capita personal income. It is calculated by dividing per capita tax revenue (property, nonproperty) by per capita personal income. Figures in parentheses indicate number of municipalities.

Sources: U.S. Department of Commerce, Bureau of the Census, Census of the Population 1970; Census of Governments: 1972.

governmental character is more closely related to property than nonproperty tax burden differentials. Reformed suburbs also have lighter property tax burdens but heavier nonproperty tax burdens than unreformed suburbs. Lastly, reformed suburbs, like reformed central cities, are more balanced in their property and nonproperty tax burdens. In summary, there appears to be conclusive evidence that the reform characteristics have produced similar results in both cities and suburbs located throughout the United States.

Tax Burden Patterns by Functional Responsibility

Central City Differences by Functional Responsibility

The findings reported in Table 4.6 suggest that of all the classificatory schemes utilized in studying tax burden differences in central

TABLE 4.6: Tax Burdens for Central Cities and Suburbs, by Functional Responsibility, 1972
(percent)

Functional Responsibilities	Total Tax Burden	Property Tax Burden	Nonproperty Tax Burden
Central cities			
Education (76)	8.3	6.9	1.4
No education (167)	3.1	1.9	1.2
Hospitals (78)	6.2	4.8	1.4
No hospitals (165)	4.0	2.9	1.1
Welfare (80)	7.7	6.2	1.5
No welfare (163)	3.2	2.1	1.1
Education, hospitals, welfare (33)	9.9	8.4	1.5
None of these functions (116)	3.0	1.9	1.1
Suburbs			
Education (49)	7.5	7.1	0.4
No education (291)	1.9	1.2	0.7
Hospitals (45)	5.8	5.1	0.7
No hospitals (295)	2.3	1.5	0.8
Welfare (89)	5.3	4.7	0.6
No welfare (251)	1.9	1.1	0.8
Housing and urban renewal (43)	3.8	3.0	0.8
No housing and urban renewal (297)	2.6	1.9	0.7
Education, hospitals, welfare, housing and urban renewal (4)	8.0	7.6	0.4
None of these functions (218)	1.7	1.0	0.7

Note: Tax burden is the relationship between per capita tax revenue and per capita personal income. It is calculated by dividing per capita tax revenue (property, nonproperty) by per capita personal income. A city is regarded as having functional responsibility for a service if it has primary financial responsibility for provision of the service. If it does not have primary financial responsibility, it is regarded as not having functional responsibility for that service. Figures in parentheses indicate number of municipalities.

Sources: U.S. Department of Commerce, Bureau of the Census, Census of the Population 1970; Census of Governments: 1972.

cities, classification by functional responsibility is superior. The most dramatic differences in tax burdens (total, property, and non-property) appear when cities performing all three least common municipal functions are compared with cities performing none of these functions. Total tax burdens of cities providing education, hospitals, and welfare for their residents are more than three times heavier (9.9 percent) than those borne by residents of cities having the responsibility for none of these costly functions (3.0 percent). When the specific least common functions are examined in relation to total tax burdens, it is found that education is the function that has the greatest impact of total tax burdens (followed by welfare, then hospitals). These figures seem to justify property owner claims of having to support the costs of education for the entire municipal population.

When an examination is made of the property tax burden differences by functional responsibility, the differences between cities with least common functional responsibilities and those without are much more striking. For example, property tax burdens in cities providing all three least common functions are nearly four and one-half times heavier than those in cities providing none of the least common functions. Again, the specific functional responsibility which is most related to heavier property tax burdens is education.

The relationship between nonproperty tax burdens and functional responsibility is much weaker. However, the relationship is still the same; nonproperty tax burdens are heavier in cities with responsibility for the least common functions than in cities not having such financial responsibilities.

Relatedly, the balance in property and nonproperty tax burdens is much greater in cities not responsible for education, welfare, and/or hospitals. This lends weight to property owner complaints of bearing an unequal portion of the costs of education, welfare, and hospitals in municipalities providing these services to their populaces.

Suburban Differences by Functional Responsibility

Differences in total tax burdens between suburbs with financial responsibility for least common functions (education, welfare, hospitals, housing and urban renewal) and those without are even greater than those between central cities with such functional responsibilities and those without. Residents of suburbs with financial responsibility for all four least common functions bear total tax burdens that are 4.7 times greater (8.0 percent) than those borne by residents of suburbs not providing any of these services (1.7 percent). Even more marked is the difference in property tax burdens between suburbs with heavy functional responsibilities and those without (7.6 times heavier in suburbs with heavy functional responsibilities). Similar to the pattern observed in central cities, education is the function that has the greatest impact on tax burdens. The suburban pattern does deviate from the central city pattern in that hospitals, rather than welfare, have the second greatest impact on tax burdens.

Another suburban difference in tax burden patterns, when contrasted with central city patterns, occurs in the relationship between nonproperty tax burdens and functional responsibilities. Although there is far less nonproperty tax burden disparity between suburbs with and without least common functional responsibilities, nonproperty tax burdens appear to be slightly higher in suburbs without these responsibilities (the reverse of the central city pattern).

Suburban municipalities in general have lighter nonproperty tax burdens than central cities. But, as pointed out in previous observations, suburbs do resemble central cities in their balance between property and nonproperty tax burdens. Suburbs without responsibility for education, welfare, hospitals, and/or housing and urban renewal are more balanced than suburbs with such functional responsibilities that have much heavier property than nonproperty tax burdens.

The results of analyzing tax burdens of cities and suburbs by functional responsibility confirm the theory that greater explanation of central city/suburban differences in tax burden structures is possible when municipalities are grouped according to whether they provide functions not usually provided by most other municipalities—functions that place a greater strain on their tax structures (and taxpayers) than is felt in municipalities without such financial obligations.

Summary

Through this comparison of means analysis, it has been found that tax burdens (property and nonproperty) are characteristically heavier in both central cities and suburbs located in the Northeast, with large populations, complex economic bases, unreformed governmental characters, and bearing financial responsibilities for education, welfare, hospitals, and/or housing and urban renewal. These same types of cities and suburbs also have much heavier property than nonproperty tax burdens.

The results also indicate that when property and nonproperty tax burdens are analyzed separately, there is much greater variation in property tax burdens than in nonproperty tax burdens. This pattern holds true not only for variations among central cities and suburbs but also between the two municipal types.

Suburban municipalities in general show less variation in their tax burdens (property and nonproperty) than do central cities. Similarly, suburban municipalities have more nearly equal property and nonproperty tax burdens than central cities, which generally have much heavier property than nonproperty tax burdens.

DETERMINANTS OF PROPERTY AND NONPROPERTY TAX BURDENS

The earlier tax burden determinant studies,[10] while limited, suggest that measures of social status (income, employment), ethnicity, population size, and governmental character will be significant determinants of city and suburban tax burdens.

Determinants of Property Tax Burdens

Central City Property Tax Burden Determinants

The results reported in Table 4.7 support many of the findings of the comparison of means analysis. Indeed, the significant determinants of central city property tax burdens include measures of region, population size, economic base, governmental character, and functional responsibility. The findings also strengthen those of Kee and Sanders in that measures of ethnicity and social status are among the significant determinants as well.

The heaviest property tax burdens are found among older, larger, more densely populated cities located in the Northeast, with declining populations, complex economic bases, unreformed governments, and more functional responsibilities due to greater proportions of ethnic minorities, aged persons, renters, noncollege-educated persons, and antiquated housing structures.

An interesting result of the analysis is that land area density turns out to be much more strongly related to property tax burdens than mere population size. Previous research has shown that land area density is strongly related to social pathologies and economic class measures (in a positive direction).[11] It will subsequently be shown that these measures are also related to heavier tax burdens, thus helping to explain the strong relationship between land area density and property tax burdens.

Mobility is another significant determinant of city property tax burdens. The results show that mobility measures are negatively related to central city property tax burdens, which lends credence to the argument that migration of capable central city taxpayers results in heavier tax burdens for remaining central city residents.

The proportion of aged persons in the city population is another significant determinant of property tax burdens. The elderly repre-

TABLE 4.7: Determinants of Property Tax Burdens of Central Cities and Suburbs

Variable	r	β	R^2
Central cities			
Ethnicity	.55	.38	.30
Least common functional responsibility	.49	.21	.42
Region	-.42	-.24	.46
Aged persons	.30	.22	.50
College graduates	-.14	.19	.53
Homeownership	-.48	-.13	.54
Economic base	-.24	-.14	.55
Housing antiquity	.32	-.10	.55
Population land area density	.43	.18	.56
Population size	.17	-.12	.56
Governmental character—reformism	-.21	.04	.56
Growth rate	-.14	.05	.57
Age of city	.39	.01	.57
Suburbs			
Least common functional responsibility	.55	.40	.30
Region	-.45	-.36	.37
Residential crowding	.12	.23	.41
Ethnicity	.15	.06	.42
Per capita personal income	-.12	-.05	.42
Governmental character—reformism	-.14	.06	.42
Centralization of central city	-.13	-.04	.43
Aged persons	.14	.03	.43
Mobility (different house)	-.18	-.01	.43
Housing antiquity	.19	.01	.43

Source: Compiled by the author.

sent a dependent segment of the population, a segment that is a heavy resource user.

The proportion of college graduates in a city is negatively associated with central city property tax burdens and understandably so. The greater the educational level of the populace, the less will be the need for the governing body to provide costly, poverty-related services such as health care, hospitals, welfare, or housing and urban renewal, which have the effect of increasing property tax burdens.

The relationship between percent foreign born (ethnicity) and property tax burden turns out to be significant, as predicted by Kee. The explanation for this pattern probably centers on the fact that ethnics come to central cities virtually unskilled and contribute to the demand for provision of poverty-related services.

The age of the city is another measure found to be a significant determinant of central city property tax burdens. The older central cities are those most characterized by outmigration of capable tax-payers and disproportionate numbers of ethnics, blacks, elderly, and poor—the nonrevenue producing, but high-service-using residents. The older central cities are also those that tend to provide the least common municipal functions (education, welfare, and hospitals) for their residents. The figures shown in Table 4.8 further highlight the important predictive power of the variable labeled least common functional responsibility. The functional responsibilities that most affect property tax burdens in a positive direction are education, welfare, housing and urban renewal, and health.

TABLE 4.8: Functional Responsibility Determinants of Property Tax Burdens of Central Cities and Suburbs

Variable	r	β	R^2
Central cities			
Education	.57	.40	.33
Welfare	.48	.16	.36
Housing and urban renewal	.29	.17	.39
Water	-.11	-.11	.40
Health	.23	.09	.41
Libraries	.22	.06	.41
Parks and recreation	.06	.02	.41
Sewerage	-.02	-.01	.41
Hospitals	.22	.01	.41
Highways	.06	.01	.41
Suburbs			
Welfare	.61	.35	.37
Hospitals	.47	.14	.42
Education	.27	.74	.44
Highways	.06	-.46	.47
Sanitation	.26	.26	.49
Fire	.09	-.47	.53
Libraries	.07	-.18	.55
Sewerage	.15	.15	.56
Parks and recreation	.26	.15	.56
Health	.36	.10	.57
Water	.10	.17	.57
Housing and urban renewal	-.00	.05	.57

Source: Compiled by the author.

In summary, poverty-related measures (demographic, socio-economic, and governmental) are the best predictors of property tax burdens among central cities.

Suburban Property Tax Burden Determinants

The best predictors of suburban property tax burdens are measures of functional responsibility, regional location, residential crowding, and ethnicity, which account for 41 percent of the variance. Additional significant predictors of suburban property tax burdens include measures of age, mobility, housing antiquity, income, governmental character, and central city domination of the SMSA (see Table 4.7).

Suburban property tax burdens are heaviest among suburbs located in the SMSAs not overly dominated by their central cities, usually in the Northeast, and characterized by unreformed governments, declining populations, greater proportions of elderly, ethnic minorities, and poorer persons, living in older, more crowded housing conditions. resulting in financial responsibilities for provision of the least common, most costly suburban functions.

It is very interesting to find that mobility is a significant determinant of suburban property tax burdens, in a negative direction. In other words, property tax burdens increase as population growth declines. This should serve as a warning to suburbs that population out-migration has the same impact on suburban tax burdens as it has on central city property tax burdens.

Other variables have similar impacts on suburban property tax burdens as on central city property tax burdens. Greater proportions of the aged, poor, and ethnic minorities, living in older, more crowded homes, increase suburban property tax burdens, as do the number of least common functions for which the suburb has primary financial responsibility.

The domination of the SMSA by its central city is another significant determinant of suburban property tax rates, but in a negative direction. This negative relationship between the domination of an SMSA by its central city and a suburb's property tax burden is understandable when it is considered that suburbs located outside of a large, dominating central city are much more likely to be exclusive than suburbs located outside a central city that does not so greatly dominate the SMSA. That is, citizens of the exclusive suburbs are likely to represent the economic elite, and consequently, such suburbs would not face the need for heavy property tax burdens because of the lesser service demands made by more affluent citizens (who generally prefer to utilize nonproperty or user-related revenues). This explanation will become even more plausible when the relationship between central city domination of the SMSA and suburban nonproperty tax burden is examined.

As the figures shown in Table 4.8 reveal, the functional responsibility determinants of suburban property tax burdens resemble those of central cities. In suburbs, education is the function that has the greatest impact on suburban property tax burdens. Welfare and hospitals are two other services that very significantly increase property tax burdens.

In summary, the results of this analysis of the impact of various demographic, socioeconomic, and governmental variables on suburban property tax burdens indicate that, as in central cities, poverty-related measures are the best predictors of suburban property tax burdens.

Determinants of Nonproperty Tax Burdens

Central City Nonproperty Tax Burden Determinants

Table 4.9 reports the results of the analysis of the determinants of central city nonproperty tax burdens. Nonproperty tax burdens are higher among older cities, located in the Midwest, with larger, more dense populations, more functional responsibilities, greater proportions of governmental employees, and characterized by segregated housing patterns and heavy concentrations of the aged and nonwhites.

One difference between determinants of property tax burdens and nonproperty tax burdens in central cities is the strength of population size as a predictor. Population size is a more powerful determinant of nonproperty tax burdens than land area density (the reverse is true of property tax burdens). The strength of population size as a determinant of nonproperty tax burden is understandable when it is recalled that nonproperty taxes (sales, alcoholic beverage, cigarette, business and occupational licenses) are taxes that are collected from individual sales, meaning that the larger the population, the larger the nonproperty tax burden is likely to be. The crowded condition of the population is not as significant a factor as the size of the population.

Relatedly, the significance of age of the city as a determinant of property tax burden can be explained by the fact that the oldest cities are usually the largest cities and can thus reap more from nonproperty taxes than smaller cities. Likewise, cities with greater proportions of government employees are likely to be larger cities— cities attracting numbers of nonresidents (for business or pleasure purposes), which, of course, stimulates collection of sales, liquor, cigarette, and business-type taxes.

TABLE 4.9: Determinants of Nonproperty Tax Burdens of Central Cities and Suburbs

Variable	r	β	R^2
Central cities			
Population size	.48	.35	.23
Race (nonwhites)	.35	.22	.29
Region	.14	.23	.32
Aged persons	.22	.13	.35
Total functional responsibility	.18	.16	.36
Residential segregation	.31	.13	.37
Age of city	.30	-.12	.37
Land area density	.35	.10	.37
Government employment	.03	.01	.37
Suburbs			
Mortality ratio	.51	.50	.26
Governmental character—reformism	.11	.13	.27
Region	-.12	-.06	.27
Homeownership	-.27	-.06	.27
Residential crowding	-.29	-.05	.27
Total functional responsibility	.29	-.01	.27

Source: Compiled by the author.

Another interesting result of this analysis is that age, race, and social pathology measures are better determinants of nonproperty tax burdens than are education, class, or ethnicity measures, although these measures are certainly interrelated. Usually cities with heavy proportions of elderly persons and nonwhites are the most financially distressed, meaning that their property tax base is narrow, which necessitates heavy usage of nonproperty taxes to supplement property taxes.

The results shown in Table 4.10 reveal that the specific services that are the best determinants of central city nonproperty tax burdens are sewerage and housing and urban renewal. These services tend to stimulate assessment of nonproperty taxes, namely, business taxes and occupational license taxes, due to the heavy capital improvement costs and related business construction opportunities involved in each. However, it should be noted that the specific functional responsibilities of central cities account for very little of the difference in central city nonproperty tax burdens.

In general, demographic and governmental characteristics (population size, age of city, regional location, government employment, and total functional responsibilities) are the better determinants of central city nonproperty tax burdens.

Suburban Nonproperty Tax Burden Determinants

The figures in Table 4.9 show that the most significant determinants of suburban nonproperty tax burdens are regional location, governmental character, functional responsibility, homeownership, residential crowding, and mortality ratios.

Suburbs with fewer functional responsibilities, reformed governments, usually located in the South, and characterized by proportionately fewer homeowners, less residential crowding, and higher mor-

TABLE 4.10: Functional Responsibility Determinants of Nonproperty Tax Burdens of Central Cities and Suburbs

Variable	r	β	R^2
Central cities			
Housing and urban renewal	.14	.13	.02
Sewerage	.13	.15	.04
Welfare	.12	.13	.05
Water	.10	.08	.06
Sanitation	-.00	-.09	.06
Libraries	.07	.04	.06
Health	.02	-.03	.06
Hospitals	.08	.03	.06
Highways	.06	.02	.06
Education	.09	-.02	.06
Suburbs			
Education	.69	.50	.47
Police	.64	1.04	.57
Highways	.35	-.60	.74
Parks and recreation	-.10	-.21	.83
Welfare	-.06	-.09	.85
Health	-.06	-.09	.86
Sanitation	-.09	-.10	.86
Sewerage	.32	-.12	.87
Hospitals	-.03	-.04	.87
Housing and urban renewal	.41	.05	.87
Fire	.66	.08	.87
Water	.39	-.03	.87

Source: Compiled by the author.

tality rates, have heavier nonproperty tax burdens than other suburbs. In other words, satellite suburbs (more business-dominated) rather than bedroom suburbs (more heavily residential) have higher nonproperty tax burdens.

The significance of residential crowding as a determinant of suburban nonproperty tax burdens (a negative determinant) is easily explainable. Residential crowding in a suburban setting indicates the existence of a familistic life style—a style that is less likely to contribute heavily to nonproperty tax revenues, since the community is probably more residential than commercial in nature.

The negative impact of homeownership on suburban nonproperty tax burdens is also explainable by the nature of the suburb. A greater proportion of homeowners would be characteristic of a bedroom suburb rather than a satellite suburb. The negative impact of homeownership is also congruent with theories of suburban service demands. Suburban dwellers, particularly in bedroom communities, are less demanding and, more important, less in need of poverty-related services such as welfare, housing and urban renewal, and so on. Suburban governments then can concentrate more heavily on efficiency-type services (services with payments in direct proportion to services used) rather than equity-type services (services provided on the basis of need). Nonproperty taxes, then, are not likely to be as lucrative a revenue source as are nontax revenues (special assessments, charges) in bedroom suburbs.

An explanation for the particularly strong predictive powers of mortality ratios is also related to the residential-commercial mix of the suburb. Many retirement-type suburbs (usually located in the South or West) with higher mortality ratios, are self-contained communities with both residential and commercial properties. These communities are more likely to minimize property tax burdens and rely more heavily on nonproperty taxes for revenue (sales, alcoholic beverage, and cigarette taxes).

The positive impact of reformism on suburban nonproperty tax burdens demonstrates the influence of the reform call for de-emphasis of the property tax as a source of municipal revenue. Reformed governments (council-manager governments) are also more characteristic of satellite suburbs than of bedroom suburbs.

As the results shown in Table 4.10 reveal, specific functional responsibilities are extremely important in predicting suburban nonproperty tax burdens. Education, police, fire, parks and recreation, and welfare responsibilities account for 86 percent of the variance in suburban nonproperty tax burdens. Education and police responsibilities have a positive impact on nonproperty tax burdens, whereas highways, parks and recreation, and welfare have a negative impact. The explanation for the varying impacts of these services centers around economies of scale in service provision, the lack of which necessitates greater tax effort. To begin with, suburbs are characterized by more equal property and nonproperty tax burdens than central cities; therefore nonproperty tax burdens must be heavier to support the costs of expensive services such as education. In addition, police protection, in particular, is a municipal service that suffers from diseconomies of scale, thereby explaining the positive impact of police responsibility on nonproperty tax burdens. Other services that also suffer from diseconomies of scale are highways, fire, sewerage, housing and urban renewal, and libraries. [12]

In summary, determinants of suburban nonproperty tax burdens are generally measures that are related to the demographic and socioeconomic make-up of the suburb. Suburbs of a more nonresidential nature are characterized by higher nonproperty tax burdens.

SIGNIFICANCE OF THE FINDINGS

Tax burdens are characteristically heaviest among cities located in the Northeast, with large populations, complex economic bases, unreformed governmental characters, and bearing heavy financial responsibility for education, welfare, and hospitals. These densely populated areas, with high concentrations of aged, nonwhite, foreign born, and economically disadvantaged persons and greater incidences of social pathology (greater public assistance, crime, fertility, and poverty rates as well as more female-headed households, greater income inequalities, and older, more run-down housing) are also characterized as having the heaviest service demands placed upon them by their constituents.

In attempting to explain central city/suburban tax burden differences, it is necessary to recall that a major suburban advantage thus far has been the ability to exclude undesirable residents (nonwhites, ethnics, aged, poor) through zoning regulations, rental and real estate transactions, and so on. The result of these exclusionary practices on the part of suburbs is the continued concentration within central cities of socioeconomic groups that impose heavy service demands, yet are incapable of supporting the costs of these services. As Sacks and Callahan found in their study, "It is the very 'sorting out' of different types of population groups that is one of the initial and continuing factors in the existence of fiscal disparities."[13]

While demographic and socioeconomic measures are extremely important in accounting for central city/suburban tax burden disparities, results of this analysis have indicated that functional responsibility measures are extremely important in accounting for tax burden variations among central cities and suburbs, respectively. It is critical to analyze not only the total functions performed, but the specific types of functions performed, particularly the least common, most costly functions in the case of property tax burdens. For example, it is the pattern of service provision that largely explains the severe fiscal crises of cities like New York and Detroit—cities that are financially responsible for providing education, welfare, hospitals, and housing and urban renewal services to their residents, services generally provided by other governmental units such as counties or states. The less financially troubled cities and suburbs should continue to let those other governmental units provide such services.

NOTES

1. See Richard P. Nathan, Allen D. Manvel, and Susannah E. Calkins, Monitoring Revenue Sharing (Washington, D.C.: The Brookings Institution, 1975).

2. Charles M. Tiebout, "A Pure Theory of Local Expenditures," Journal of Political Economy 64 (October 1956): 416-24.

3. Robert B. Pettengill and Jogindar S. Uppal, Can Cities Survive? The Fiscal Plight of American Cities (New York: St. Martin's Press, 1974), p. 75.

4. See Alan K. Campbell and Seymour Sacks, Metropolitan America: Fiscal Patterns and Governmental Systems (New York: The Free Press, 1967); Seymour Sacks and John Callahan, "Central City-Suburban Fiscal Disparity," in Advisory Commission on Intergovernmental Relations, City Financial Emergencies: The Intergovernmental Dimension (Washington, D.C.: U.S. Government Printing Office, 1973); and Pettengill and Uppal, op. cit.

5. Woo Sik Kee, "City-Suburban Differentials in Local Government Fiscal Effort," National Tax Journal 21 (June 1968): 183-89.

6. Heywood T. Sanders, "Policies, Populations, and Governmental Structures," The Municipal Yearbook 1972 (Chicago: ICMA, 1973).

7. Robert C. Wood, 1400 Governments (Cambridge, Mass.: Harvard University Press, 1961).

8. R. B. Andrews and Jerome J. Dasso, "The Influence of Annexation on Property Tax Burdens," National Tax Journal 14 (March 1961): 96.

9. Robert L. Lineberry and Ira Sharkansky, Urban Politics and Public Policy, 2nd ed. (New York: Harper & Row, 1974), p. 207.

10. Kee, op. cit.; Sanders, op. cit.

11. Thomas R. Dye, "Population Density and Social Pathology," Urban Affairs Quarterly 11 (December 1975): 265-75.

12. See Werner Z. Hirsch, The Economics of State and Local Government (New York: McGraw-Hill, 1970), pp. 176-97; Harvey Shapiro, "Economies of Scale and Local Government Finance," Land Economics 39 (May 1963): 135-86; and Robert E. Will, "Scalar Economics and Urban Service Requirements," Yale Economic Essays 5 (Spring 1965): 1-62.

13. Sacks and Callahan, op. cit., p. 92.

Chapter 5

Effective Property Tax Rates:
Comparable Measures of Property
Tax Rates Across Communities

INTRODUCTION

Weaknesses of Nominal Property
Tax Rate Measures

Until recently, comparisons of property tax rates across communities were somewhat futile because the only available rates to be compared were nominal rates. Nominal rates are statutory rates, usually set by the state legislature, which are expressed in terms of mills (one-tenth of one cent). According to the U.S. Bureau of the Census, "one cannot use [compare] the nominal property tax rate because the wide variation in assessment ratios across communities implies that the actual rate at which communities tax property is not likely to bear a systematic relationship to the nominal rate."[1] For example, even though two cities may have identical property tax (millage) rates, they may differ tremendously in their levels of assessment. One community may assess property at 100 percent of its market value, whereas the other community may assess property at only 50 percent of its value. In other words, communities differ in their levels of assessment (the proportion of the total value of the property that is assessed for tax purposes). To complicate the situation even further, the assessment procedures may vary within the same municipality. There are numerous accounts of incidences in which the property owned by certain powerful people in the community is assessed quite differently (usually lower) than similar property owned by the average citizen. At any rate, for these reasons, nominal rates are not comparable across communities.

122

Advantages of Effective Property
Tax Rate Measures

To overcome the inadequacies and inaccuracies of the nominal tax rate as a comparative measure, the Bureau of the Census began in 1967* to use a measure known as the effective property tax rate, which is defined as "the relationship derived by dividing total tax billed by sales price of the property."[2] Thus, in calculating an effective property tax rate, "the tax bill is related to what the property would be worth in the market (as indicated by the sales price), rather than to what the property is worth in terms of prevailing level of assessment. Effective rates usually lie substantially below nominal rates because the market values which condition effective rates usually are substantially above assessed values."[3] Effective property tax rates, unlike nominal rates, are comparable across communities.

Types of Property Examined

This chapter focuses on the mean effective property tax rate for all types of real property and on the median effective property tax rate for fully taxable single-family property.[†] Real property is defined as "land plus anything permanently attached to the land, appurtenant to the land, or immovable by law."[5] Residential (nonfarm) single-family property includes "all types of single-family houses not on farms, including detached houses; single-family parts of semi-detached and row or town houses if separately assessed; rural and suburban estates and residences not primarily used for farming; and single family units of a condominium."[6]

The analysis concentrates on fully taxable single-family property instead of "all single-family" or "partially exempt-single-family" property because previous research has indicated that owners of fully taxable single-family dwellings are not only the most "taxed" of all community residents, but are also the most vociferous in their resistance to increased property tax rates. In the ACIR study of public opinion toward taxes, the findings showed that homeowners, much

---

*Effective property tax rate data were collected for cities of 100,000 population and above in 1967. There are also limitations with the 1972 data which were collected for municipalities over 50,000. Thus, the suburban data is size-biased, unavoidably, toward the largest suburbs.

†The median is defined as "the value in an array above and below which lie an equal number of values."[4]

more than renters, were hostile to the property tax and regarded it as the most unfair of all the taxes levied by different levels of government.[7]

Framework of Analysis

Central city and suburban effective property tax rates (for all types of real property and for fully taxable single-family residential property) will be compared by region, population size, economic base, governmental character, and functional responsibility. Then an analysis will be made of the impacts of various demographic, socioeconomic, and governmental conditions on both types of effective property tax rates, for central cities and suburban municipalities.

The results of this analysis will be interesting especially in view of the fact that previous research has indicated that municipalities that increase their property tax rates and/or currently have relatively high tax rates are likely to be experiencing fiscal strain. (Witness New York City, which already has one of the highest effective property tax rates in the country.) "Any city would be reluctant to increase their property tax rates unless it is absolutely necessary. Such increases would tend to accelerate the flow of population and economic activity to locations beyond the city boundaries."[8] Mieszkowski reached a similar conclusion: "Unless increases in property tax rates in a particular city are accompanied by improvements in the quality of public services, residents will have an incentive to move, the size and quality of the housing stock will deteriorate, and the location of industrial activities in high tax jurisdictions will be discouraged."[9]

Besides the economic ramifications of high effective property tax rates, there are also political costs to recommending further increases. The cities that are currently under fiscal pressure and that have higher effective property tax rates than other municipalities cannot realistically consider raising such tax rates to relieve these pressures, if the governmental officials who make such decisions want to remain in office.

PREVIOUS RESEARCH

Several studies have examined the variance in the effective property tax rate but most have looked only at variance in the effective property tax rate within a single city or a single SMSA. These studies, while limited, can provide clues as to what determines variation in effective property tax rates. Most of them have found a relationship between population characteristics, housing characteristics, and effective property tax rates within a municipality or SMSA.

An excellent study of effective property tax rate variation within a single city was conducted in the city of Boston by David Black.[10] Black looked at 18,000 individual residential property transactions, as well as the existing population and housing characteristics in Boston in 1950 and 1960. He found that four variables (median family income, percent population nonwhite, percent deteriorated and dilapidated housing, and mean value of owner-occupied property) could explain 61 percent of the variance in the effective property tax rate within Boston. His results indicated that assessment ratios were negatively related to family income, but positively related to racial composition, density of low-quality housing, and value of owner-occupied property. In other words, he found that the lowest effective property tax rates tend to prevail in the better sections of the city (predominantly single-family-property neighborhoods that have relatively high property values and family incomes, show little or no evidence of physical deterioration, and are inhabited by whites). Highest effective rates, on the other hand, tend to be levied against properties in slums and ghetto areas.

Peterson and Solomon came to similar conclusions in their study:

> There is mounting evidence that local assessments are carried out in such a way that low-income properties are assessed at a substantially greater proportion of true market value than high income properties. This means that within the same city, poor homeowners often are saddled with higher effective property tax rates than homeowners who are better off.[11]

In a broader study, Morris Beck compared the effective property tax rates of 279 taxing districts in the northeastern New Jersey metropolitan area.[12] He chose to study variation in the state of New Jersey because of its relatively heavy reliance on local property taxes. Beck initially used nine independent variables (density, full value of real property per square mile, median family income, all taxable property per capita, all real property per capita, business real property per capita, municipal expenditures per capita, and school expenditures per capita) to attempt to explain variation in effective property tax rates. However, the results of his multivariate regressional analysis indicated that the strongest determinants of effective property tax rates within that SMSA were density, the variety and quality of local services, size and composition of the tax base, and the availability of nonproperty revenues from state and local sources. Perhaps Beck's most significant finding was that "density of real property, although far less powerful than population density as a predictor variable, proves to be a more significant determinant of tax rates than the per capita value of taxable property—often cited as the key to variation in tax rates."[13]

In summary, these earlier studies suggest that demographic (population size, density, land use) and socioeconomic (income, housing) measures are the most significant determinants of effective property tax rates within and among municipalities. The sole governmental variable that is suggested as being a significant determinant is that of functional responsibilities—the number and type of services financed by a municipality.

GENERAL EFFECTIVE PROPERTY
TAX RATE PATTERNS

Caution must be taken in comparing central city and suburban effective property tax rates. The suburban figures represent only the very largest suburbs since the Census Bureau did not collect such data for cities under 50,000 in 1972. Thus, it should be kept in mind that the suburban figures are size-biased (toward the largest suburbs) and, in comparison with central cities, are much more homogeneous in their make-up (although the largest suburbs are the most heterogeneous of all suburbs).

The figures shown in Table 5.1 generally indicate that among central cities, effective property tax rates are higher for fully taxable single-family property than for all types of real property. This highlights one of the oft-cited problems of core cities—very high tax rates on residential property that in turn stimulate more affluent central city taxpayers to move to the suburbs.

The results are very different in suburbs. The effective tax rates are higher for all types of real property than for single-family residential property. This finding suggests that suburban governmental officials are well aware of the political costs of high property tax rates on residential property, particularly in the light of the motive prompting many suburbanites to move to the suburbs in the first place.

By examining the effective property tax rates for the first quartile* and the third quartile, it is possible to get a feel for the progressivity of the tax structure. In other words, if the tax rate is relatively higher for the more valuable property (third quartile) than for the less

---

*The U.S. Bureau of the Census defines a quartile as "the value which identifies the boundary between two consecutive intervals in a frequency distribution of four intervals, each containing one-quarter of the total array."[14]

TABLE 5.1: Effective Property Tax Rates: All Central Cities and Suburbs, 1972

Type of Property	Central Cities	Suburbs
All types of real property	2.12	2.33
Fully taxable single-family dwellings		
First quartile	1.68	1.71
Median	2.24	2.16
Third quartile	2.38	2.06

Note: Effective property tax rate is the relationship derived by dividing total tax billed by the sales price of the property. It is the ratio of sales price to tax bill of a piece of property. The data were available only for cities with populations over 50,000. Therefore the data for suburbs represents only 44 (13 percent) of the suburbs in the study and cannot be interpreted as representative of suburban municipalities in general.

Source: Calculated from U.S. Department of Commerce, Bureau of the Census, Census of Governments: 1972, vol. 2 (Washington, D.C.: Government Printing Office), pt. 2, Table 12.

valuable property (first quartile), then the effective property tax rate can be said to be progressive (based on ability to pay). If, on the other hand, the effective tax rate for lower-valued property is nearly equal to or greater than the tax rate for the higher-valued property, then the tax structure can be said to be regressive.

Comparing the effective property tax rates for the first and third quartiles, it can be observed that the tax rate structures of central cities are more progressive, or more equitable, than those of the suburbs. Among suburbs, there is less difference between tax rates for lower-valued property and higher-valued property, thus making their tax structures more regressive than those of the central cities. This is consistent with the efficiency goal of most suburban governments.

Effective Property Tax Rates by Region

The initial analysis by the Census of Governments: 1972 indicated that a relationship existed between effective property tax rates and regional location.[15] The findings of this study, reported in Table 5.2, confirm those made by the Census of Government study.

TABLE 5.2: Effective Property Tax Rates for Central Cities and Suburbs, by Region, 1972

		Types of Property		
		Fully Taxable Single-Family Dwellings		
	All Types of Real Property	First Quartile	Median	Third Quartile
Region				
Central cities				
Northeast (44)	3.26	2.32	3.66	3.46
South (72)	1.35	1.14	1.46	1.64
North Central (54)	2.37	2.01	2.38	2.79
West (37)	1.91	1.47	1.88	1.92
Suburbs				
Northeast (6)	3.25	1.97	3.27	2.67
South (20)	1.20	1.10	1.20	1.30
North Central (20)	2.23	1.88	2.22	2.40
West (46)	2.24	1.47	1.79	1.50

Note: Effective property tax rate is the relationship derived by dividing total tax billed by the sales price of the property. It is the ratio of sales price to tax bill of a piece of property. Figures in parentheses indicate number of municipalities. The data were available only for cities with population over 50,000. Therefore the data for suburbs represent only 44 (13 percent) of the suburbs in the study and cannot be interpreted as representative of suburban municipalities in general. Central city figures do not add to 243 due to missing data, most of which is for cities in the 50,000–99,999 category.

Source: Calculated from U.S. Department of Commerce, Bureau of the Census, Census of Governments: 1972, vol. 2 (Washington, D.C.: Government Printing Office), pt. 2, Table 12.

Central City Differences by Region

Effective property tax rates for all types of property are highest among central cities located in the northeastern and midwestern regions and are lowest among southern and western central cities. This finding is consistent with prevailing notions that fiscal strain is greatest among cities located in the Northeast—the older, more poverty-stricken cities, with more functional responsibilities. A high effective property tax rate (one of the signs of fiscal strain) is both a cause and an effect of the outmigration of more affluent central city residents. For example, the median effective property tax rate for fully taxable single-family property is 2.5 times higher in northeastern central cities than in southern central cities.

There is also a regional pattern in the progressivity of the tax structure. Tax structures in the Northeast and Midwest are much more progressive than those in the South and West. These governments by necessity must be more responsive to the vast income differentials of their residents by constructing more progressive tax structures. Among cities in the Northeast and Midwest, the effective tax rate for the third quartile is 1.2 times greater than that for the first quartile. In contrast, in southern central cities, the difference between effective tax rates for the first and third quartiles is minimal (.50).

The relatively low effective tax rates for all types of property have prompted not only residents, but businesses and industries as well, to migrate to the South and West at the expense of cities in the Northeast and Midwest. The result is an even greater increase in the effective property tax rates within those suffering cities—a devastating, never-ending cycle.

Suburban Differences by Region

Suburban effective property tax rates show regional variations similar to those of central cities, particularly rates for all types of real property. Northeastern suburbs are characterized by effective property tax rates that are almost three times higher than those of southern suburbs. However, western suburbs, unlike western central cities, do not resemble southern suburbs, but are more like midwestern suburbs in their effective property tax rates.

Looking at the median effective tax rates for fully taxable single-family property, it appears that northeastern suburbs (like northeastern cities) have much higher residential property taxes (2.8 times higher) than southern suburbs. Relatedly, tax structures are much more progressive in northeastern and midwestern suburbs.

In summary, tax rate structures of central cities and suburbs show similar regional variations, thereby suggesting that perhaps it is not regional location so much as other demographic and socioeconomic factors that explain variation in central city and suburban effective property tax rates.

Effective Property Tax Rates
by Population Size

The relationship between population size and effective property tax rates does not appear to be as strong as might have been expected (see Table 5.3).

TABLE 5.3: Effective Property Tax Rates for Central Cities and Suburbs, by Population Size, 1972

| | | Types of Property | | |
| Population Size | All Types of Real Property | Fully Taxable Single-Family Dwellings | | |
		First Quartile	Median	Third Quartile
Central cities				
Over 1,000,000 (6)	2.15	1.80	2.15	2.52
500,000-999,999 (18)	2.11	1.76	2.19	2.51
250,000-499,999 (27)	2.15	1.79	2.09	2.57
100,000-249,999 (65)	2.17	1.87	2.27	2.71
Below 100,000 (91)	2.08	1.48	2.29	2.05
Suburbs				
Over 100,000 (8)	2.21	1.71	2.16	2.06
50,000-99,999 (36)	2.35	1.77	2.11	2.11

Note: Effective property tax rate is the relationship derived by dividing total tax billed by the sales price of the property. It is the ratio of sales price to tax bill of a piece of property. Figures in parentheses indicate number of municipalities. The data were available only for cities with populations over 50,000. Therefore the data for suburbs represents only 44 (13 percent) of the suburbs in the study and cannot be interpreted as representative of suburban municipalities in general. Central city figures do not add to 243 due to missing data, most of which is for cities in the 50,000-99,999 category.

Source: Calculated from U.S. Department of Commerce, Bureau of the Census, Census of Governments: 1972, vol. 2 (Washington, D.C.: Government Printing Office), pt. 2, Table 12.

Central City Differences by Population Size

Table 5.3 shows that effective property tax rates for all types of real property actually differ little across population size categories. The clearest distinction is between cities with populations over 100,000 and those with populations below 100,000; the larger cities have higher effective property tax rates.

A slightly different pattern emerges when effective property tax rates for single-family property are compared. Tax rates for cities with populations below 250,000 are higher than tax rates for cities with larger populations (although the lowest rates are found in

cities with populations of 250,000–499,999). Part of the explanation
for higher tax rates on single-family property, coupled with lower-tax
rates on all types of real property in the smaller central cities, may
very well be related to the growth policies of these smaller cities.
Smaller, growing cities tend consciously to formulate tax structures
characterized by lower tax rates for commercial property in an effort
to entice such development into city limits.

Suburban Differences by Population Size

The figures shown in Table 5.3 indicate that smaller suburbs
(like smaller central cities) have higher effective property tax rates
for all types of real property and for the first and third quartiles of
fully taxable single-family residential property than larger suburbs.
One possible explanation for this pattern was suggested by Oldman
and Aaron. They found that the more a government relies on nonproperty taxes, the lower need be its property tax rate.[16] Among suburbs,
it has already been observed that the larger suburbs rely more on
nonproperty taxes than the smaller ones, thus explaining the lower
property tax rates among the larger suburbs.

Effective Property Tax Rates
by Economic Base

Effective property tax rates differ significantly by economic
base, as can be seen by the figures shown in Table 5.4. Generally,
the more diversified economic-based cities have higher effective property tax rates than municipalities with more specialized economic
bases (with the exception of suburban rates for single-family residential property).

Central City Differences by Economic Base

Cities with more complex economic bases (manufacturing, industrial, diversified manufacturing) have higher effective property
tax rates for all types of real property than cities with less complex,
more specialized economic bases (retailing, diversified retailing,
other). However, when the effective property tax rates for fully taxable single-family property are analyzed, industrial-based cities drop
out of the group of cities characterized by the heaviest tax rates. The
assumption that can be made here is that industrial-based central
cities have much higher effective tax rates for land and improvements
on it (industrial property) than for single-family dwelling property (of
which there is probably very little). Thus, it is the cities with manu-

TABLE 5.4: Effective Property Tax Rates for Central Cities and Suburbs, by Economic Base, 1972

		Types of Property		
		Fully Taxable Single-Family Dwellings		
	All Types of Real Property	First Quartile	Median	Third Quartile
Economic Base				
Central cities				
Manufacturing (72)	2.51	1.89	2.81	2.68
Industrial (2)	2.75	1.35	1.60	1.75
Diversified manufacturing (57)	2.08	1.78	2.11	2.59
Diversified retailing (41)	1.74	1.51	1.83	2.11
Retailing (22)				
Other (13)	1.75	1.09	1.56	1.49
Suburbs				
Manufacturing (15)	2.39	1.53	2.11	1.84
Industrial (1)	2.10	—	—	—
Diversified manufacturing (3)	2.60	0.90	2.00	1.27
Diversified retailing (7)	2.44	2.13	2.49	2.83
Retailing (12)	2.23	1.93	2.30	2.11
Other (2)	1.50	1.35	1.50	1.65

Note: Effective property tax rate is the relationship derived by dividing total tax billed by the sales price of the property. It is the ratio of sales price to tax bill of a piece of property. Figures in parentheses indicate number of municipalities. The effective property tax rate data were available only for cities with populations over 50,000. Therefore the data for suburbs represent only 44 (13 percent) of the suburbs in the study and cannot be interpreted as representative of suburban municipalities in general. Central city figures do not add to 243 due to missing data, most of which is for cities in the 50,000-99,999 category. The first five economic base types are the five basic economic types (collected on the basis of place of work). The Other category represents cities with very specialized economic bases: wholesaling, mining, transportation, resort, government and armed forces, professional, hospital, education, or science.

Sources: International City Management Association, The Municipal Yearbook 1963, 1957 (Chicago: ICMA, 1963, 1957) (the economic base classification data have not been reported since 1963); calculated from U.S. Department of Commerce, Bureau of the Census, Census of Governments: 1972, vol. 2 (Washington, D.C.: Government Printing Office), pt. 2, Table 12.

facturing and diversified manufacturing economic bases that are characterized by the highest effective property tax rates, and also the most progressive property tax rate structures.

Suburban Differences by Economic Base

Generally, suburbs with more complex economic bases have higher effective property tax rates for all types of property than the more specialized economic-based suburbs. However, diversified-retailing- and retailing-based suburbs do have higher effective property tax rates for single-family dwellings than suburbs with other economic bases. One possible explanation for this is that these two types of suburbs usually provide services, such as education, hospitals, and housing and urban renewal, that are not provided by other economic-based suburbs. Black found in his study that "rate variation among different tax jurisdictions is highly correlated with variation in the quality and quantity of locally financed public services. Thus, in a Tiebout-like world, these rates represent public service prices paid by residents at different locations."[17]

Effective Property Tax Rates
by Governmental Character

Central City and Suburban Differences

Effective property tax rates show a strong relationship to governmental character in both central cities and suburbs, as indicated in Table 5.5. Unreformed municipalities (cities and suburbs) are characterized by the highest effective tax rates, both for all types of real property and for single-family residential property. Reformed municipalities, on the other hand, have the lowest such rates; mixed governments fall between the two. These findings further substantiate reformer claims of lower taxes with council-manager governments, nonpartisan elections, and at-large plans of council-member selection.

Effective Property Tax Rates
by Functional Responsibility

David Black's discovery of a correlation between quantity of locally financed public services and effective property tax rate variation is confirmed in this analysis of cities and suburbs by their functional responsibilities.[18] As the figures in Table 5.6 reveal, effective property tax rates on all types of property are higher across each least common functional responsibility category (welfare, education, hospitals, housing and urban renewal) in both central cities and suburbs. This pattern is even more marked when the effective property tax rates in central cities and suburbs having responsibility for all the least common functions are contrasted with the rates in central cities and suburbs having responsibility for none of these costly functions.

Central City Differences by Functional Responsibility

Table 5.6 shows that central cities with fiscal responsibility for education, welfare, or hospitals, have higher effective property tax rates on all types of property than cities without such financial responsibility. Cities with the very highest effective property tax rates (also those conceded to be in the greatest fiscal crises) are those stuck with financial responsibility for all three of these functions. For example, the effective property tax rate for all types of real property in cities with all three functions is 2.88 percent; for cities with none of these functional responsibilities, it is 1.95 percent. Looking at the specific functional responsibility categories, it is found that the greatest difference in effective property tax rates is found between cities with educational responsibilities and those without. This finding can only serve to reinforce convictions of property owners that they are footing the bill for education.

Generally, then, it appears that among central cities, higher effective property tax rates are accompanied by a greater quantity of services. (No comment can be made, however, about the quality of the services provided.) But it does appear that Mieszkowski's warning that higher tax rates not accompanied by greater public services will cause outmigration has been heeded, although perhaps not consciously.

Suburban Differences by Functional Responsibility

Generally, as in central cities, suburbs with more of the least common functional responsibilities have higher effective property tax rates than suburbs without such fiscal responsibilities, for all types of real property and for single-family residential property.

There is one slightly different pattern that emerges among suburbs when the specific functional categories are examined more closely. The greatest difference among suburbs, by functional responsibility, is between suburbs having primary financial responsibility for hospitals and suburbs having no such responsibility. The other patterns, however, are identical to those observable in central cities:

TABLE 5.5: Effective Property Tax Rates for Central Cities and Suburbs, by Governmental Character, 1972

Governmental Character	All Types of Real Property	Types of Property		
		Fully Taxable Single-Family Dwellings		
		First Quartile	Median	Third Quartile
Central cities				
Unreformed[a] (20)	2.56	1.95	2.51	2.69
Mixed[b] (126)	2.15	1.66	2.36	2.43
Reformed[c] (61)	1.92	1.63	1.92	2.16
Suburbs				
Unreformed[a] (1)	2.50	2.10	2.50	2.80
Mixed[b] (24)	2.38	1.98	2.36	2.56
Reformed[c] (19)	2.25	1.33	1.89	2.39

[a]Unreformed cities are all those with a mayor-council form of government, partisan elections, and a single-member district council member selection plan.

[b]Mixed cities are all those having at least one reformed characteristic and one unreformed characteristic.

[c]Reformed cities are those with a council-mayor form of government, nonpartisan elections, and an at-large council member selection plan.

Note: Effective property tax rate is the relationship derived by dividing total tax billed by the sales price of the property. It is the ratio of sales price to tax bill of a piece of property. The data were available only for cities with populations over 50,000. Therefore the data for suburbs represents only 44 (13 percent) of the suburbs in the study and cannot be interpreted as representative of suburban municipalities in general. Central city figures do not add to 243 due to missing data, most of which is for cities in the 50,000-99,999 category. Figures in parentheses indicate number of municipalities.

Sources: International City Management Association, The Municipal Yearbook 1968, 1958 (Chicago: ICMA, 1958, 1968); calculated from U.S. Department of Commerce, Bureau of the Census, Census of Governments: 1972, vol. 2 (Washington, D.C.: Government Printing Office), pt. 2, Table 12.

TABLE 5.6: Effective Property Tax Rates for Central Cities and Suburbs, by Functional Responsibility, 1972

Functional Responsibility	All Types of Real Property	Types of Property		
		Fully Taxable Single-Family Dwellings		
		First Quartile	Median	Third Quartile
Central cities				
Education (68)	2.56	2.04	2.49	2.89
No education (139)	1.91	1.50	2.12	2.13
Hospitals (68)	2.34	1.85	2.27	2.61
No hospitals (139)	2.01	1.59	2.23	2.26
Welfare (75)	2.41	1.91	2.35	2.69
No welfare (132)	1.96	1.55	2.18	2.20
All three least common functions (30)	2.88	2.16	2.68	3.04
None of the least common functions (94)	1.95	1.50	2.26	2.12
Suburbs				
Education (7)	2.63	1.60	2.67	2.61
No education (37)	2.27	1.72	2.07	2.14
Hospitals (6)	2.87	2.10	2.95	2.67
No hospitals (38)	2.24	1.64	2.04	1.96
Welfare (13)	2.50	1.80	2.52	2.32
No welfare (23)	2.25	1.67	2.01	1.95
Housing and urban renewal (10)	2.52	1.86	2.59	2.29
No housing and urban renewal (34)	2.17	1.53	1.73	1.58
All four least common functions (1)	3.10	—	3.50	—
None of these least common functions (23)	2.24	1.51	1.88	1.80

Note: Effective property tax rate is the relationship derived by dividing total tax billed by the sales price of the property. It is the ratio of sales price to tax bill of a piece of property. The data were available only for cities with populations over 50,000. Therefore the data for suburbs represent only 44 (13 percent) of the suburbs in the study and cannot be interpreted as representative of suburban municipalities in general. Central city figures do not add to 243 due to missing data, most of which is for cities in the 50,000-99,999 category. A city is regarded as having functional responsibility for a service if it has primary financial responsibility for provision of the service. If it does not have primary financial responsibility, it is regarded as not having functional responsibility for that service. The service areas analyzed in this table are all services that are among those for which municipalities least often have primary financial responsibility. Figures in parentheses indicate number of municipalities.

Source: Calculated from U.S. Department of Commerce, Bureau of the Census, Census of Governments: 1972, vol. 2 (Washington, D.C.: Government Printing Office), pt. 2, Table 12.

the greatest difference in effective property tax rates for single-family property among suburbs is found in tax rates for the more expensive homes (third quartile); and suburbs with the least common functional responsibilities have more progressive tax rate structures for single-family properties than do suburbs without such functional responsibilities.

DETERMINANTS OF EFFECTIVE PROPERTY TAX RATES

Having found that effective property tax rates are generally higher in municipalities located in the Northeast, with larger populations, complex economic bases (except for suburban single-family residential property tax rates), unreformed governments, and responsibilities for raising the revenue to provide education, welfare, hospital, and housing and urban renewal services to their constituencies, the remainder of the chapter will focus on the impact of demographic, socioeconomic, and governmental conditions on city and suburban effective property tax rates. As in previous chapters, of specific interest is whether the same kinds of conditions are significant determinants of effective property tax rates (for all types of real property and for fully taxable single-family residential property) in both cities and suburbs.

Central City Effective Property Tax Rate Determinants: All Types of Real Property

Table 5.7 reports the results of the analysis of the determinants of effective property tax rate variation for all types of real property. The model significantly explains 90 percent of the variance among central cities in effective property tax rates for all types of real property.

Higher effective property taxes (all types of real property) are associated with older cities, located in the Northeast, with negative growth rates, higher public assistance rates, poorer housing conditions, greater proportions of females in the labor force, more ethnic minorities, less familistic life styles, and a greater proportion of taxable property than other central cities.

In summary, among central cities, the significant determinants are primarily found to be measures of income, familism, life style, and social pathologies, all of which have the net effect of increasing governmental expenditures for poverty-related services, which puts a tremendous strain on the financial structures of these cities.

TABLE 5.7: Determinants of Central City Effective Property Tax Rates: All Types of Real Property, 1972

Variable	r	β	R^2
Ethnicity	.43	-.58	.19
Taxable real property	.39	2.52	.27
Age of city	.40	-.07	.34
Female-headed households	-.12	-.32	.39
Taxable state property	-.03	1.83	.45
Median family income	.29	.51	.49
Cumulative fertility ratio	.09	-.32	.51
Females in labor force	.25	-.32	.53
Public assistance rate	.20	.39	.55
Manufacturing employment	.27	.78	.56
Condition of housing	-.15	-.30	.58
Mortality rate	-.15	-.74	.60
Growth rate	-.10	1.09	.61
Domination of central city	-.09	.75	.63
Region	-.13	-.75	.66
Mobility	.05	-.75	.72
Crime rate	.10	.84	.90

Source: Compiled by the author.

Suburban Effective Property Tax Rate Determinants:
All Types of Real Property

The figures shown in Table 5.8 reveal that among these larger suburbs, the best predictors of effective property tax rates (all types of real property) are measures of population size, land use, income, and education.

Suburbs with the highest effective property tax rates are the larger suburbs with lesser proportions of taxable real and personal property, and containing more highly educated residents with more homogeneous incomes (less concentration of wealth in the hands of a few). As has previously been pointed out, such larger suburbs usually have more tax-exempt property within their boundaries due to the greater proportion of cultural, educational, governmental, and religious properties—properties that are more likely to be supported by higher income, better-educated suburbanites.

In summary, one of the major distinctions between central cities and suburbs with regard to the determinants of effective property tax rates for all types of real property is that among central cities, poverty-related indicators are the best predictors of effective tax rates, whereas among suburbs, measures of wealth are the best predictors of effective property tax rates for all types of real property.

TABLE 5.8: Determinants of Suburban Effective Property Tax Rates: All Types of Real Property, 1972

Variable	r	β	R^2
Population size	.48	.16	.23
Index of income concentration	-.13	-.54	.27
Taxable real property	-.24	-5.17	.33
Taxable personal property	.14	-4.60	.42
Median school years completed	-.03	1.00	.73

Source: Compiled by the author.

Central City Effective Property Tax Rate Determinants: Fully Taxable Single-Family Residential Property

As the figures shown in Table 5.9 indicate, the determinants of central city variation in effective property tax rates for fully taxable single-family property resemble the determinants of tax rates for all types of real property. However, they do include more housing-related variables.

Higher effective property tax rates on single-family residential property are associated with greater proportions of taxable property, a more familistic life style (fewer female-headed households, greater cumulative fertility ratios), newer and less crowded housing, greater proportions of persons employed in manufacturing, but also with higher crime rates, less mobile populations, and greater proportions of aged persons.

These findings are evidence that central cities, with more social problems, which in turn create the need for more poverty-related expenditures, respond by increasing the residential property tax rate, which, of course, further stimulates outmigration of those capable of paying central city taxes. Such actions rapidly reach the point of diminishing returns.

Suburban Effective Property Tax Rate Determinants: Fully Taxable Single-Family Residential Property

The determinants of suburban effective property tax rates for single-family residential property are, again, similar to the deter-

TABLE 5.9: Determinants of Central City Effective Property Tax Rates: Fully Taxable Single-Family Dwellings (Median), 1972

Variable	r	β	R^2
Taxable real property	.27	1.04	.07
Manufacturing employment	.23	.56	.13
Taxable state property	-.03	.83	.16
Crime rate	.08	.67	.19
Female-headed household	-.07	.01	.22
Mobility	-.01	-.53	.24
Median age	.02	-3.43	.25
Aged	.22	3.66	.31
Cumulative fertility ratio	.02	-1.78	.37
Age of housing	.22	1.06	.46
Residential crowding	-.19	-1.23	.66

Source: Compiled by the author.

minants of tax rates for all types of real property—primarily measures of population size, land use, and income (see Table 5.10).

The highest effective property tax rates (single-family residential property) are characteristic of suburbs with large populations, greater proportions of tax-exempt property, more lower-income families, but with greater proportions of white-collar workers, and more valuable housing. This finding suggests that what is happening among these suburbs is that low-income properties are assessed at a substantially greater proportion of the true market value than are the more valuable residential properties, confirming what Peterson and

TABLE 5.10: Determinants of Suburban Effective Property Tax Rates: Fully Taxable Single-Family Dwellings (Median), 1972

Variable	r	β	R^2
Population size	.46	.33	.21
Index of income concentration	-.09	-2.96	.24
Taxable real property	-.22	-1.05	.28
Taxable state property	-.02	-.44	.32
White-collar occupations	.05	1.37	.35
Median family income	.00	-3.02	.44
Housing value	.05	2.02	.83

Source: Compiled by the author.

Solomon found—higher effective property tax rates for poorer homeowners, a most inequitable situation.

SIGNIFICANCE OF THE FINDINGS

This analysis of the effective property tax rates of municipalities would not have been possible several years earlier. Until recently, comparison of property tax rates across communities was
somewhat futile because the available data were all nominal rates
(statutory rates) which could not meaningfully be compared because
of the wide variation in assessment ratios across communities.

Effective property tax rates are higher among cities located in
the Northeast, with larger populations, more diverse economies, unreformed governmental characters, and financial responsibility for
the least common municipal functions. These rates are largely determined by measures of income, familism, life style, and social pathologies. In other words, the determinants of effective property tax rates
in central cities are largely poverty-related measures.

Among the larger suburbs (since data is available for cities of
50,000 and above only), effective property tax rates are generally
highest in the very largest suburbs, located in the Northeast, with
diverse economies, unreformed governmental characters, and responsibility for the least common, most costly municipal functions. Thus
far it appears that suburban patterns are identical to those of central
cities. However, there are some distinctions between suburban effective property tax rate patterns for all types of real property and for
single-family residential property. Generally, the effective tax rate
is higher for all types of real property than for single-family residential property. This is perhaps indicative of the pressure brought to
bear upon suburban politicians by suburban homeowners, pressure to
keep residential property taxes relatively low.

Another difference between central cities and suburbs in their
effective property tax rate patterns is that the determinants of suburban
rates differ from those of central city rates. The results show that
the determinants of effective property tax rates in suburbs are generally measures of wealth as opposed to measures of poverty (as is
the case in central cities).

The results of this study also show that there is a significant
central city/suburban differential in tax rate structures, particularly
for single-family residential property. Property tax rate structures
for central city homeowners are much more progressive (graduated)
than similar structures affecting suburban homeowners.

The significance of the results reported in this chapter is that
the effective property tax rate is an accurate indicator of fiscal strain,

particularly in central cities. As suburbs become more like central cities in their demographic and socioeconomic make-up, it can be expected that their tax rate structures will more closely resemble those existing in central cities today. Suburbs would do well to take heed of the causes and consequences of higher effective property tax rates.

NOTES

1. Wallace E. Oates, "The Effects of Property Taxes and Local Public Spending on Property Values: An Empirical Study of Tax Capitalization and the Tiebout Hypothesis," Journal of Political Economy 77 (December 1969): 957-71.

2. U.S. Bureau of the Census, Census of Governments: 1972, vol. 2, Taxable Property Values and Assessment-Sales Price Ratios, Part 2: Assessment-Sales Price Ratios and Tax Rates (Washington, D.C.: Government Printing Office, 1973), p. 16.

3. Ibid.

4. U.S. Bureau of the Census, op. cit., p. 26.

5. Ibid.

6. Ibid.

7. Advisory Commission on Intergovernmental Relations, Public Opinion and Taxes (Washington, D.C.: U.S. Government Printing Office, 1972).

8. Mordecai S. Feinberg, "The Implications of Core-City Decline for the Fiscal Structure of the Core City," National Tax Journal 17 (September 1964): 216.

9. Peter Mieszkowski, "The Property Tax: An Excise Tax or a Profits Tax?" Journal of Public Economics 1 (1972): 74.

10. David E. Black, "The Nature and Extent of Effective Property Tax Rate Variation within the City of Boston," National Tax Journal 25 (June 1972): 203-10.

11. George E. Peterson and Arthur P. Solomon, "Property Taxes and the Populist Reform," Public Interest 30 (Winter 1973): 60-75.

12. Morris Beck, "Determinants of the Property Tax Level: A Case Study of Northeastern New Jersey," National Tax Journal 18 (March 1965): 74-77.

13. Ibid.

14. U.S. Bureau of the Census, op. cit., p. 26.

15. Ibid.

16. Oliver Oldman and Henry Aaron, "Assessment-Sales Ratios under the Boston Property Tax," National Tax Journal 18 (March 1965): 36-49.

17. Black, op. cit., p. 230.

18. Ibid.

Chapter 6

Tax Efficiency Patterns
of U.S. Cities and Suburbs:
Differing Patterns
of Community Choice

INTRODUCTION

Tax efficiency (the service/tax burden ratio) is defined in terms of the relationship between the benefits an individual or household receives from the expenditures of the government and the tax burden he/she bears as a result of the government's taxation policies.[1] Political economists have long hypothesized about the importance of tax efficiency in citizen locational decisions. According to the economic model of locational choice, "the consumer-voter may be viewed as picking that community which best satisfies his preference pattern for public goods."[2] More specifically, the "individual household when deciding on a place to live (or move to) will weigh the income which can be earned against the services which will be supplied, and the tax bill which must be paid in a particular location. As income opportunities and services rise, or as the tax bill falls, a location will become relatively more attractive."[3] Tax efficiency is an important measure in that it serves as an approximation of citizen perception of the relationship between taxes paid and services received.*

The purpose of this chapter is to determine whether cities and suburbs differ in the service packages offered to their residents; whether cities and suburbs differ in the efficiency of provision of services to their residents; and which demographic, socioeconomic, and governmental conditions most affect variations in the efficiency of service provision both among and between central cities and suburban municipalities.

---

*See Chapter 1 for an in-depth discussion of the shortcomings of tax efficiency as a comparative measure.

The results of the analysis should help determine whether the necessary conditions for such locational choices exist (that is, differences in service packages and tax efficiency) and, consequently, whether central city claims regarding the impact of such choices are justified. Specifically, central cities have attributed their financial difficulties to massive outmigration of those able to pay for services.[4] "Services deteriorate and the tax burden increases leading to the exodus of those able to move who find the public service to tax burden ratio more attractive in the suburbs."[5] City officials maintain that this exodus leaves the cities with both a disproportionate share of those unable to pay for services provided and a disproportionate responsibility for providing costly poverty-related services to these persons.

In addition to reflecting the differences in community choice with regard to service package offerings, the results of this analysis should reflect differences in community choice with regard to the basic goals of governmental revenue and expenditure policy—equity versus efficiency. It is important to note that equity and efficiency are often incompatible values: a city or suburb would find difficulty in having both equitable and efficient taxing systems or both equitable and efficient service delivery (expenditure) systems. What often happens is that a "city optimizes within constraints which so limit its options that it knowingly chooses for efficiency reasons policies which must be condemned on equity grounds" and vice versa.[6] The outmigration (from central city to suburb) theory suggests that suburban governmental bodies more often make efficiency choices than do central city governmental bodies.

PREVIOUS RESEARCH

The primary weakness of previous tax-efficiency-related studies is that they have been theoretical in nature. To date, there have been no attempts to examine these theories in a comparative context, using local governments as the units of analysis. This is particularly unfortunate in the light of the general hypothesis that tax efficiency is an important component of locational (migrational) decisions.

The groundwork for such theorizing was laid down by Charles Tiebout. Tiebout viewed persons as consumers "surrounded by a government whose objective it is to ascertain his wants for public goods and tax him accordingly."[7] As previously stated, a "consumer-voter when making a locational choice, will move to that community which best satisfies his preference pattern for public goods."[8] Several subsequent studies have hypothesized that rational consumers to some extent do weigh the benefits from local public services against the cost of their tax liability in choosing a community in which to reside.[9]

Miller and Tabb were the first to suggest an empirical measure of tax efficiency—a "tax-service ratio."[10] However, they did not operationalize this measure. Rather, they theoretically analyzed tax-service ratios at different locations in the metropolitan area and hypothesized as to their impacts on locational decisions.

Virtually all locational choice studies have claimed that differences in tax burdens have stimulated movement out of the central cities into the suburbs, a process that is seen as a reinforcing one. Perhaps this phenomenon is best characterized by William Baumol who labeled it the "process of dynamic deterioration."[11] According to Baumol,

Individuals move to the suburbs, which causes per capita income in the suburbs to exceed per capita income in the city. The higher incomes in the suburbs permit a higher level of public service in the suburban areas than in the city. More services in the suburbs lure more high-income individuals into the suburbs. At the same time, the tax base of the city is being eroded. This process may continue until the quality of services provided in the city is so poor relative to the quality of services provided elsewhere that outside aid or consolidation is necessary.

A related finding is that once these people have moved into the suburbs, they continue to use services for which they are no longer footing the bill or are at least only partially footing the bill. John Kasarda found that suburban population, in particular the commuting suburban population, exerts especially strong pressures on police, fire, highway, sanitation, and recreation functions of central cities.[12] He concluded that "the obvious and important inference suggested by this finding is that the suburban population has at least as great an impact on public services provided by the central city government as does the central city population itself."[13] Roy Bahl also addressed this central city/suburban problem: "This nonreciprocal, suburb-on-city influence on public service levels together with the relatively greater public goods choice of suburbanites, tends to widen the resources-requirements gap in core cities and to reduce it in the suburbs."[14]

A natural response to the problem of outmigration of central city residents is to maintain that the tax loss to the city is equal to the value of the public services that the city would have to provide for these people. However, this response has been attacked for the following reasons: the high income groups that are migrating to the suburbs surely supported public services that were primarily for others; many public services are such that consumption by one individual does not reduce the amount available for others; and suburban residents continue to consume most of the services of the city when returning to the city for work or for recreational activities.[15]

The consumption of central city services by suburbanites is referred to as the problem of externalities or spillovers.[16] Hirsch recognized the significance of spillovers for governmental efficiency. "There are several defects in our economy that prevent the attainment of efficiency—most noticeably, external effects or spillovers."[17] There are two different theories with regard to the capacity to deal with externalities or spillovers. Hirsch expresses a somewhat optimistic theory; he suggests that spillovers can be adjusted for by intergovernmental fiscal measures.[18] On the other hand, Alan Williams expresses a general pessimism about alleviation of such problems.[19] "No foreseeable restructuring of local government boundaries is likely to reduce intercommunity spillovers very substantially, still less render them insignificant, so that the problems posed here are likely to persist for some time."[20] Regardless of the theory embraced, the externality problem continues to exist and to limit the efficiency choices available to central city decision makers.

GENERAL TAX EFFICIENCY PATTERNS

As the results shown in Table 6.1 indicate, greater general tax efficiency is found among suburban municipalities than among central cities. Suburban residents receive 1.6 times more for their tax dollars in services than do central city residents. It is appropriate, however, to note that this comparison is in no way a commentary on the quality of the services. Likewise, general tax efficiency figures do not include monies paid in taxes to other governments that are eventually returned to the local government. While these figures cannot account for intergovernmental transfers, they do demonstrate the capacity of the local government tax structure to cover the costs of service expenditures legitimated by the local governing body. Thus, they reflect the additional pressure to rely upon intergovernmental transfer payments to meet local service needs.

Among central cities, tax-service ratios are highest for police, fire, and highways, and are lowest for health and libraries. Among suburbs, the tax efficiency pattern is slightly different. Police ranks highest, highways second, and sewerage third. Health and housing and urban renewal reflect the lowest efficiency scores among suburbs.

When central city/suburban differences are examined, the results show that central city residents get more for their tax dollars than suburban residents in health and housing and urban renewal services only. This confirms what has been suggested in other studies

TABLE 6.1: General Tax Efficiency of Central Cities and Suburbs: All Services and by Specific Service Area

Service Area	Central Cities	Suburbs
All services	.458	.727
Highways	.052	.110
Health	.006	.004
Fire	.043	.047
Police	.054	.119
Sewerage	.037	.090
Sanitation	.022	.044
Parks and recreation	.030	.039
Housing and urban renewal	.023	.002
Libraries	.007	.010

Note: Tax efficiency (the service/tax burden ratio) is the relationship between the benefits an individual or household receives from the government's expenditure policies and the tax burden he/she bears as a result of the government's taxation policies (per capita expenditures/per capita total tax burden). The larger the figure, the more efficient is the return on the tax dollar.

Source: Compiled by the author.

contrasting central city and suburban expenditure patterns—that is, that central cities have much higher expenditures for poverty-linked services (welfare, health and hospitals, and education) than do suburbs.[21] Housing and urban renewal can also be considered a poverty-linked service. The figures in Table 6.1 show that there is greater central city/suburban disparity in housing and urban renewal/tax burden ratios than in any other service/tax burden ratio. On the other hand, central city/suburban service/tax burden disparities are least for fire protection, parks and recreation, and library services.

If central cities and suburbs are contrasted in terms of their service packages, it appears that suburbs have the more attractive package for the higher income persons. Suburban residents are offered a service package characterized by these efficiency priorities: police, highways, sewerage, fire, sanitation, parks and recreation, libraries, health, and housing and urban renewal. (Notice that the last two services are those classified by Kee as poverty-linked services.) Central city residents are offered a service package with these priorities: police, highways, fire, sewerage, parks and recreation, housing and urban renewal, sanitation, libraries, and health.

On the basis of these general tax efficiency figures and service priorities, it appears that suburbs stand a much better chance of attracting residents from the central cities than vice versa. The most distressing part of all of this is that higher tax rates in central cities are not the answer. Miller and Tabb discussed this dilemma in their study of local government expenditures:

> If upper income families pay more taxes than lower income families, logically a community composed of more upper income units would offer more in the way of public services with the same tax rate as would a jurisdiction composed of a larger group of low income persons. In fact, empirical evidence indicates that expenditure levels are higher in jurisdictions with lower tax rates.[22]

This is congruent with earlier findings of Haskell and Leshinski that the "community which discourages in-migration by low income families so as to keep its tax rate low, ceteris paribus, is most attractive to the high income family trying to maximize its fiscal residuum."[23]

Tax Efficiency by Region

Central City Differences by Region

The figures shown in Table 6.2 reveal that central cities located in the South and the West have the most efficient tax structures. This finding is consistent with earlier findings of this study that central cities in the Northeast and Midwest, the larger cities, are more equity-oriented in their taxing and service distribution because they contain greater proportions of persons in poverty conditions.

Suburban Differences by Region

Suburban regional tax efficiency patterns are different from those of central cities. Midwestern suburbs have the most efficient tax structures. Much of the explanation for this finding lies in the size of the suburbs (midwestern suburbs are among the medium-sized suburbs).

Tax Efficiency by Population Size

Central City Differences by Population Size

Table 6.3 indicates that medium-sized cities are the most efficient in tax utilization and, as predicted by Shapiro, the least effi-

TABLE 6.2: Tax Efficiency for Central Cities and Suburbs, by Region (service/tax burden ratio)

	All Services	Highways	Health	Fire	Police	Sewerage	Sanitation	Parks and Recreation	Housing and Urban Renewal	Libraries
Central cities										
Northeast (53)	.303	.019	.003	.022	.026	.013	.010	.011	.023	.004
South (87)	.516	.052	.006	.048	.060	.036	.033	.033	.021	.006
North Central (62)	.474	.075	.008	.045	.056	.052	.017	.023	.024	.007
West (41)	.512	.057	.005	.055	.073	.046	.021	.054	.022	.013
Suburbs										
Northeast (96)	.598	.067	.006	.032	.082	.033	.033	.024	.009	.015
South (50)	.648	.073	.002	.053	.093	.056	.068	.043	.001	.008
North Central (109)	.858	.135	.005	.063	.134	.149	.043	.038	.004	.011
West (85)	.678	.127	.002	.061	.133	.043	.023	.074	.004	.014

Note: Figures in parentheses indicate number of municipalities.

Source: Compiled by the author.

TABLE 6.3: Tax Efficiency for Central Cities and Suburbs, by Population Size (service/tax burden ratio)

	All Services	Highways	Health	Fire	Police	Sewerage	Sanitation	Parks and Recreation	Housing and Urban Renewal	Libraries
Central cities										
Over 1,000,000 (6)	.375	.027	.009	.029	.064	.022	.019	.017	.020	.006
500,000-999,999 (20)	.504	.070	.011	.039	.065	.039	.022	.035	.019	.009
250,000-499,999 (27)	.539	.055	.008	.043	.056	.046	.025	.041	.036	.008
100,000-249,999 (69)	.507	.056	.006	.047	.058	.039	.023	.035	.026	.007
50,000-99,999 (121)	.409	.047	.004	.041	.048	.034	.021	.025	.018	.006
Suburbs										
Over 100,000 (12)	.704	.089	.005	.067	.098	.036	.019	.070	.019	.018
50,000-99,999 (43)	.695	.120	.003	.074	.111	.038	.032	.051	.011	.021
25,000-49,999 (77)	.669	.085	.003	.055	.099	.065	.031	.049	.007	.013
Below 25,000 (208)	.727	.110	.004	.047	.119	.090	.044	.039	.002	.010

Note: Figures in parentheses indicate number of municipalities.

Source: Compiled by the author.

cient tax utilization is characteristic of the very largest and the very smallest cities.[24] In fact, the results of the ACIR tax opinion survey show that residents of the largest cities (over one million) accurately perceive their cities' inefficiency.[25] In that survey, these residents were the least confident of their city government's ability to "give them their money's worth" in terms of municipal services.

Much of the central city variation in tax efficiency by population size can be explained by the economic principle of economy of scale. Statistical analyses of average unit costs (AUC) indicate that the cost curves for highways, fire, sewerage, sanitation, parks and recreation, housing and urban renewal, and libraries are U-shaped, meaning that the costs are higher per person in the very largest and very smallest cities but are lowest in the medium-sized cities.[26] To examine one particular example of the close correlation of the findings of this study with earlier economy-of-scale research, let us look at a study of fire protection service distribution. Robert E. Will estimated per capita service requirements for fire protection for 38 cities of 50,000-1,000,000 population.[27] He regressed these per capita figures against city population and concluded that there are significant economies of scale associated with provision of municipal fire protection services. Major economies of scale were found among cities with populations up to 300,000; very little evidence was found that such economies exist for larger populations. In yet another study, Hirsch found that the AUC (average unit cost) for fire protection is U-shaped with the trough at about 110,000.[28] Comparing general tax efficiency data for fire protection, it can be observed that fire/tax burden ratios are greatest in central cities of 100,000-249,999. In summary, tax efficiency is greatest among medium-sized central cities because of their ability to benefit from economies of scale.

Suburban Differences by Population Size

This analysis is the first attempt to study efficiency among local governmental units below 50,000 population. (It should be noted that the results cannot literally be compared to those of central cities because of the differences in size categories.) The results here show that tax efficiency is greatest among the smallest suburbs, which at first appears to be a rather surprising finding, until it is recalled that the smallest suburbs provide the fewest services and depend more on tax revenues than larger suburbs.

Tax Efficiency by Economic Base

Central City Differences by Economic Base

The figures in Table 6.4 suggest that economic base is related to tax efficiency in central cities. The most complex economic-based cities (manufacturing) are the least efficient, whereas the least complex economic-based cities are the most efficient in their tax structures. This finding is probably attributable to variations in the number and kind of functional responsibilities provided by the municipality. Functional responsibilities are more efficiency-oriented (in terms of both financing and provision) among smaller, more homogeneous cities, with more specialized economic bases.

Suburban Differences by Economic Base

Economic-base tax efficiency patterns are much more marked in suburbs than in central cities, although the pattern is identical in nature. Suburbs with more specialized economic bases (and usually more socioeconomically homogeneous populations) are characterized by the most efficient tax structures—again attributable to the number and type of services provided to their residents. Such a finding in both cities and suburbs can only serve to reinforce more affluent central city residents' notions that fewer services, but of a higher quality, are sometimes better than a lot of services, none of which is of quality calibre.

Tax Efficiency by Governmental Character

An examination of general tax efficiency by governmental character is especially significant in light of reform theory. The whole premise of the reform movement is that certain structural arrangements (council-manager governments, nonpartisan elections, and at-large plans for electing council members) will provide for more efficient governmental operations. To date there have been no studies that have empirically analyzed tax efficiencies by governmental character. However, Hirsch does allude to the possibility that such a relationship exists. "The nature and structure of the government have a direct bearing on the extent to which officials are responsive to the desires of their constituents and supply them with the services they want or should have."[29] He also acknowledges that local government officials can affect service distribution by trading off costs and benefits they as politicians are likely to incur as a result of their endorsement of a particular service distribution. Hirsch warns that serious

TABLE 6.4: Tax Efficiency for Central Cities and Suburbs, by Economic Base (service/tax burden ratio)

	All Services	Highways	Health	Fire	Police	Sewerage	Sanitation	Parks and Recreation	Housing and Urban Renewal	Libraries
Central cities										
Manufacturing (86)	.402	.038	.006	.034	.043	.033	.015	.020	.025	.004
Industrial (3)	.511	.055	.003	.045	.028	.103	.015	.019	.031	.007
Diversified manufacturing (60)	.543	.065	.007	.050	.063	.041	.025	.031	.024	.008
Diversified retailing (50)	.448	.054	.006	.045	.056	.034	.026	.038	.026	.008
Retailing (29)	.411	.054	.002	.047	.056	.036	.027	.042	.018	.010
Other (15)	.559	.064	.006	.050	.076	.041	.028	.037	.001	.007
Suburbs										
Manufacturing (87)	.690	.086	.004	.057	.102	.065	.035	.038	.010	.011
Industrial (12)	.578	.079	.005	.052	.075	.047	.032	.020	.000	.010
Diversified manufacturing (19)	.600	.093	.004	.059	.078	.024	.038	.043	.007	.013
Diversified retailing (41)	.720	.097	.005	.069	.124	.115	.046	.047	.009	.013
Retailing (61)	.699	.117	.004	.054	.124	.050	.049	.042	.000	.015
Other (24)	.723	.087	.004	.062	.108	.043	.044	.066	.003	.016

Note: Figures in parentheses indicate number of municipalities.
Source: Compiled by the author.

TABLE 6.5: Tax Efficiency for Central Cities and Suburbs, by Governmental Character (service/tax burden ratio)

	All Services	Highways	Health	Fire	Police	Sewerage	Sanitation	Parks and Recreation	Housing and Urban Renewal	Libraries
Central cities										
Unreformed cities (20)*	.461	.044	.008	.038	.045	.024	.020	.016	.024	.008
Mixed cities (147)	.467	.053	.006	.044	.055	.039	.022	.030	.023	.006
Reformed cities (76)	.440	.051	.005	.041	.054	.037	.022	.035	.022	.008
Suburbs										
Unreformed suburbs (11)	.636	.076	.004	.055	.091	.084	.027	.020	.005	.008
Mixed suburbs (241)	.687	.098	.005	.048	.106	.070	.037	.034	.006	.011
Reformed suburbs (116)	.756	.120	.002	.061	.128	.086	.044	.065	.004	.014

*Figures in parentheses indicate number of municipalities.
Source: Compiled by the author.

diseconomies of scale "can accompany a large local government that loses efficiency because of political patronage and administrative top-heaviness"[30] (both characteristics most often associated with unreformed governments).

As the results reported in Table 6.5 reveal, there is less variation in tax efficiencies of both cities and suburbs when contrasted by governmental character than when contrasted by region, population size, or economic base.

Central City Differences by Governmental Character

Mixed cities are the most efficient of all governmental types. At first glance, it appears that unreformed cities are more efficient than reformed cities. However, when mixed cities are excluded and reformed and unreformed cities are contrasted with regard to efficiencies for specific services, it appears that reformed cities are more efficient (except for health and housing and urban renewal services).

These findings may be interpreted as consistent with reform theory since reformed cities are the most efficient in service provision for all but the two poverty-linked services—those least important to their citizens. (These services are said to be least important on the basis of socioeconomic characterisitcs of reformed city residents as opposed to those of unreformed city residents who tend to be of lower social status.) At any rate, governmental character does not appear to be as strongly related to tax efficiency as has previously been theorized.

Suburban Differences by Governmental Character

A much stronger relationship between governmental character and tax efficiency is evident among suburbs. Reformed suburbs, as hypothesized, are characterized by the most efficient tax structures, whereas unreformed suburban tax structures are the least efficient. Thus, it appears that reformism has had a greater impact on suburban tax efficiency patterns than on central city efficiency patterns. Much of this could be attributable to the relative ages of central cities and suburbs at the advent of the reform movement.

Tax Efficiency by Functional Responsibility

By classifying central cities and suburbs by their responsibility or nonresponsibility for financing services that are least often financed by municipalities, it is possible to analyze the financial effects of providing these least common functions on the municipality's provision of the more common municipal functions.

On the basis of Hirsch's findings that citizen pressures result in low average unit cost functions for education, welfare, and housing and urban renewal services, and on the basis of his finding that both hospitals and welfare can be more efficiently provided by other levels of government, one should expect to find lower, more inefficient, service/tax burden ratios among cities and suburbs responsible for providing these functions.[31]

Central City and Suburban Differences by Functional Responsibility

The results shown in Table 6.6 indicate that central cities providing education, hospitals, or all the least common functions are characterized by more efficient tax structures than cities without such financial responsibilities. This result comes as somewhat of a surprise, but suggests that further outmigration of central city residents in such cities (if one accepts Tiebout's thesis) is somewhat counteracted by the provision of these more visible services (schools, hospitals).

Among suburbs, the reverse situation occurs; suburbs without responsibility for the least common functions are considerably more efficient in their provision of all services than suburbs with such burdensome financial responsibilities. The answer to central city/suburban differences probably lies in diseconomies of scale that most affect the provision of these relatively expensive services among the smaller suburban municipalities.

DEMOGRAPHIC, SOCIOECONOMIC, AND
GOVERNMENTAL CORRELATES
OF TAX EFFICIENCY

Correlates of Central City Tax Efficiency

The results shown in Table 6.7 indicate that among central cities, the most significant demographic correlates of tax efficiency are measures of mobility (population growth and population mobility). Somewhat unexpected is the finding that population size and density are not among the significant correlates of tax efficiency. This is surprising in view of the many studies that suggest that size and density, as important determinants of economies of scale, might be important determinants of tax efficiency.[32] Although this may contra-

TABLE 6.6: Tax Efficiency for Central Cities and Suburbs, by Functional Responsibility (service/tax burden ratio)

	All Services	Highways	Health	Fire	Police	Sewerage	Sanitation	Parks and Recreation	Housing and Urban Renewal	Libraries
Central cities										
Education (76)*	.473	.032	.006	.031	.040	.027	.016	.023	.019	.006
No education (167)	.451	.061	.006	.048	.060	.041	.025	.034	.024	.007
Hospitals (78)	.507	.044	.007	.039	.053	.029	.019	.025	.021	.005
No hospitals (165)	.435	.055	.005	.044	.054	.041	.023	.033	.023	.008
Welfare (80)	.448	.033	.007	.033	.042	.028	.017	.020	.023	.005
No welfare (163)	.464	.061	.005	.047	.060	.041	.025	.035	.022	.008
Education, hospitals, welfare (33)	.498	.025	.008	.028	.037	.028	.011	.019	.020	.005
None of these functions (116)	.433	.062	.005	.048	.059	.043	.024	.036	.023	.008
Suburbs										
Education (49)	.633	.037	.005	.034	.045	.069	.017	.019	.004	.007
No education (291)	.722	.116	.004	.056	.125	.077	.043	.048	.005	.013
Hospitals (45)	.681	.057	.006	.044	.070	.045	.027	.021	.004	.009
No hospitals (295)	.713	.112	.004	.054	.120	.081	.041	.047	.005	.013
Welfare (89)	.624	.064	.007	.041	.077	.058	.028	.029	.006	.011
No welfare (251)	.739	.119	.003	.057	.126	.082	.043	.049	.005	.013
Housing and urban renewal (43)	.684	.072	.004	.066	.103	.004	.037	.041	.029	.018
No housing and urban renewal (297)	.712	.110	.004	.051	.114	.081	.039	.044	.002	.012
All four functions (4)	.530	.024	.004	.029	.035	.007	.007	.008	.013	.007
None of these functions (218)	.724	.124	.003	.053	.127	.078	.043	.049	.002	.012

*Figures in parentheses indicate number of municipalities.

Source: Compiled by the author.

TABLE 6.7: Demographic, Socioeconomic, and Governmental Correlates of Tax Efficiency: Central Cities and Suburbs

Environmental Characteristics	Tax Efficiency	
	Cities	Suburbs
Demographic Characteristics		
Population size	.02	-.07
Population density		
Land area density	-.10	-.05
Residential crowding	.09	.25[a]
Room crowding	-.06	.01
Mobility		
Moving to different house	.18[b]	.17[a]
Population growth	.19[b]	.08
Region	.19[b]	.19[a]
Socioeconomic Characteristics		
Age		
Aged persons	.25[a]	-.02
Median age	-.07	.07
Youth	.34[a]	.19[a]
Education		
Median school years completed	.25[a]	-.10
College graduates	.35[a]	.03
Class (economic status)		
Median family income	.13[c]	-.03
Per capita personal income	.57[a]	-.11[c]
Homeownership	.02	.22[a]
Housing value	.16[b]	.21[a]
Affluence	.24[a]	.20[a]
White-collar employment	.31[a]	.20[a]
Government employment	.20[b]	
Manufacturing employment	-.15[c]	
Females in labor force	.14[c]	-.02

Race		
Nonwhites	$.21^a$	$-.17^b$
Ethnicity		
Foreign born	$-.23^a$	$-.07$
Social pathology		
Mortality ratio	$-.08$	$-.22^a$
Public assistance rate	$-.11$	$-.18^a$
Poverty	$.04$	$-.19^a$
Crime rate	$.07$	$-.01$
Fertility ratio	$.35^a$	$.15^b$
Female-headed households	$-.10$	$-.09$
Income inequality	$.20^b$	$-.02$
Run-down housing	$-.06$	$-.09$
Housing antiquity	$-.22^a$	$-.23^a$
Governmental Characteristics		
Age		
Age of central city	$.04$	
Domination of central city		
Central city proportion of SMSA		
Economic base	$.14^c$	$-.12^c$
Form of government	$.00$	$-.06$
Type of election	$.07$	$.11^c$
Type of council-member selection plan	$.02$	$.11^c$
Governmental character—reformism	$-.03$	$-.05$
Functional responsibilities		$.09$
Total functional responsibility	$.10$	$-.23^a$
Responsibility for least common functions	$.08$	$-.03$

[a] Significant at .001 level.
[b] Significant at .01 level.
[c] Significant at .05 level.

Note: Figures are simple correlation coefficients.

Source: Compiled by the author.

dict theoretical notions with regard to economies of scale, it is congruent with locational choice theory. Cities that are still attracting population are less apt to suffer from fiscal problems than are those cities that are losing population. In other words, economic growth is related to population growth of central cities.

An examination of the socioeconomic correlates of tax efficiency among central cities shows that those cities characterized by more educated, more affluent, youthful populations are characterized by more efficient tax structures. On the contrary, cities with the least efficient tax structures are likely to be those characterized by more needy and less affluent populaces, a predicament that mandates governmental provision of poverty-related services and further erodes the effectiveness of the existing tax structure in providing needed services. A change in the tax structure to accommodate provision of services of a redistributive (need) nature ends up further damaging the efficiency of the tax structure, and certainly stimulates locational choices on the part of persons capable of moving.

Governmental variables, particularly institutional or structural variables, do not turn out to be very strongly or very significantly related to tax efficiency of central cities. This finding is also somewhat surprising in the light of existing theoretical notions regarding the impact of reform institutions on fiscal patterns of cities.[33] Specifically, many have theorized that certain structural arrangements (council-manager governments, nonpartisan elections, and at-large council-member selection plans) provide for a more efficient governmental operation. However, the results indicate that the impact of reformed institutional structures on taxing and spending policies of central cities has been vastly overestimated.

In summary, among central cities, socioeconomic measures are more strongly and significantly related to tax efficiency than are demographic or governmental measures.

Correlates of Suburban Tax Efficiency

Among suburbs, patterns emerge nearly identical to those observed in central cities. Demographic and socioeconomic variables are more strongly and significantly related to suburban tax efficiency than are governmental variables (Table 6.7).

As in the case of central cities, an important demographic correlate of suburban tax efficiency is population mobility. However, population mobility among suburbanites may be more a measure of upward mobility (moving to a better house) since population growth is not significantly related to efficiency. This interpretation is strengthened by examining the correlation of economic status variables with general tax efficiency. The significant correlates include homeownership, housing value, and white-collar employment.

Several other significant socioeconomic correlates of tax efficiency are more indicative of the familistic life style associated with suburban living. Residential crowding (median number of persons per dwelling unit) is positively related to suburban tax efficiency. Similarly, there is a positive relationship between youth and tax efficiency.

Significant social pathology measures are negatively related to tax efficiency. This suggests that suburbs having to provide poverty-related services (like central cities) will tend to be more inefficient in the provision of all services as contrasted with suburban governments that do not have to provide these services. This is reflective of the previously mentioned dilemma facing governmental decision makers: efficiency versus equity.

Governmental conditions, particularly structural arrangements, are only weakly related to suburban tax efficiency (the same pattern as observed in central cities). The strongest governmental correlate of suburban tax efficiency is more a measure of governmental responsibility than of structure: the total number of services provided. As the number of services to be provided increases, suburban tax efficiency decreases. This seems to strengthen the argument that persons moving to suburban areas often prefer that the government undertake only the most basic services and provide them in the most efficient manner possible. The list of most basic services tends not to include the costly poverty-related services.

Central City/Suburban Differences

The difference between central city and suburban correlates of tax efficiency is primarily one of strength rather than one of direction. Generally, mobility measures are positively related to tax efficiency in both cities and suburbs, indicating the relationship between population growth and economic growth. Similarly, class or economic status variables are positively related to tax efficiency, whereas social pathology indicators are negatively related. Governmental variables, particularly institutional arrangement variables, are only weakly related to tax efficiency, with the relationship being a weak positive one between reform structural arrangements and tax efficiency.

The results do show that education variables are much more strongly and significantly related to tax efficiency in central cities than in suburbs. On the other hand, total functional responsibilities performed is a much more important correlate of suburban tax efficiency than of central city tax efficiency. Central cities do, however, vary much less in the number of services provided than suburbs. This suggests that as suburbs become more like central cities with regard to service packages offered and demographic, socioeconomic, and governmental characteristics, there will be less opportunity for locational choice based on efficiency criteria.

DETERMINANTS OF TAX EFFICIENCY

Determinants of Central City Tax Efficiency

The results of the analysis of the determinants of central city tax efficiency (Table 6.8) strengthen the results of the earlier comparison of means and correlational analyses. The variables having the greatest impact on central city tax efficiency are economic-related (or wealth) indicators. The results show that tax efficiency is greatest among the more fiscally sound cities.

Growing cities, with proportionately wealthier, more educated residents, a more familistic life style, and fewer incidences of social pathology (crime, poverty, older housing structures) are characterized by more efficient tax structures.

In summary, it appears that tax efficiency is a fairly accurate measure of central city residents' perceptions of the relationship between taxes paid and services received, since cities with the greatest tax efficiency are characterized by population mobility and growth (translated to mean economic growth as well), whereas cities with inefficient tax structures are characterized by declining populations.

Determinants of Suburban Tax Efficiency

Among suburbs, the significant determinants of variation in tax efficiency are measures of income, housing, and land use. Wealthier suburbs, with newer housing structures, and more tax-exempt property (indicative of the presence of more cultural, religious, governmental, and education-related property, which, among suburbs, is also indicative of wealth), have the most efficient tax structures.

In summary, among suburbs, as among central cities, tax efficiency is largely determined by economic-status measures. Affluence affords the luxury of efficient tax structures, whereas poverty mandates equitable or redistributive tax structures and service distribution.

TABLE 6.8: Determinants of General Tax Efficiency (All Services): Central Cities and Suburbs

Variables	r	β	R^2
Central cities			
Per capita personal income	.52	.33	.27
College-educated persons	.34	.52	.32
Population size	.18	.61	.34
Cumulative fertility ratio	.01	.88	.36
Youth	-.15	-.87	.37
Age of housing	-.25	-.55	.39
Age of city	.03	.12	.41
Taxable real property	-.17	-1.95	.42
Mobility (different house)	.16	.97	.42
Economic base	.14	-.03	.43
Poverty	.02	-.15	.44
Taxable state property	.12	-1.76	.45
Housing value	.14	-.69	.46
Domination of central city	.10	-1.28	.48
Crime rate	.07	-.92	.60
Suburbs			
Per capita personal income	.39	.56	.15
Taxable state property	-.00	-1.31	.20
Age of housing	.17	.85	.25
Taxable real property	-.24	-1.32	.32

Source: Compiled by the author.

SIGNIFICANCE OF THE FINDINGS

The results of this comparative analysis of the tax efficiency patterns of central cities and suburbs have shown that there is a difference among and between them. This is largely attributable to differences in service packages, reflective of the impact of demographic, socioeconomic, and governmental conditions on locational choices of citizens and goal choices of governmental decision makers, particularly with regard to taxing and spending policies.

The results suggest that the greater tax efficiency of suburban municipalities can serve to further stimulate outmigration from the central cities, which in turn can force cities to make inefficient decisions. On the other hand, the fact that various demographic, socioeconomic, and governmental variables affect cities and suburbs in similar ways (differing primarily in strength rather than direction) suggests that as central city/suburban disparities decrease, the opportunity for such locational and goal choices will diminish.

NOTES

1. Werner Z. Hirsch, The Economics of State and Local Government (New York: McGraw-Hill, 1970).

2. Charles Tiebout, "A Pure Theory of Local Expenditures," Journal of Political Economy 64 (October 1956): 418.

3. Stephen M. Miller and William K. Tabb, "A New Look at a Pure Theory of Local Expenditures," National Tax Journal 26 (June 1973): 163.

4. See Woo Sik Kee, "Suburban Population Growth and Its Implications for Core City Finance," Land Economics 43 (May 1967): 202-11; and David F. Bradford and Harry H. Kelejian, "An Econometric Model of the Flight to the Suburbs," Journal of Political Economy 81 (May/June 1973): 566-89.

5. Miller and Tabb, op. cit., p. 102.

6. Ibid., p. 161.

7. Tiebout, op. cit., p. 417.

8. Ibid., p. 418.

9. See W. E. Oates, "The Effects of Property Taxes and Local Public Spending on Property Values: An Empirical Study of Tax Capitalization and the Tiebout Hypothesis," Journal of Political Economy 77 (November/December 1969): 957-71.

10. Miller and Tabb, op. cit.

11. William Baumol, "Urban Services: Interactions of Public and Private Decisions," in Public Expenditure Decisions in the Urban Community, ed. Howard Schaller (Washington, D.C.: Resources for the Future, 1965).

12. John D. Kasarda, "The Impact of Suburban Population Growth on Central City Service Functions," American Journal of Sociology 77 (May 1972): 1111-24.

13. Ibid., p. 1116.

14. Roy W. Bahl, "Public Policy and the Urban Fiscal Problem: Piecemeal Versus Aggregate Solutions," Land Economics 46 (February 1970): 41-50.

15. A. G. Holtmann, "Migration to the Suburbs, Human Capital, and City Income Tax Losses: A Case Study," National Tax Journal 21 (September 1968): 326-31.

16. For discussions of the effects of externalities, see Jay W. Forrester, Urban Dynamics (Cambridge, Mass.: MIT Press, 1969);

James M. Buchanan and Charles J. Goetz, "Efficiency Limits of Fiscal Mobility: An Assessment of the Tiebout Model," Journal of Public Economics 1 (April 1972): 25-43; W. E. Oates, E. P. Howrey, and W. J. Baumol, "The Analysis of Public Policy in Dynamic Urban Models," Journal of Political Economy 79 (January/February 1971): 142-53; and Kenneth V. Greene and Claudia D. Scott, "Suburban-Central City Spillovers of Tax Burdens and Expenditure Benefits," Northeast Regional Science Review, vol. 3 (1973).

17. Hirsch, op. cit., p. 202.

18. Ibid., p. 189.

19. Alan Williams, "The Optimal Provision of Public Goods in a System of Local Government," Journal of Political Economy 74 (February 1966): 18-33.

20. Ibid., p. 189.

21. See Kee, op. cit.; and Thomas F. Stinson, "Poulation Changes and Shifts in Local Government Finance," Municipal Finance 42 (August 1969): 134-39.

22. Miller and Tabb, op. cit., p. 167.

23. Mark A. Haskell and Stephen Leshinski, "Fiscal Influences on Residential Choice: A Study of the New York Region," Quarterly Review of Economics and Business 9 (Winter 1969): 47-56.

24. Harvey Shapiro, "Economics of Scale and Local Government Finance," Land Economics 9 (May 1963): 135-86.

25. Advisory Commission on Intergovernmental Relations, Public Opinion and Taxes (Washington, D.C.: U.S. Government Printing Office, 1972).

26. Hirsch, op. cit.

27. Robert E. Will, "Scalar Economics and Urban Service Requirements," Yale Economic Essays 5 (Spring 1965): 1-62.

28. Hirsch, op. cit.

29. Ibid., p. 194.

30. Ibid., p. 177.

31. Kasarda also found that public housing, public health, and other welfare services imposed a heavy burden on the operating budgets of cities. Kasarda, op. cit.

32. See Alvin H. Hansen and Harvey S. Perloff, State and Local Finance in the National Economy (New York: Norton, 1944); Shapiro, op. cit.; Will, op. cit.; Hirsch, op. cit.; and G. Ross Stephens and Henry J. Schmandt, "Revenue Patterns of Local Government," National Tax Journal 15 (December 1962): 423-37.

33. See Bernard H. Booms, "City Governmental Form and Public Expenditure Levels," National Tax Journal 19 (June 1966): 187-99; Robert L. Lineberry and Edmund P. Fowler, "Reformism and Public Policy in American Cities," American Political Science Review 58 (September 1967): 701-16; John C. Weicher, "Aid, Expenditures, and

Local Government Structure," National Tax Journal 25 (December 1972): 473-84; and Heywood T. Sanders, "Policies, Populations, and Governmental Structures," in International City Management Association, The Municipal Yearbook 1972 (Chicago: ICMA, 1973).

Part II

Special Investigations:
Present and Future
Implications of Current
Revenue Patterns

The Impact of Tax Structures on Women and Other Minorities: Inefficiencies and Inequalities

INTRODUCTION

Due at least partially to the passage of the Equal Pay Act of 1963, to Title VII of the 1964 Civil Rights Act, and to the entire women's movement, a considerable amount of literature has been produced over the past decade discussing the economically disadvantaged positions of women and blacks.[2] Much research has also been done regarding the fiscal structures of local governments, which have become increasingly strained.[3] These studies have primarily focused attention on the inadequacies of local government tax structures, particularly the regressivity of local property taxes. To date, however, there have been virtually no attempts to determine whether the economically disadvantaged position of women and blacks, especially in the large metropolitan areas of the United States, affects local government tax structures or, conversely, whether local government tax structures affect the economic positions of women and minorities.

The purposes of this chapter are several. First, a comparison of the per capita personal incomes of women and men (both within the total population and within the black population) will be made to determine the extent of income inequality. Second, a comparison will be made of the tax burdens borne by each of these groups in an attempt to establish whether there is a linkage between income inequalities and local government tax structures. Finally, an examination of the relationship between tax burdens and levels of service provision will be made to determine the efficiency (or inefficiency) of local government tax structures on each of these groups. The results of this analysis should provide some insights into the effects of inequitable and inefficient local government tax structures on existing economic imbalances between males and females, blacks and whites, in U.S. society.

This chapter is coauthored by Nikki R. Van Hightower, Women's Advocate, City of Houston, Texas, and is an expansion of a jointly authored article.[1]

Framework of Analysis

The units of analysis are the 125 SMSAs with populations of 250,000 or more. Control groups utilized in the study were selected on the basis of race, region, and population size. Statistics on the black population were gathered for purposes of comparison. As a group, they tend, like women, to fall disporportionately into lower income categories. However, it was felt that it would be interesting to discover whether disparities, if they exist, between male and female tax burdens and tax efficiencies, are sustained within this racial group.

Since cost-of-living adjustments are not available by SMSA, the closest approximation to such an adjustment can be made by analyzing the data by region. The regional classification scheme adopted is the standard Bureau of the Census classification: Northeast, South, North Central (Midwest), and West.

Similarly, controls for differences in economies of scale are virtually unobtainable for SMSA units of analysis. Consequently, the best surrogate measure for economies of scale is population size. The 125 SMSAs have been grouped into three population size categories: one million and over; 500,000-999,999; and 250,000-499,999. The exclusion of SMSAs under 250,000 population is solely a function of data availability. The Census Bureau does not report income by sex and household status for SMSAs under 250,000 population. The time frame within which the analysis is performed is a single time point— 1972.

Types of Household-Status Groups

One of the early results of this study was the discovery that the U.S. Bureau of the Census categorization of income earners is somewhat sexist. The major categories of household status are male heads of household (married males living with wives and other family members); primary males (single males); female heads of household (women living without spouse but with other family members); wives of heads (women living with spouse and other family members); and primary females (single females). It should be noted that with the exception of the primary group designation, the male and female household status groups are not comparable. This results from the U.S. Census Bureau's usage of the term "head of household," of which there can be only one per family and, if there is a male present, the male must be so designated. As stated by the Census Bureau, "One person in each household is designated as the 'head,' that is, the person who is regarded as the head by the members of the household. However, if a married woman living with her husband was reported as the head, her husband was considered the head for the purpose of simplifying the tabulations."[4] Thus, male heads of household include all males living with family members whether or not a spouse is present. Since by Census Bureau definition there can be only one head, the comparable group of females must be divided into two categories: wife of head, for those women living with spouses; and female heads of household, for those women living without their spouses but with other members of their families.

PATTERNS OF PER CAPITA PERSONAL INCOME

The fact that women and minorities generally earn significantly lower wages than men has been well documented. The report of the Twentieth Century Fund Task Force on Women and Employment indicates that:

1. Working women earn, on the average, only 58 per cent of what working men earn; black women earn even less.

2. Women who want to work are much more likely than men to be employed.

3. Most women work in "female occupations" (such as stenographers, teachers, waitresses, household workers) which are often neither unionized nor protected by strong federal legislation.

4. Over a third of the families headed by women live in poverty, compared to only about 12 percent of all families.

5. Women's chances for top management jobs are slim, regardless of their abilities. [5]

What has not been well documented is the extent of income inequality between males and females, particularly within the various household groups. The reason for this lack of data is the failure of the U.S. Census Bureau to report per capita income figures by household status or by sex for SMSAs. To obtain these per capita personal income figures, it is necessary to make extensive calculations. Per capita income is computed by taking the median (in terms of dollars) for each of the 11 categories of income, then multiplying the median figure by the total number of persons in each income category, adding the total income earned by each household-status group, and dividing this total earned income by the total number of persons in each household-status group. Consequently, even these per capita income figures are approximations (though it can be argued they are close approximations) of the actual per capita incomes of these various household-status groups. An intentional choice was made to analyze only employed persons, since they bear the tax burdens, whereas unemployed persons do not.

The figures shown in Table 7.1 indicate that a strong relationship exists between sex and per capita income, or, in other words, between sex and income inequality.

Within the total population, males have higher per capita incomes than do females. Specifically, male heads of household have per capita incomes twice those of female heads of household. The disparity in per capita incomes for single males and females is somewhat less, single male per capita incomes being, on the average, one and one-half times greater than those of single female wage earners. The explanation for this, of course, is directly related to the type of employment of each group. It has been well established that differential employment is the basis of economic sex discrimination.

When per capita income differentials are examined within the black population, the relationship between sex and per capita income still holds. Black male heads of household have per capita incomes that are 1.8 times greater than per capita incomes of black female heads of household. Similarly, the differential between the per capita incomes of black single males and black single females is almost identical to the pattern observed within the total population: black single male per capita incomes are 1.6 times greater than those of black single females.

The results in Table 7.1 also indicate that per capita income is related not only to sex, but also to household status within each gender group. Both male and female heads of household have higher per capita incomes than single (primary) individuals. The explanation for this lies in the median age of the different groups: single individuals are no doubt younger than heads of household, less experienced in the labor market, and are more subject to periodic unemployment and temporary layoffs.

The most surprising result of the comparison of per capita incomes is that female heads of household are found to have a higher per capita income than other female household-status groups. Much of the previous research on the economic plight of women has indicated that families headed by women are much more apt to be poverty-stricken than other families.[6] The seeming inconsistency here probably results from the fact that poverty levels are calculated taking into consideration not only income but also the number of family members. Per capita income, on the other hand, reflects only the average income earned by a certain group, not the number of people who are being supported by the income. Therefore, although female heads of household have a higher per capita income as a group than wives of heads

TABLE 7.1: Per Capita Income of Employed Persons Living in SMSAs over 250,000, by Household Status, Race, and Gender

Household Status, Sex, Race	Per Capita Income (dollars per year)	Percent Difference in Income*
Total population		
Male heads of household	8,526	—
Males—primary (single)	5,796	-32
Female heads of household	4,407	-48
Females—primary (single)	3,892	-54
Females—wives of heads	3,307	-61
Black population		
Male heads of household	5,947	—
Males—primary (single)	4,182	-30
Female heads of household	3,284	-45
Females—wives of heads	3,198	-46
Females—primary (single)	2,637	-56

*Percent differences in income figures are based on the per capita personal incomes of male heads of household.

Note: Per capita income is computed by taking the median (in terms of dollars) for each of the 11 categories of income, then multiplying the median figures by the total number of persons in each income category, adding the total income earned by each household-status group, and dividing this total earned income by the total number of persons in each household-status group.

Source: Calculated from U.S. Bureau of the Census, Census of Population, 1970 (Washington, D.C.: Government Printing Office), Table 194.

or primary (single) females, they are in reality relatively poorer due to the number of persons that income must support. Also to be considered is the fact that need is undoubtedly an incentive to seek higher-paying jobs. Although the income of wives of heads (married females) may be critical to the family's overall standard of living, it may not be as critical for meeting basic needs. Wives may not be as willing to make the same sacrifices (irregular shifts, overtime, and so on) as female heads of household in order to earn higher salaries. It stands to reason that any person in a household where there are two earners, as opposed to one, has much more flexibility in choosing conditions of employment. [7]

When the relationship between per capita income and household status within each gender group is analyzed by race, the results are nearly identical to those observed through a similar observation of the total population. The single difference is that black wives of heads are at the bottom of the economic ladder when the entire population is considered, whereas primary (single) black females are at the bottom in the per capita income rankings within the black population. These figures suggest that among the black race, young single females are the most economically disadvantaged, whereas among the entire (primarily white) population, married females are the most economically disadvantaged. Certain prevalent stereotypes of females in the labor force might account for this difference. Married women face a certain stigma in the labor market—they will not last, they are not reliable, they quit, they get pregnant, and they have child-care responsibilities that take them off the job an inordinate amount of time. Black females, on the other hand, are not perceived by employers in the same fashion as are white females. First, black females are not considered as "feminine" but rather as "nonfeminine" whereas white females are considered to be the "real women" and are consequently looked at differently in the labor market. Married black females are considered more responsible than single black females. Since blacks are generally considered to be economically deprived, the income of black married females is viewed as essential to the survival of the family; therefore she is not considered to be working solely "to fill up the afternoons." Employers, thus, see married black females as better risks in terms of stability and staying on the job. In other words, the combination of racism and sexism works differently for black females than for white females. [8]

In summary, the results of the comparison of means analysis of per capita personal incomes by household status and sex, show that income inequalities do exist between males and females, among different household-status groups, and between blacks and the predominantly white population. These findings are evidence that linkages exist among income inequalities, household status, gender, and race.

GENERAL TAX BURDEN PATTERNS

Tax burdens are defined in terms of the relationship between per capita tax revenue and per capita personal income. By definition, then, the focus is on the equity of the tax structure—the relationship between the taxes paid and the ability of certain groups to pay. The analysis focuses not only on the total tax burden, but on each of its components as well—the property tax burden and the nonproperty tax burden.

The property tax has long been recognized as the most regressive of all local government taxes. A property tax is a "government levy on certain physical or tangible assets that are claims to future services."[9] While the common tendency is to characterize the local government property tax as a tax on homeowners, it is important to recognize that nonhomeowners also bear a property tax burden as a result of landlords shifting forward property taxes in the form of rents charged. Since poorer people spend greater percentages of their incomes for housing than well-to-do persons, property taxes are much more burdensome for the poor than for the rich. That is, they are highly regressive taxes.

The two most commonly used nonproperty taxes at the local level are the income tax and the sales tax, both regressive taxes. Sales taxes take larger shares of the incomes of poor people who must spend most of their incomes buying basic necessities that are subject to tax. Income taxes at the local level, unlike those at the state or national level, tend to take fixed proportions of personal incomes, typically 1 percent.[10]

It is appropriate at this point to comment on the limitations of the data. It is impossible to disaggregate taxes paid by each household-status group and each gender group from total taxes collected from all persons within an SMSA. By necessity, tax burden must be calculated by dividing per capita tax revenue for all residents of an SMSA by the per capita personal income figures for each of the designated control groups. This discrepancy between actual taxes paid by each group and the per capita tax revenue figures that are, by necessity, used in the tax burden calculations, can be somewhat compensated for by taking into account the highly regressive nature of local government tax structures (property and nonproperty). These figures, imperfect as they are, aid in determining whether linkages exist among tax burdens, household status, and sex. If these linkages are found to exist, it will confirm one of the earlier hypotheses, namely, that local government tax structures are inequitable. That is, local tax structures place undue stress on the finances of those least able to bear the strain.

The figures shown in Table 7.2 support earlier hypotheses suggesting linkages among tax burdens (total, property, and nonproperty), household status, and gender, both within the total population and within the black population.

Tax Burden Patterns by Household Status

Examining first the linkage between tax burdens and household status, it is found that heads of household generally bear a much lighter tax burden than do single (primary) individuals. This is, of course, related to the differences in income levels of heads of household as compared with single persons. (The results of the previous comparison of per capita personal income by household status show that a perfect inverse relationship exists between per capita income and tax burdens.)

The linkage between tax burdens and gender is also very clear. The disparity in tax burdens borne by the various household-status groups is less for females than for males. This can be explained by the tendency of female incomes not to vary greatly, regardless of household status. A word of caution must be expressed regarding comparison of the tax burdens of males and females, particularly those of male and female heads of household. As previously stated, the two groups are not comparable; male heads of household may have their tax burdens lightened by the presence of a working wife, whereas female heads of household must bear the entire tax burden for themselves and their dependents. By definition, these dependents do not include an adult male residing in the home. Since the two head-of-household groups are not comparable, the result is a false inflation of the tax burden borne by wives of heads of household. The effect of combining the incomes of male heads of household and their working wives would be to generally deflate the high tax burdens of working wives, while somewhat inflating the burdens of male heads of household. However, the disparity between tax burdens borne by male and female heads of household still exists as a result of the regressive nature of local government tax structures and the differences in per capita personal incomes. In fact, female heads of household having no male with whom to share the tax burden bear a much heavier tax burden than either married or single males.

The only truly comparable tax burden figures are those of single males and females, both self-supporting. When a comparison is made of the total tax burdens borne by each of these groups, it is observed that tax burdens borne by single females are one and one-half times heavier than those borne by single males. Even if the weaknesses of the data (the difference between actual taxes paid and per capita taxes) were eliminated, it would not diminish the linkage between tax burdens and gender, due to the differences in per capita income and the regressiveness of local tax structures.

Tax Burden Patterns by Race

The same patterns observed within the total population are also observable within the black population (Table 7.2). This further lends credence to the theory that the most critical linkages are those among

Table 7.2: Tax Burdens of Employed Persons Living in SMSAs over 250,000, by Household Status, Race, and Gender (percent)

Household Status, Race, Gender	Total Tax Burden[a]	Increase in Total Tax Burden[b]	Property Tax Burden	Increase in Property Tax Burden	Nonproperty Tax Burden	Increase in Nonproperty Tax Burden
Total population						
Male heads of household	3.0	—	2.5	—	0.5	—
Males—primary (single)	4.0	+33.0	3.4	+36.0	0.6	+20.0
Female heads of household	5.4	+56.0	4.6	+84.0	0.9	+80.0
Females—primary (single)	6.0	+100.0	5.1	+104.0	1.0	+100.0
Females—wives of heads	7.0	+133.0	6.0	+140.0	1.1	+120.0
Black population						
Male heads of household	3.9	—	3.2	—	0.7	—
Males—primary (single)	6.1	+56.0	5.0	+56.0	1.2	+71.0
Female heads of household	7.4	+90.0	6.1	+91.0	1.4	+100.0
Females—wives of head	7.3	+87.0	6.1	+91.0	1.4	+100.0
Females—primary (single)	8.8	+126.0	7.2	+125.0	1.6	+129.0

[a]Tax burden is the relationship between per capita tax revenue and per capita personal income. Tax burden is calculated by dividing per capita tax revenues by per capita personal income (per capita tax revenue/per capita personal income).

[b]Based on the tax burden of male heads of household.

Source: Calculated from U.S. Department of Commerce, Bureau of the Census, Census of Governments: 1972, vol. 5, Local Government in Metropolitan Areas (Washington, D.C.: Government Printing Office), Table 12.

tax burdens, gender, and household status. However, the fact remains that blacks bear heavier tax burdens than whites.

Tax Burden Patterns by Region

The figures shown in Table 7.3 indicate that when a control is made for region (as a surrogate measure of cost-of-living differences among SMSAs), the relationships among tax burdens (total, property, and nonproperty), household status, and sex still exist. Tax burdens are generally found to be heaviest for all persons (regardless of household status or sex) who live in northeastern SMSAs and are lightest for persons living in southern SMSAs. This finding will become even more important in the subsequent analysis of tax efficiencies.

Tax Burden Patterns by Population Size

The figures shown in Table 7.4 indicate that when a control is made for differences in population size (to compensate for differences in economies of scale and in number of services provided), the relationships among tax burdens of all types, household status, and sex are still observable. Generally, tax burdens are heaviest for all persons living in the largest metropolitan areas (over one million). Previous research has indicated that tax burdens are generally heavier in larger metropolitan areas than in smaller metropolitan areas due to the provision of a wider range of services and a greater expectation of and need for provision of poverty-related services (welfare, health, hospitals, housing and urban renewal)—another point to be reemphasized in the analysis of local government tax efficiency.

In summary, crude as the figures may be, they do demonstrate that local government tax structures are, because of their regressiveness, inequitable. This inequity affects females more than males, single persons more than married persons, and blacks more than whites. These findings may be interpreted as evidence of the bias of local government officials who write tax laws that reflect a society that stresses the values of a family structure, headed by males, specifically white males.

TAX EFFICIENCY PATTERNS

Tax efficiency is defined in terms of the relationship between the services an individual or household receives from the expendi-

TABLE 7.3: Tax Burdens of Employed Persons Living in SMSAs over 250,000, by Region, Household Status, Race, and Gender (percent)

Household Status, Race, Gender	Total Tax Burden Region				Property Tax Burden Region				Nonproperty Tax Burden Region			
	NE	S	NC	W	NE	S	NC	W	NE	S	NC	W
Total population												
Male heads of household	4.3	2.2	2.7	3.2	3.4	1.7	2.5	2.8	0.9	0.5	0.3	0.5
Males—primary (single)	4.5	3.2	4.2	4.8	3.8	2.4	3.8	4.1	0.7	0.8	0.4	0.7
Female heads of household	6.0	4.8	5.5	6.0	5.2	3.5	5.1	5.2	0.9	1.1	0.6	0.9
Females—primary (single)	6.7	4.8	6.4	6.8	5.7	3.6	5.9	5.8	1.0	1.1	0.7	1.0
Females—wives of heads	7.9	5.3	7.7	8.3	6.8	4.1	7.0	7.1	1.2	1.3	0.8	1.2
Black population												
Male heads of household	4.6	3.5	3.7	4.7	4.0	2.7	3.4	3.9	0.6	0.8	0.5	0.7
Males—primary (single)	6.2	5.0	8.2	6.7	5.4	3.8	7.0	5.7	0.8	1.2	1.4	1.0
Female heads of household	8.5	6.7	7.2	8.5	7.4	5.0	6.6	7.2	1.2	1.7	0.9	1.3
Females—wives of heads	8.7	6.5	7.3	9.0	7.5	4.9	6.6	7.7	1.9	1.4	1.0	1.4
Females—primary (single)	9.4	8.3	8.8	10.0	8.1	6.3	7.9	8.5	1.3	2.0	1.2	1.5
All males	4.9	3.5	4.7	4.9	4.2	2.7	4.2	4.1	0.8	0.8	0.7	0.7
All females	7.8	6.0	7.2	8.1	6.8	4.6	6.5	6.9	1.3	1.4	0.9	1.2

*The regional classification is NE for Northeast, S for South, NC for North Central (Midwest), and W for West.

Note: Tax burden is the relationship between per capita tax revenue and per capita personal income (per capita tax revenue/per capita personal income).

Source: Calculated from U.S. Department of Commerce, Bureau of the Census, Census of Governments: 1972, vol. 5, Local Government in Metropolitan Areas (Washington, D.C.: Government Printing Office), Table 12.

TABLE 7.4: Tax Burdens of Employed Persons Living in SMSAs over 250,000 by Population Size, Household Status, Race, and Gender (percent)

	Total Tax Burden Population Size			Property Tax Burden Population Size			Nonproperty Tax Burden Population Size		
	1,000,000 and over	500,000–999,999	250,000–499,999	1,000,000 and over	500,000–999,999	250,000–499,999	1,000,000 and over	500,000–999,999	250,000–499,999
Total population									
Male heads of household	3.4	2.8	3.5	2.9	2.2	2.8	0.5	0.5	0.7
Males—primary (single)	4.7	4.1	3.8	4.1	3.3	3.2	0.8	0.8	0.6
Female heads of household	6.5	5.5	5.2	5.7	4.4	4.4	1.0	1.1	0.8
Females—primary (single)	7.0	6.0	5.8	6.1	4.8	4.9	1.1	1.2	0.9
Females—wives of heads	8.7	7.1	6.9	7.6	5.8	5.8	1.4	1.4	1.0
Black population									
Male heads of household	4.6	3.8	3.6	4.0	3.0	3.0	0.8	0.8	0.6
Males—primary (single)	8.8	5.5	5.1	7.4	4.3	4.2	1.7	1.2	0.9
Female heads of household	8.3	7.3	7.2	7.3	5.7	5.9	1.3	1.6	1.3
Females—wives of heads	8.3	7.4	7.1	7.3	5.8	5.9	1.7	1.5	1.3
Females—primary (single)	9.6	8.8	8.4	8.4	6.8	6.8	1.6	2.0	1.5
All males	5.4	4.1	4.0	4.6	3.2	3.3	1.0	0.8	0.7
All females	8.1	7.0	6.8	7.1	5.6	5.6	1.4	1.5	1.1

Note: Tax burden is the relationship between per capita tax revenue and per capita personal income (per capita tax revenue/per capita personal income).

Source: Calculated from U.S. Department of Commerce, Bureau of the Census, Census of Governments: 1972, vol. 5, Local Government in Metropolitan Areas (Washington, D.C.: Government Printing Office), Table 12.

tures of the government and the tax burden he or she bears as a result of the government's taxation policies. This is also referred to as the service/tax burden ratio. To date, the best available measure of the benefits an individual receives from the expenditures of his or her local government is per capita expenditures, both for total services provided and for specific services provided.

An examination is made of not only the general tax efficiency for all services, but also of the efficiency of the tax structure in providing for the so-called poverty-linked services (welfare, health, hospitals, and housing and urban renewal). If greater benefit, as shown by tax efficiency figures, is received by those most in need of aid, the inequities created by a highly regressive local government structure will be at least partially alleviated. If linkages are found among tax inefficiency, household status, and gender, it will demonstrate the costs of inequitable tax structures, for those persons most unfairly taxed in relation to their ability to pay place a greater strain than others on the system, by demanding and requiring increased governmental services, usually the poverty-linked services. Even more basically, it will demonstrate the costs to the entire economic and governmental system of poorer, often unequal, pay for employed minorities (women and blacks).

Again, it is necessary to comment on the imperfections of the data. First, it is impossible to disaggregate the service-level figures. No precise determination could be made of how much is spent per capita on each household-status, gender, or racial group. Consequently, service-level measures are for the entire population. One consolation is that certain groups receive more of certain types of services than other groups. Thus, by comparing the general efficiency of the tax structure for all services, it is possible to get a general feel for the overall efficiency of local government tax structures.

General Tax Efficiency (All Services)

The figures shown in Table 7.5 indicate that the efficiency of local government tax structures is indeed related to household status, sex, and race. When a specific focus is made on the tax efficiency of all services provided by the local governments, it is found that males (in both the total and black populations) receive greater returns on their tax dollars through services than females. Similarly, blacks receive a substantially lesser return on their tax dollars than whites. When analyzed by household-status group, it is found that heads of household receive the most in return for taxes paid. However, these figures may be somewhat misleading, since their proportion of services received is diminished by the number of dependents who must

TABLE 7.5: General Tax Efficiency (All Services) for Employed Persons Living in SMSAs over 250,000, by Region, Population Size, Household Status, Race, and Gender

Household Status, Race, Gender Group	General Tax Efficiency	Region*				Population Size		
		NE	S	NC	W	1,000,000 and over	500,000– 999,999	250,000– 499,999
Total population								
Male heads of household	18.874	17.790	19.694	18.463	19.315	18.349	19.489	17.948
Males—primary (single)	12.809	12.167	13.570	12.210	13.057	12.966	13.267	12.544
Female heads of household	9.670	9.121	9.382	10.067	10.313	10.773	9.829	9.197
Females—primary (single)	8.602	8.137	9.035	7.950	9.234	8.807	9.034	8.330
Females—wives of heads	7.359	6.897	8.127	6.637	7.540	7.104	7.610	7.084
Black population								
Male heads of household	8.208	6.690	11.496	7.951	4.755	12.708	11.232	8.253
Males—primary (single)	5.774	4.973	8.006	5.484	3.303	9.108	7.749	5.898
Female heads of household	4.505	3.617	6.212	4.563	2.593	7.723	5.847	4.159
Females—wives of heads	4.411	3.567	6.244	4.286	2.461	7.341	5.821	4.235
Females—primary (single)	3.616	3.276	4.870	3.396	2.169	6.086	4.857	3.585
All males	11.416	10.405	13.192	11.027	10.108	13.282	12.934	11.161
All females	6.361	5.769	7.315	6.150	5.718	7.972	7.166	6.098

*The regional classification is NE for Northeast, S for South, NC for North Central (Midwest), and W for West.

Note: Tax efficiency (the service/tax burden ratio) is the relationship between benefits an individual or household receives from the government's expenditure policies and the tax burden he or she bears as a result of the government's taxation policies (per capita expenditures/total tax burden).

Source: Compiled by the author.

share the proportion of services received for the entire household. Even so, female heads of household get less in return for taxes paid than male heads of household, many of whom are further aided by working wives. These results seem to indicate that local government tax structures are not only inequitable, but also inefficient in delivering services to those most in need of the services within their populations.

Table 7.5 also indicates that the relationships among tax efficiency, household status, sex, and race hold when region and population size, respectively, are held constant. Tax structures are most inefficient for all persons, regardless of group, living in the northeastern SMSAs and are most efficient for persons living in southern SMSAs. Much of this can be explained by the eroding tax base of northern SMSAs, coupled with the necessity of providing a greater number of services as a result of tradition.

Similarly controlling for population size, it is found that tax structures are most efficient for all persons living in the medium-sized SMSAs (500,000-999,999). This is very closely related to economies of scale. Tiebout was very much concerned with population size and its relation to service provision. "For every pattern of community services . . . there is an optimal community size. This optimum is defined in terms of the number of residents for which this bundle of services can be produced at the lowest average cost."[11] In a later study, Shapiro found that the most serious financial problems occur in units with very large or very small numbers of people residing within their jurisdictions.[12] Subsequent research has shown that the real concern is not with economy of scale in production of the services, but rather with the distribution of costs and benefits of the goods and services produced.[13] The findings do demonstrate the existence of economies of scale in service provision within these 125 SMSAs.

Tax Efficiency: Poverty-Related Services

If it is assumed, as it was by Netzer, that services received are progressive in relation to income,[14] then one would expect to find that local government tax structures are efficient in the provision of poverty-related services—that is, they are delivered to those in the greatest need. Again, a note of caution must be made regarding the disaggregation of service-level figures. However, as the results shown in Table 7.6 indicate, the tax structures of these 125 SMSAs over 250,000 population are inefficient in their provision of welfare, hospitals, health, and housing and urban renewal services, particularly to females and blacks. It might properly be argued that female

TABLE 7.6: Tax Efficiency (Poverty-Related Services) for Employed Persons Living in SMSAs over 250,000, by Household Status, Race, and Gender

| Household Status, Race, Gender | Tax Efficiency | | | |
	Welfare	Hospitals	Health	Housing and Urban Renewal
Total population				
Male heads of household	1.066	.858	.231	.577
Males—primary (single)	.718	.582	.156	.394
Female heads of household	.539	.433	.118	.290
Females—primary (single)	.491	.390	.106	.264
Females—wives of heads	.413	.343	.090	.229
Black population				
Male heads of household	.455	.415	.231	.268
Males—primary (single)	.330	.294	.075	.189
Female heads of household	.244	.231	.058	.140
Females—wives of heads	.243	.227	.057	.144
Females—primary (single)	.212	.181	.047	.117

Note: Tax efficiency (the service/tax burden ratio) is the relationship between the benefits an individual or household receives from the expenditures of the government and the tax burden he or she bears as a result of the government's taxation policies (per capita expenditures/total tax burden). Tax efficiency for each of the poverty-related services (welfare, hospitals, health, housing and urban renewal) is calculated by dividing the per capita expenditures for each service by the total tax burden (per capita expenditure for each service/total tax burden). The larger the figure, the more efficient is the return on the tax dollar.

Source: Compiled by the author.

heads of household receive greater proportions of the funds spent on these services, especially health and welfare services, than male heads of household. But it might also be argued that hospitals and housing and urban renewal services would be equally likely to benefit males and females, blacks and whites. Yet it can be observed that these services, too, are inefficiently provided for by the tax structures of metropolitan governments.

In summary, local government tax structures, in addition to being inequitable, are also inefficient. The effects of these weaknesses of local tax structures have the greatest impacts on females, single persons, and blacks. Thus, it is possible to observe that linkages exist among tax efficiency, household status, gender, and race.

SIGNIFICANCE OF THE FINDINGS

The results of this study indicate that linkages exist among per capita personal income, local government tax burdens, tax efficiencies, household status, gender, and race. The existence of these linkages suggests that the economically disadvantaged position of women and blacks, especially in the large metropolitan areas of the United States, affects local government tax structures and, conversely, that local government tax structures affect the economic positions of women and minorities. Local government tax structures are found to be both inequitable and inefficient.

The data indicate that males, averaging higher per capita incomes than females, have lighter tax burdens and benefit from greater tax efficiencies. In other words, men, who have higher average earnings, pay a lower proportion of those earnings to local taxes and, at the same time, receive greater benefits on their tax dollars, than do women and blacks. Although the household-status groups in the black population have lower per capita incomes, heavier tax burdens, and suffer from tax inefficiencies more than their counterparts in the total population, the relative position of the gender groups remains the same as in the total population. Specifically, women are consistently more economically disadvantaged than men. Not only are they handicapped within the society by lower per capita incomes, but they are additionally penalized by heavier local tax burdens and lower returns on their tax dollars.

Certain household-status groups also bear a heavier brunt of local taxation policies than others. Male and female heads of household have consistently lower tax burdens and benefit from greater tax efficiencies than do single males and females.

In summary, the findings indicate that persons who are most penalized by the inequalities and inefficiencies of local government tax structures are females, low-income earners, blacks, unmarried persons, and working wives. As Heather Ross, in her recent study of poverty, indicated, "There is nothing in the nature of economic progress which assures that all people will benefit equally. Indeed, one of the important functions of humane government policy is to correct major imbalances that occur when economic activity rewards some people much more than others."[15] If Ross's statement is accepted, it must be concluded that with regard to humanitarianism, local tax policy is in every respect a dismal failure. Rather than helping to alleviate economic imbalances, local government tax policies serve to further aggravate these imbalances. Local tax policy has been largely neglected insofar as its impact on women and blacks is concerned. It has been obscured under the guise of neutral impact on males and females, in particular. This illusion needs to be stripped away and local tax policy must take its rightful place on the list of economic discriminators.

NOTES

1. Susan Ann MacManus and Nikki R. Van Hightower, "The Impacts of Local Government Tax Structures on Women: Inefficiencies and Inequalities," Social Science Journal 14 (April 1977): 103-16.

2. See U.S. Department of Labor, Manpower Administration, Manpower Report of the President (Washington, D.C.: Government Printing Office, April 1971); U.S. Women's Bureau, 1969 Handbook on Women Workers (Washington, D.C.: Government Printing Office, 1969); U.S. Department of Labor, Economic Report of the President (Washington, D.C.: Government Printing Office, 1973), chap. 4; Victor Fuchs, "Differences in Hourly Earnings between Men and Women," Monthly Labor Review 94 (May 1971): 9-15; Barbara Bergmann and Irman Adelman, "The 1973 Report of the Council of Economic Advisors: The Economic Role of Women," American Economic Review 63 (September 1973): 509-14; Jessie Bernard, Women and the Public Interest, An Essay on Policy and Protest (Chicago: Atherton, 1971); Juanita Kreps, Sex in the Marketplace: American Women at Work (Baltimore: Johns Hopkins University Press, 1971); Twentieth Century Fund Task Force on Women and Employment, Exploitation from 9 to 5 (Lexington, Mass.: Lexington, 1975); and Maxine C. Johnson, "Women and Public Policy: The Search for Equity in the Labor Market," Paper presented at the 1976 Annual Meeting of the Southwestern Political Science Association, Dallas, Texas, April 7-10, 1976.

3. See Alan K. Campbell and Seymour Sacks, Metropolitan America: Fiscal Patterns and Governmental Systems (New York: The Free Press, 1967); Seymour Sacks and John Callahan, "Central City-Suburban Disparity," in Advisory Commission on Intergovernmental Relations, City Financial Emergencies: The Intergovernmental Dimension (Washington, D.C.: U.S. Government Printing Office, 1973); and Robert B. Pettengill and Jogindar S. Uppal, Can Cities Survive? The Fiscal Plight of American Cities (New York: St. Martin's Press, 1974).

4. Department of Commerce, Bureau of the Census, Census of Population, 1970 (Washington, D.C.: U.S. Government Printing Office), Appendix B, p. 23.

5. Twentieth Century Fund Task Force on Women and Employment, op. cit., p. 3.

6. Economic Report of the President, op. cit., p. 108.

7. For an interesting discussion of working mothers, see Jessie Bernard, The Future of Motherhood (New York: Dial, 1974), chap. 10.

8. Cynthia Fuchs Epstein, "Positive Effects of the Multiple Negative: Explaining the Success of Black Professional Women," in Women in a Changing Society, ed. Joan Huber (Chicago: University of Chicago Press, 1973), pp. 150-73.

9. Werner Z. Hirsch, The Economics of State and Local Government (New York: McGraw-Hill, 1970), p. 25.

10. Robert L. Lineberry and Ira Sharkansky, Urban Politics and Public Policy (New York: Harper & Row, 1971), p. 193.

11. Charles M. Tiebout, "A Pure Theory of Local Expenditures," Journal of Political Economy, 64 (October 1956): 416-24.

12. Harvey Shapiro, "Economies of Scale and Local Government Finance," Land Economics 39 (May 1963): 135-86.

13. Hirsch, op. cit., p. 198.

14. Dick Netzer, Economics of the Property Tax (Washington, D.C.: The Brookings Institution, 1966), pp. 33-66.

15. Heather Ross, "Poverty: Women and Children Last," in Economic Independence for Women: The Foundation for Equal Rights, ed. Jane Roberts Chapman (Beverly Hills: Sage Publications, 1976), p. 137.

Chapter 8

Changing Revenue Patterns
in U.S. Suburbs:
A Potential Fiscal Crisis?

INTRODUCTION

"Suburbs are rich, and getting richer; cities are poor, and getting poorer." "Suburban residents are wealthy, highly educated, white, middle-aged, Protestants; city residents are poor, unskilled, uneducated, blacks, browns, ethnics, and elderly." As over-simplistic as these descriptions may appear, they represent common perceptions of the financial and socioeconomic conditions of cities and suburbs within the SMSAs of the United States.

To date, much attention has been focused on changes in the financial conditions of large central cities,[1] primarily because of the fiscal crises experienced by New York, Philadelphia, and Detroit. Fiscal conditions are gauged as nearing crisis levels when revenue structures are increasingly incapable of raising enough revenue to meet current operating expenditure needs. There has not, however, been much discussion about the changes in the fiscal conditions of U.S. suburbs. Yet it is a fact that suburbs experience maturation processes similar to those of central cities. "Cities beget suburbs, which grow into small cities, which then show the vigor of youth, the stability of middle age, and eventual decline."[2] Suburbs are already beginning to face the problems caused by rapid growth that cities have felt for decades:

> While not experiencing the drastic changes in the socio-economic character of their population, they are faced with the prospect of developing an urban infra-structure which carries with it substantial expenditure demands. Thus, while tax levels and tax rates remain higher in central cities, suburbs have experienced percentage in-

creases in taxes and expenditures which are remarkably similar to those of central cities.[3]

Until recently, most studies have focused on changes in the expenditure patterns of municipalities at the expense of examining changes in the revenue side of the budgetary ledger. Now it is becoming apparent that changes in revenue patterns are important predictors of financial crises.[4] Increasing reliance on intergovernmental revenues and on nonproperty tax revenues, combined by a fairly stable reliance on property taxes, are often signs that a city's revenue structure is becoming strained.

The purpose of this chapter is to describe and contrast patterns of change in the revenue structures of 340 U.S. suburban municipalities over a ten-year period (1962-72). Specifically, the study examines the changes in both revenue levels (per capita) and revenue reliance patterns (the proportion of total general revenue received from each particular revenue source). The sources of revenue analyzed include intergovernmental (federal, state), tax (property and nonproperty), and nontax (charges and miscellaneous general revenues). Additionally, the linkages between changes in various demographic, socioeconomic, and governmental conditions and changes in suburban revenue patterns are examined.

By examining the determinants of change in suburban revenue patterns, it is possible to determine which environmental changes most affect the intake of and the reliance upon certain types of revenues. Governmental officials can thus learn to detect the conditions in their cities that are likely to necessitate changes in revenue and expenditure patterns in order to avert fiscal crises.

Framework of Analysis

Within a systems-analytic framework, the linkage between changes in demographic, socioeconomic, and governmental characteristics (inputs) and changes in revenue patterns (outputs) of these 340 suburban municipalities will be examined. In contrast to earlier chapters, the time frame within which this change analysis is performed is, by definition, longitudinal (dynamic): 1962-72.

PREVIOUS RESEARCH

Weaknesses

Previous research on changes in the revenue patterns of suburbs has been rather limited, since most fiscal research has focused attention on cities, not on suburbs. The limited suburban research that has been done is generally weak as the result of problems in definition, scope, and research design.

Suburbs have traditionally been somewhat inaccurately defined. Many studies have defined suburbs as "all the area outside the central city within an SMSA."[5] However, there are severe consequences when suburbs are so defined. As has been pointed out in earlier chapters, the lumping together of all the governmental units outside the central city into a broad category labeled suburbs represents a failure to recognize that there are different types of suburbs; suburbs are not homogeneous in their demographic, socioeconomic, or governmental characteristics. They are separate governmental units with taxing, spending, and borrowing powers; they are separate policy-making units.

Those studies that have correctly defined suburbs suffer from the problem of limited scope. They have merely contrasted suburbs within a single metropolitan area.[6] In other words, these studies have been of a descriptive (case study) nature rather than of a comparative nature. Consequently, the results of these studies are not generalizable and it cannot be inferred that they characterize suburban municipalities throughout the United States.

Another problem with previous research efforts has been that many of the studies were designed for the purpose of contrasting central city and suburban changes in revenue patterns rather than for comparing and contrasting change patterns among suburbs. The bulk of these studies have analyzed the impacts of outmigration on[7] or suburban exploitation of[8] central city finances. Even those studies that have made general contrasts of central city and suburban fiscal disparities[9] suffer from a previously identified problem—the lumping together of all suburbs as homogeneous units of analysis. In summary, research designed to contrast revenue patterns of cities and suburbs, while providing information regarding revenue patterns of suburbs collectively, does not, however, delineate change patterns among suburbs—suburbs that are at different stages in the maturation process.

CHANGES IN SUBURBAN REVENUE LEVELS

As the figures shown in Table 8.1 indicate, suburbs experienced the greatest changes between 1962 and 1972 in their tax revenue levels (+$62), followed by changes in intergovernmental revenue levels (+$26), and changes in nontax revenue levels (+$19).

A comparison of the changes in the levels of the two types of intergovernmental revenue indicates that state aid levels increased

TABLE 8.1: Change in Revenue Level and Reliance of 340 Suburbs, by Revenue Source, 1962–72

Source	Change in Level[a] (dollars)	Change in Reliance[b] (percent)
Total general revenue	106	
Intergovernmental revenue	26	11.5
Federal	6	4.3
State	20	7.2
Tax revenue	62	17.2
Property	43	5.2
Nonproperty	19	12.0
Nontax revenue	19	-28.7

[a]Level is the per capita dollar amount from a particular revenue source.

[b]Reliance is the percentage of the total general revenue received from a particular source.

Sources: U.S. Department of Commerce, Bureau of the Census, Census of Governments: 1962, 1972 (Washington, D.C.: Government Printing Office), vol. 4, Table 21 (1962), Table 22 (1972).

(+$20) much more than federal aid levels (+$6). However, if one examines the proportional increases in levels, federal aid levels have increased the most. Similarly, comparing changes in tax revenue levels, it is found that the greatest dollar increases per capita were in property tax levels (+$43) as contrasted with nonproperty tax level changes (+$19). However, the greatest proportional increases were in nonproperty tax levels. These two findings alone suggest that the potential for a fiscal crisis does indeed exist among U.S. suburbs. They are headed down the same financial paths that cities have already trod.

While such figures are indicative of the general revenue level changes for suburbs collectively, comparison-of-means analysis by region, population size, economic base, governmental character (reformism), and functional responsibility enables a more in-depth contrast of changes among suburbs (Tables 8.2–8.6).

TABLE 8.2: Change in Revenue Level and Reliance of 340 Suburbs, by Revenue Source and Region, 1962-72

	Northeast (96)[a]	South (50)[a]	North Central (109)[a]	West (85)[a]
Change in Level[b] (dollars)				
Intergovernmental revenue	35	15	25	21
Federal	6	8	5	5
State	29	7	20	16
Tax revenue	105	44	46	43
Property	97	23	29	13
Nonproperty	8	21	17	30
Nontax revenue	6	31	26	16
Total general revenue	146	91	97	82
Change in Reliance[c] (percent)				
Intergovernmental revenue	7.1	5.4	8.5	12.0
Federal	0.5	3.8	2.3	2.9
State	6.6	1.6	6.2	9.1
Tax revenue	10.8	17.2	14.3	11.1
Property	9.6	4.7	4.6	0.2
Nonproperty	1.2	12.5	19.7	10.9
Nontax revenue	-17.8	-22.7	-22.7	-23.1

[a]Number of suburbs.

[b]Level is the per capita dollar amount for a particular revenue source.

[c]Reliance is the percentage of the total general revenue received from a particular source.

Note: Figures may not add to total due to rounding.

Sources: U.S. Department of Commerce, Bureau of the Census, Census of Governments: 1962, 1972 (Washington, D.C.: Government Printing Office), vol. 4, Table 21 (1962), Table 22 (1972).

TABLE 8.3: Change in Revenue Level and Reliance of 340 Suburbs, by Revenue Source and Population Size, 1962-72

	Over 100,000 (12)[a]	50,000- 100,000 (43)[a]	25,000- 50,000 (77)[a]	Below 25,000 (208)[a]
Change in Level[b] (dollars)				
Intergovernmental revenue	33	24	26	24
Federal	11	4	6	5
State	22	19	21	19
Tax revenue	23	43	67	60
Property	3	23	54	40
Nonproperty	20	20	23	20
Nontax revenue	11	13	16	21
Total general revenue	74	81	109	104
Change in Reliance[c] (percent)				
Intergovernmental revenue	8.7	7.2	4.2	9.1
Federal	2.9	2.1	1.4	2.2
State	5.7	5.1	2.8	7.0
Tax revenue	-11.6	-7.6	-1.0	18.6
Property	-21.0	-11.8	-1.2	8.8
Nonproperty	10.4	4.2	0.2	9.8
Nontax revenue	2.9	0.3	-3.2	-27.7

[a]Number of suburbs.

[b]Level is the per capita dollar amount for a particular revenue source.

[c]Reliance is the percentage of the total general revenue received from a particular source.

Note: Figures may not add to total due to rounding.

Sources: U.S. Department of Commerce, Bureau of the Census, Census of Governments: 1962, 1972 (Washington, D.C.: Government Printing Office), vol. 4, Table 21 (1962), Table 22 (1972).

TABLE 8.4: Change in Revenue Level and Reliance of 340 Suburbs, by Revenue Source and Economic Base, 1962-72

	Economic Base[a]					
	Manufacturing (87)[b]	Industrial (12)[b]	Diversified Manufacturing (19)[b]	Diversified Retailing (41)[b]	Retailing (61)[b]	Other (24)[b]
Change in Level[c] (dollars)						
Intergovernmental revenue	33	15	27	19	15	30
Federal	9	-2	6	4	2	4
State	24	17	21	15	12	25
Tax revenue	63	79	88	49	34	63
Property	47	55	70	32	16	48
Nonproperty	16	24	18	17	18	15
Nontax revenue	8	32	3	20	4	20
Total general revenue	104	55	116	88	52	113
Change in Reliance[d] (percent)						
Intergovernmental revenue	8.8	-3.8	3.5	5.9	5.7	2.5
Federal	3.5	-7.2	1.1	1.2	1.2	0.8
State	5.3	3.4	2.5	4.7	4.6	1.7
Tax revenue	-1.1	13.8	17.6	-9.3	-1.0	-2.0
Property	-6.3	9.5	9.9	-8.8	-8.1	-3.4
Nonproperty	5.2	4.3	7.7	0.5	7.1	1.4
Nontax revenue	-7.6	-10.1	-21.1	3.4	-4.7	4.1

[a]The first five economic-base types are the five basic economic types (collected on the basis of place of work. Other represents suburbs with very specialized economic bases: wholesaling, mining, transportation, resort, government and armed forces, professional, hospital, education, or service. Figures do not add to total due to missing data.

[b]Number of suburbs.

[c]Level is the per capita dollar amount for a particular revenue source.

[d]Reliance is the percentage of the total general revenue received from a particular source.

Sources: U.S. Department of Commerce, Bureau of the Census, Census of Governments: 1962, 1972 (Washington, D.C.: Government Printing Office), vol. 4, Table 21 (1962), Table 22 (1972). International City Management Association, The Municipal Yearbook, 1963 (Chicago: International City Management Association, 1963).

TABLE 8.5: Change in Revenue Level and Reliance of 340 Suburbs, by Revenue Source and Governmental Character, 1962-72

	Governmental Character[a]		
	Unreformed (11)[b]	Mixed (213)[b]	Reformed (116)[b]
Change in Level[c] (dollars)			
Intergovernmental revenue	31	29	18
Federal	2	6	5
State	29	23	13
Tax revenue	66	70	42
Property	49	53	23
Nonproperty	17	17	19
Nontax revenue	18	17	25
Total general revenue	186	93	85
Change in Reliance[d] (percent)			
Intergovernmental revenue	8.8	9.1	6.1
Federal	1.0	2.1	2.0
State	7.8	7.0	4.1
Tax revenue	-4.0	18.8	-1.0
Property	-2.1	9.9	-5.4
Nonproperty	1.9	8.9	4.4
Nontax revenue	-4.8	-28.0	-5.2

[a]Unreformed suburbs are those with a mayor-council form of government, partisan elections, and a ward council member selection plan. Reformed suburbs are those with a council-manager form of government, nonpartisan elections, and at-large council member selections plans. Mixed suburbs are those having at least one "reformed" characteristic and one "unreformed" characteristic.

[b]Number of suburbs.

[c]Level is the per capita dollar amount for a particular revenue source.

[d]Reliance is the percentage of the total general revenue from a particular source. Figures may not add to total due to rounding.

Sources: U.S. Department of Commerce, Bureau of the Census, Census of Governments: 1962, 1972 (Washington, D.C.: Government Printing Office), vol. 4, Table 21 (1962), Table 22 (1972).

TABLE 8.6: Change in Revenue Level and Reliance of 340 Suburbs, by Revenue Source and Functional Responsibility, 1962–72

	Functional Responsibility									
	Education (49)[a]	No Education (291)[a]	Hospitals (45)[a]	No Hospitals (295)[a]	Welfare (89)[a]	No Welfare (251)[a]	Housing and Urban Renewal (43)[a]	No Housing and Urban Renewal (297)[a]	All Four Functions (4)[a]	None of Functions (218)[a]
Change in Level[b] (dollars)										
Intergovernmental revenue	58	20	37	24	41	20	36	24	83	21
Federal	10	5	8	5	7	1	9	5	21	4
State	48	16	29	19	33	20	27	19	61	17
Tax revenue	160	45	120	53	110	45	64	61	146	42
Property	149	25	107	33	97	24	46	42	142	24
Nonproperty	11	20	13	20	13	21	18	19	4	18
Nontax revenue	21	19	20	19	12	21	18	19	19	20
Total general revenue	239	84	176	95	161	86	118	104	247	85
Change in Reliance[c] (percent)										
Intergovernmental revenue	5.6	9.0	3.9	9.2	7.0	9.1	7.7	8.6	8.6	10.1
Federal	1.6	2.2	1.0	2.2	1.1	2.6	1.7	2.1	-0.3	2.6
State	4.0	6.8	2.8	7.0	6.0	6.5	6.0	6.5	8.8	7.4
Tax revenue	4.5	14.4	2.0	14.6	3.1	16.4	-3.0	15.2	-9.5	15.2
Property	3.6	5.2	-0.3	5.8	1.4	6.2	-8.4	6.9	-7.8	8.4
Nonproperty	0.9	9.2	2.3	8.8	1.7	10.2	5.4	8.3	1.7	6.8
Nontax revenue	-10.1	-23.4	-5.9	-23.8	-10.2	-25.5	-4.8	-23.8	1.0	-29.1

[a]Number of suburbs.

[b]Revenue level is the per capita dollar amount for a particular revenue source.

[c]Revenue reliance is the percentage of the total general revenue from a particular source.

Note: Figures may not add to total due to rounding.

Sources: U.S. Department of Commerce, Bureau of the Census, Census of Governments: 1962, 1972 (Washington, D.C.: Government Printing Office), vol. 4, Table 21 (1962), Table 22 (1972).

Changes in Intergovernmental Revenue Levels

Changes in Federal Aid Levels

The greatest changes in federal aid levels occurred among southern suburbs (+$8), suburbs with populations exceeding 100,000 (+$11), manufacturing-based suburbs (+$9), suburbs with mixed governmental characters (+$6), and suburbs with financial responsibilities for all of the least common suburban functions—education, hospitals, welfare, housing and urban renewal—(+$21).

Federal aid, since the 1930s and the advent of grants-in-aid, has been distributed on the basis of need with the goal being that of redistribution and equalization. Consequently, the formulas allocating such monies have been constructed inversely to a governmental unit's ability to pay—an equity choice rather than an efficiency choice. Jack and Reuss comment on the significance of this increasing aid. "The major significance of these patterns is that higher levels of government with access to flexible, progressive taxes have assumed a greater responsibility for provision of public wants via grants to localities thus partially redressing existing fiscal disparities."[10]

It is not surprising that greater increases in federal aid per capita have occurred among southern suburbs over the past ten years. The South, being the poorest region, thus benefited the most since federal formulas were and still are constructed inversely to a government's ability to pay.

Likewise, larger suburbs that were characterized by increasing proportions of poor, minority populations over this same ten-year period increased their federal aid dollars per capita much more than did smaller suburbs.

The greatest contrasts in changes in federal aid levels can be observed when suburbs are grouped according to functional responsibilities. Suburbs providing functions such as education, welfare, hospitals, and housing and urban renewal—functions that place a greater strain on their revenue structures—increased federal aid levels much more than did suburbs without such functional responsibilities. Suburbs having such costly responsibilities are typically the larger suburbs with poorer populations. Thus, they are more likely to be eligible for federal funding, particularly for these poverty-related services. Relatedly, suburbs with manufacturing economic bases are also the larger suburbs and consequently are more likely to have financial responsibility for these least common suburban functions than suburbs with specialized economic bases.

Changes in State Aid Levels

Changes in state aid levels among these 340 suburbs were most marked among northeastern suburbs (+$29), suburbs with populations over 100,000 (+$22), suburbs with manufacturing (+$24) and "other" (+$25) economic bases, suburbs with unreformed governmental characters (+$29), and suburbs with all four least common functional responsibilities (+$61). Of the four least common suburban functions, education appears to be the one that most stimulated increases in state aid per capita, consistent with earlier statements regarding the nature of state categorical grants.

The fact that state aid levels increased the most among northeastern suburbs (+$29) and the least among southern suburbs (+$7) is perhaps explainable by the fact that southern suburbs are generally smaller. Many state aid formulas are based on mere population size rather than solely on the basis of the income level of the population; that is, they are efficiency-related rather than equity-related. This would also explain why the larger suburbs have increased state aid levels more than smaller suburbs, and why manufacturing-based suburbs and suburbs with functional responsibilities for education, welfare, hospitals, and housing and urban renewal have all experienced greater per capita increases in state aid than suburbs not so characterized. It also explains why suburbs with unreformed governmental characters increased per capita state aid more than reformed suburbs, since unreformed suburbs are typically larger.

As to the explanation for the comparatively larger increases in state aid per capita to suburbs with "other" economic bases, one needs only to turn to the type of program likely to be funded by state aid. Many of these more specialized suburbs have economic bases that make them eligible for large, state block grants: governmental, education, hospitals, resort (tourism), and so on. It is often in the best interests of the entire state economy to stimulate growth of these specialized suburbs.

Changes in Tax Revenue Levels

Changes in Property Tax Levels

Property tax level changes were greatest among suburbs located in the Northeast (+$97), suburbs with populations between 25,000–50,000 (+$54), suburbs with diversified-manufacturing economic bases (+$70), suburbs with unreformed governmental characters (+$49), and suburbs with responsibilities for performing all of the least common functional responsibilities (+$142). Education is the particular least common function that most results in increases in property tax levels (+$149).

One obvious explanation for the comparatively greater increases in property tax levels among northeastern suburbs involves legal constraints, in this case the lack thereof. Eighty percent of the states in the Northeast place no restrictions upon municipal use of the property tax. In contrast, 90 percent of the states outside the Northeast do place such restrictions on their municipal governments. It has also been suggested that southern and western municipalities have been more able to use annexation or consolidation methods to incorporate more taxable property into their governmental jurisdictions and thereby to keep property tax level increases relatively low in comparison with the older, more locked-in suburbs in the Northeast and Midwest.

The finding that property tax levels increased most among smaller-sized suburbs is not surprising in the light of the results of an earlier study that found a curvilinear relationship between population size and property tax levels.[11] In other words, higher per capita property taxes are characteristic of smaller and larger suburbs; lower per capitas are characteristic of middle-sized municipalities. Another explanation for greater increases in property tax levels among smaller suburbs may be that since states place greater restrictions upon their usage of nonproperty taxes, they have had no alternative but to increase property tax levels.

The greater increases in property tax levels by suburbs with diversified-manufacturing economic bases was also to be expected. Wood[12] suggested that tax assessors in communities with large industrial or commercial bases typically make extensive use of that tax base.

The finding that property tax levels increased most among unreformed suburbs is also congruent with earlier theories. Reform theory is premised on efficiency, or "getting the most out of the government with the least amount of money" through operating the government in a businesslike manner. It has been stated that "much of the rhetorical thunder in support of reform (manager governments, nonpartisan elections, and at-large constituencies) claims that lower taxes . . . will follow their adoption."[13]

Finally, it is to be expected that suburbs with financial responsibilities for providing education, welfare, hospitals, and housing and urban renewal will have increased their property tax levels much more than suburbs without such responsibilities. Looking specifically at the relationship between educational responsibility and property tax level increases, it can be observed that as educational costs have escalated, so have property tax levels—by necessity, since education is a function that is almost totally supported by property tax levies.

Changes in Nonproperty Tax Levels

Nonproperty tax level changes were greatest among western suburbs (+$30), suburbs with industrial economic bases (+$24), suburbs with reformed governmental characters (+$19), suburbs with populations of 25,000-50,000 (+$23), and suburbs without responsibilities for any of the least common suburban functions (+$18).

The property tax has traditionally been the main source of tax revenue for municipalities. Nonproperty taxes are relatively new sources of income for municipalities and are still prohibited at the local level in many states. As was stated earlier, municipal use of nonproperty taxes is much more restricted than is use of the property tax.

Part of the explanation for the greater per capita nonproperty tax increases among western suburbs is that western states have tended to place few restrictions on municipal use of nonproperty taxes. For example, 60 percent of the western states (as opposed to 37 percent of the nonwestern states) allow their municipalities to levy a general sales tax; 75 percent (as opposed to 39 percent) allow their municipalities to levy additional selective sales or excise taxes. The extensive use of nonproperty taxes among western suburbs also helps explain why property tax levels did not increase as much among western suburbs as among northeastern suburbs.

Larger, older suburbs, with industrial bases, unreformed governmental characters and with financial responsibilities for education, welfare, hospitals, and housing and urban renewal, have traditionally been characterized by greater increases in property tax than nonproperty tax levels. Younger, smaller suburbs, being aware of the increasing unpopularity of the heavily regressive property tax, have turned to nonproperty tax sources much more quickly than have the older, larger suburbs, largely due to state enabling legislation.

Changes in Nontax Revenue Levels

Changes in nontax revenue levels were greatest among suburbs located in the South (+$41), suburbs with populations below 25,000 (+$21), suburbs with industrial economic bases (+$32), and suburbs with reformed governmental characters (+$25). Changes in nontax levels do not appear to be related to differences in functional responsibilities, at least not in this simple comparison-of-means analysis.

Use of nontax revenues has traditionally been associated with smaller municipalities.[14] Smaller municipalities, with more homogeneous populations, tend to make more efficiency-related choices in their selection of revenues and in their methods of financing municipal service delivery. Many municipal services in small cities are financed directly by the user. Each individual citizen or household pays in proportion to services received. There are very few evidences of equitably (progressively) structured revenues or of equitably delivered (on the basis of need) services among small suburbs. This explains why increases in nontax revenue levels were greatest among smaller, southern, reformed suburbs.

CHANGES IN SUBURBAN REVENUE
RELIANCE PATTERNS

Changes in revenue levels reflect changes in intensity of usage of particular revenue sources. Changes in revenue reliance patterns, however, represent changes in direction—changes in relative dependence on intergovernmental, tax, and nontax revenues. As the figures shown in Table 8.1 indicate, suburban reliance upon intergovernmental revenues (+11.5 percent) and tax revenues (+17.2 percent) increased between 1962 and 1972, whereas proportional reliance upon nontax revenues declined (-28.7 percent).

As was the case in analyzing changes in revenue levels, it is important to analyze each type of intergovernmental revenue to get an accurate picture of changes in reliance patterns. Reliance on federal aid among these 340 suburbs increased (+4.3 percent) but not as much as did reliance on state aid (+7.2 percent). It does appear though that the gap between reliance on state aid and federal aid is slowly narrowing.

A comparison of the changes in property and nonproperty tax reliance indicates that while suburbs have increased reliance on both types of tax revenue, they have increased reliance on nonproperty taxes (+12.0 percent) at a much greater rate than on property taxes (+5.2 percent). Such figures suggest that use of the property tax is at its peak, for either legal or political reasons.

Increased reliance upon intergovernmental revenues (federal and state) and upon nonproperty taxes is evidence that suburban revenue structures, not unlike city revenue structures, are becoming strained. Thus, it appears that the potential for fiscal crises exists among suburbs and, in fact, is becoming increasingly more eminent as suburbs mature.

Changes in Intergovernmental Revenue Reliance

Changes in Federal Aid Reliance

Figures shown in Tables 8.2-8.6 indicate that changes in reliance on federal aid were greatest among suburbs located in the South (+3.8 percent), suburbs with the largest populations (+2.0 percent, suburbs with industrial economic bases (-7.2 percent), suburbs with mixed governmental characters (+2.0 percent), and suburbs without responsibility for the least common functions (+2.6 percent). Housing and urban renewal and education are the two least common functions that are most associated with changes in reliance upon federal funds (positively associated).

It has been stated that "the function of grants is twofold: (1) to give to poorer municipalities a disproportionate share of these revenues to increase their capability for providing needed services in an attempt to effect stabilization, equalization, and support of such governments; and (2) to provide impetus to expansion of particular functions."[15]

Since southern suburbs have been characterized by the poorest populations and have also been undergoing the greatest growth rates, mandating expansion of services, it is not unusual to observe that they increased reliance on federal aid more than did suburbs located in other parts of the country.

Relatedly, when contrasted by population size, larger suburbs with disproportionate numbers of poor residents increased their reliance on federal aid more than did smaller suburbs for the simple reason that they were more eligible for federal aid than the smaller, higher socioeconomic-status suburbs.

Somewhat surprising is the finding that those suburbs without financial responsibility for the poverty-related services (least common services) increased reliance on federal aid more than those with such responsibilities. The explanation for this finding is likely related to the age of the suburb; older suburbs would be more likely to have been charged with such functional responsibilities for some time. Therefore, whereas their federal aid levels (per capita) increased, their proportional use of federal monies did not. On the other hand, newer suburbs do not tend to have such responsibilities primarily because they have been transferred to higher levels of government (the county and the state) and are now rarely performed at the local level. These newer suburbs are likely to apply for federal monies for capital improvement programs.

Changes in State Aid Reliance

Changes in reliance upon state aid were greatest among western suburbs (+9.1 percent), suburbs with populations under 25,000 (+7.0 percent), suburbs with manufacturing economic bases (+5.3 percent), suburbs with unreformed governmental characters (+7.8 percent), and suburbs with responsibilities for education, welfare, hospitals, and housing and urban renewal (+8.8 percent).

State aid is traditionally in the form of grants-in-aid or shared taxes. Unfortunately, the Bureau of the Census does not distinguish between the two in its reporting scheme. Likewise, it is impossible to know how much of this state aid is actually federal aid being passed through the state to local governments. State aid has "increased with the ever-increasing gap between local ability to provide services and the costs of such services."[16]

Part of the explanation for the increased reliance on state aid among western suburbs is related to the greater use of shared taxes among western states. Shared taxes (usually on tobacco, alcoholic beverages, motor fuels, sales, and so on) are returned to municipalities either on the basis of need or origin (origin being the most common method). Similarly, shared taxes make up a larger portion of the budget of a smaller suburb than of a larger suburb. Since these state-returned monies have no strings attached, smaller suburbs are not as reluctant to accept them as they tend to be with federal monies or even state grant monies with strings attached.

The other type of state aid, grants-in-aid, is usually earmarked for education, welfare, and other broad functional areas. This would explain why suburbs with financial responsibilities for these functions have increased their reliance upon state intergovernmental revenues.

Changes in Tax Revenue Reliance

Changes in Property Tax Revenue Reliance

Changes in reliance upon property taxes were greatest among suburbs located in the Northeast (+9.6 percent), suburbs with populations over 100,000 (-21.0 percent), suburbs with diversified-manufacturing (+9.9 percent) and industrial economic bases (+9.5 percent), suburbs with mixed governmental characters, and suburbs without financial responsibility for the least common suburban functions (+8.4 percent).

Increases in property tax reliance among northeastern suburbs is primarily explainable by the fact that the northeastern states still severely restrict suburban use of nonproperty taxes, yet place few or no restrictions on municipal use of property taxes.

Larger suburbs have generally reduced reliance on property taxes. This does not mean that they have reduced property tax rates or levels, but only that they now obtain a lesser proportion of their total general revenues from property taxes and a greater proportion from intergovernmental and nonproperty tax sources—both signs of strain on a local government's own revenue structures. This decreasing reliance on property taxes is partially explained by coexisting pressures for fiscal (revenue) expansion and counter political pressures not to expand use of the property tax.

The changes in property tax reliance, when analyzed by economic base, are found to be greatest among the more complex economic-based suburbs. As stated earlier, communities with a large industrial or commercial tax base tend to rely more heavily on property taxes than on other revenue sources. They are more able to do this than suburbs with other types of economic bases because industries and businesses are less likely to move, and merely pass their property tax increases on to their customers.

Suburbs without responsibility for financing education, welfare, hospitals, or housing and urban renewal programs are usually the smaller suburbs that are the most restricted in their use of revenue sources other than property taxes. Also, they tend to be the most likely to resist federal and state monies because of the strings attached. Thus, it is to be expected that they have proportionately increased reliance on the property tax.

Changes in Nonproperty Tax Reliance

Changes in reliance on nonproperty taxes were found to be the most marked among southern suburbs (+12.5 percent), the largest suburbs (+10.4 percent), diversified-manufacturing (+7.7 percent), economic-based suburbs, suburbs with mixed governmental characters (+8.9 percent), and suburbs without responsibilities for the least common suburban functions (+6.8 percent).

The tradition or age theory seems appropriate to explain greater increases in reliance on nonproperty taxes by southern and western suburbs. Their individual legislatures have tended to authorize municipal use of sales, income, and other nonproperty taxes in order to prevent the negative political and fiscal impacts associated with sole reliance upon property tax revenues. On the other hand, northeastern states have been virtually prohibitive of expanded municipal use of nonproperty taxes. The fact that suburbs with financial responsibility for the poverty-related services are almost all located in the Northeast explains why these suburbs have not increased reliance on nonproperty taxes as might have been anticipated.

There is a very strong relationship between population size and increase in reliance on nonproperty tax revenues. This finding is consistent with earlier findings of Pettengill and Uppal who found that "almost all large and medium-sized cities in the past 30 years have moved strongly in the direction of nonproperty taxes."[17]

Changes in Nontax Revenue Reliance

Changes in reliance upon nontax revenue were greatest among suburbs located in the West (-23.1 percent), suburbs with populations below 25,000 (-27.7 percent), suburbs with diversified-manufacturing economic bases (-21.1 percent), suburbs with mixed governmental characters (-28.0 percent), and suburbs without responsibility for any of the least common functions (-29.1 percent).

The older, larger suburbs of the Northeast, with more complex economic bases, unreformed governments, and poverty-related service responsibilities, reduced reliance on nontax revenues much less than the younger, faster growing suburbs of the West and South. The decrease in reliance on nontax revenues among these latter categories of suburbs was possible because they were in a better position to increase their revenue bases. They could do this by merely incorporating more taxable property into their limits (through annexation or consolidation) and by increasing property tax revenues by raising taxable property values. On the other hand, these younger suburbs were not able to expand use of charges and special assessments, since many of the services and functions usually financed by collection of these nontax revenues became the responsibility of developers rather than the municipalities (as the result of land use regulations).

DETERMINANTS OF CHANGES IN SUBURBAN REVENUE LEVELS AND RELIANCE PATTERNS

Comparison-of-means analysis employing classificatory or typological schemes such as region, population size, economic base, governmental character, and functional responsibility, stimulates data exploration—determination of convenient ways of summarizing information or development of new and potentially useful hypotheses; hypothesis testing or model fitting; and development of modes of prediction, using subgroups rather than an entire population.[18] The results of comparing suburban changes in revenue levels and reliance patterns through such analysis have provided a much more in-depth contrast of such changes among suburbs (as contrasted with earlier studies, which merely contrasted suburban change patterns with those of central cities).

TABLE 8.7: Relationships between Changes in Demographic, Socioeconomic, and Governmental Characteristics and Changes in Revenue Levels of 340 U.S. Suburbs

	Changes in Revenue Levels				
	Intergovernmental		Tax		
	Federal	State	Property	Nonproperty	Nontax
Demographic Characteristics					
Population size	$-.00$	$-.03$	$-.30^a$	$.24^a$	$.30^a$
Population density					
Land area density	$-.02$	$-.22^a$	$.77^a$	$-.67$	$-.61^a$
Residential crowding	$-.31^a$	$-.15^b$	$.63^a$	$-.62^a$	$-.38^a$
Room crowding	$-.13^c$	$-.03$	$.27^a$	$-.26^a$	$-.16^b$
Mobility					
Moving to different house	$-.01$	$-.10$	$.27^a$	$-.24^a$	$-.21^a$
Population growth	$.03$	$.03$	$-.04$	$.04$	$.02$
Socioeconomic Characteristics					
Age					
Aged persons	$-.09$	$-.01$	$.08$	$-.09$	$-.02$
Median age	$-.04$	$.02$	$.07$	$-.07$	$-.03$
Youth	$-.00$	$.06$	$.01$	$-.01$	$-.00$
Education					
Median school years completed	$-.02$	$.20^a$	$-.55^a$	$.47$	$.48^a$
College graduates	$-.08$	$-.05$	$-.17^a$	$.08$	$.42^a$
Class					
Median family income	$.02$	$-.26^a$	$-.41^a$	$.36^a$	$.33^a$
Homeownership	$-.05$	$.02$	$.12^c$	$-.12^c$	$-.06$
Housing value	$-.25^a$	$-.13^b$	$.47^a$	$-.45^a$	$-.32^a$
Affluence	$-.05$	$.02$	$.11^c$	$-.10$	$-.07$
White-collar occupations	$-.02$	$.01$	$.18^a$	$-.17^a$	$-.08$
Females in labor force	$.03$	$.04$	$-.47^a$	$.42^a$	$.33^a$
Race					
Nonwhites	$-.01$	$.08$	$.38^a$	$-.28^a$	$-.54^a$
Social pathology					
Birthrate	$.23^a$	$.15^b$	$-.42^a$	$.42^a$	$.24^a$
Mortality rate	$.39^a$	$.10^c$	$-.32^a$	$.29^a$	$.31^a$
Poverty	$-.03$	$.09$	$.18^a$	$-.13^c$	$-.22^a$
Crime rate	$-.61^a$	$-.32^a$	$.40^a$	$-.42^a$	$-.13^b$
Fertility ratio	$.00$	$.09$	$.62^a$	$-.57^a$	$-.39^a$
Run-down housing	$-.04$	$.01$	$-.07$	$.03$	$.17^a$
Governmental Characteristics					
Form of government	$-.04$	$.12^c$	$-.29^a$	$.26^a$	$.22^a$
Ballot type	$-.03$	$.04$	$.04$	$-.02$	$-.02$
Council selection plan	$-.02$	$.03$	$-.26^a$	$.23^a$	$.20^a$
Governmental character (re-formism)	$.08$	$-.00$	$.11^c$	$-.08$	$-.11^c$
Functional responsibilities (total)	$-.28^a$	$-.31^a$	$.64^a$	$-.65^a$	$-.27^a$

[a]Significant at .001 level.
[b]Significant at .01 level.
[c]Significant at .05 level.
  Source: Compiled by the author.

TABLE 8.8: Relationships between Changes in Demographic, Socioeconomic, and Governmental Characteristics and Changes in Revenue Reliance of 340 U.S. Suburbs

| | Changes in Revenue Reliance | | | | |
| | Intergovernmental | | Tax | | |
	Federal	State	Property	Nonproperty	Nontax
Demographic Characteristics					
Population size	$.27^a$	$.10$	$.01$	$.32^a$	$-.32^a$
Population density					
Land area density	$-.35^a$	$-.37^a$	$.05$	$-.60^a$	$.59^a$
Residential crowding	$-.51^a$	$-.13^b$	$.15^b$	$-.70^a$	$.56^a$
Room crowding	$-.23^a$	$-.01$	$.10$	$-.33^a$	$.22^a$
Mobility					
Moving to different house	$-.06$	$.10$	$.49^a$	$-.02$	$-.02$
Population growth	$.06$	$.06$	$.07$	$.08$	$-.09$
Socioeconomic Characteristics					
Age					
Aged persons	$-.08$	$-.03$	$.04$	$-.16^b$	$.09$
Median age	$-.02$	$.23^a$	$.59^a$	$.08$	$-.15^b$
Youth	$.01$	$.18^a$	$.24^a$	$-.02$	$-.14^b$
Education					
Median school years completed	$.22^a$	$.35^a$	$.05$	$.40^a$	$-.45^a$
College graduates	$.26^b$	$.18^a$	$.27^a$	$.33^a$	$-.37^a$
Class					
Median family income	$.33^a$	$-.08$	$.25^a$	$.17^b$	$-.23^a$
Homeownership	$-.07$	$.11^c$	$.24^a$	$-.13^c$	$.02$
Housing value	$-.40^a$	$-.04$	$.25^a$	$-.53^a$	$.39^a$
Affluence	$-.05$	$.11^c$	$.28^a$	$-.08$	$-.03$
White-collar occupations	$-.07$	$.21^a$	$.61^a$	$.01$	$-.10$
Females in labor force	$.37^a$	$.27^a$	$.18^a$	$.46^a$	$-.53^a$
Race					
Nonwhites	$-.27^a$	$-.06$	$-.07$	$-.29^a$	$.29^a$
Social pathology					
Birthrate	$.37^a$	$.31^a$	$.19^a$	$.49^a$	$-.56^a$
Mortality rate	$.50^a$	$.13^c$	$-.08$	$.62^a$	$-.55^a$
Poverty	$-.25^a$	$.11^c$	$.06$	$-.23^a$	$.14^b$
Crime rate	$.48^a$	$-.21^a$	$.06$	$-.66^a$	$.59^a$
Fertility ratio	$-.28^a$	$-.02$	$.06$	$-.31^a$	$.27^a$
Run-down housing	$.03$	$.12^c$	$.26^a$	$.08$	$-.12^c$
Governmental Characteristics					
Form of government	$.11^c$	$.13^c$	$-.11^c$	$.18^a$	$-.19^a$
Ballot type	$-.05$	$-.05$	$.05$	$-.02$	$.08$
Council selection plan	$.13^c$	$.09$	$-.06$	$.21^a$	$-.18^a$
Governmental character	$-.03$	$-.05$	$-.07$	$-.07$	$.06$
Functional responsibilities	$-.37^a$	$-.24^a$	$.27^a$	$-.58^a$	$.51^a$

[a]Significant at .001 level.
[b]Significant at .01 level.
[c]Significant at .05 level.

Source: Compiled by the author.

One of the stated purposes of this study is to examine in detail the linkages between changes in demographic, socioeconomic, and governmental characteristics of suburbs (1960–70) and changes in revenue levels (Table 8.7) and reliance patterns (Table 8.8) from 1962–72. This is accomplished through use of correlational analysis.

Correlation coefficients indicate the degree to which variation (or change) in one variable is related to variation (change) in another. A correlation coefficient summarizes the strength of association between two variables and also provides a means for comparing the strength between one pair of variables and another pair.

In order to determine which of these environmental changes most affected the intake of and the reliance upon certain types of revenues, multiple regressional analysis was performed. Those demographic, socioeconomic, and governmental change variables that were found to be significantly related to change in revenue levels and reliance patterns, as a result of the correlational analysis, were used as independent (predictor) variables in the regressional equations.

Determinants of Change in Suburban Revenue Levels

Changes in suburban demographic, socioeconomic, and governmental characteristics can better explain (predict) changes in tax and nontax revenue levels than changes in intergovernmental revenue levels. This is to be expected since tax and nontax revenues are locally raised revenues. Thus, changes in local environmental conditions can best explain changes in locally raised revenue levels.

Generally, demographic and socioeconomic changes have a much greater impact on changes in revenue levels than do changes in governmental structural arrangements. The only governmental change measure that consistently appears as a significant predictor of changes in revenue levels is that of functional responsibility, which itself is probably predictable by changes in demographic and socioeconomic conditions.

Determinants of Change in Federal Aid Levels

As the figures shown in Table 8.9 indicate, five change variables (crime rate, mortality rate, functional responsibility, birthrate, and residential crowding) can explain 51 percent of the variance in change in federal aid levels between 1962 and 1972.

It has already been shown that residential crowding (average number of persons per housing unit) is a function of youth, childrearing, population growth, and homeownership. It has also been shown that residential crowding is negatively related to crime rates and mortality rates.[19] Thus, it is not surprising that suburbs characterized by increases in residential crowding and functional responsibilities (measures of growth) experienced the greatest increases in federal aid levels. Without the benefit of categorical breakdowns of federal aid coming into these suburbs, it still seems plausible that the funds coming into suburbs experiencing growth were likely directed toward major capital outlay projects. At any rate, changes in federal aid levels among suburbs are responsive to these five change indicators.

Determinants of Change in State Aid Levels

As the figures shown in Table 8.10 indicate, changes in suburban environmental conditions can explain even less of the variance in change in state aid to suburbs (38 percent). Perhaps since it is impossible to distinguish between the proportional increases in each type of state aid (grants-in-aid and shared taxes), the prediction powers of these environmental change indicators are thereby reduced.

TABLE 8.9: Determinants of Changes in Federal Intergovernmental Revenue Levels of 340 Suburbs, 1962–72

Change Variable	r	β	R^2
Crime rate	−.61	−1.42	.37
Mortality rate	.39	−.59	.44
Functional responsibility	−.28	.23	.49
Birthrate	.23	−.11	.50
Residential crowding	−.31	.10	.51

Source: Compiled by the author.

TABLE 8.10: Determinants of Changes in State Intergovernmental Revenue Levels of 340 Suburbs, 1962–72

Change Variable	r	β	R^2
Crime rate	−.32	−.96	.10
Mortality rate	.11	−.70	.21
Median family income	−.26	−.48	.29
Median school years completed	.20	.37	.37
Residential crowding	−.15	.15	.38

Source: Compiled by the author.

The significant predictors that do emerge are: crime rate, mortality rate, median family income, median school years completed, and residential crowding. Certainly changes in the educational level and in residential crowding (reflecting increasing youth populations) would be much better predictors of state grants-in-aid, many of which are specifically directed toward educational programs. Relatedly, since certain state aid programs are somewhat redistributive, it follows that reductions in income levels would be related to increases in state aid levels.

Determinants of Change in Property Tax Levels

Changes in suburban environmental conditions turn out to be very good predictors of change in property tax levels ($R^2 = .88$). Significant predictors are land area density, fertility ratio, females in the labor force, functional responsibilities, median family income, race (percent blacks), mortality rate, poverty rate, residential crowding, homeownership, and room crowding.

Increases in land area density (population per square mile), various measures of social pathology (fertility ratio, mortality rate, poverty rate), and increases in functional responsibilities are all related to increases in property tax levels. It is likely that the influx of suburbanites of lower socioeconomic status necessitates expansion of property tax rates and/or assessment levels, primarily because these poorer residents place new demands and needs upon the suburban government—reflected by increases in functional responsibilities.

TABLE 8.11: Determinants of Changes in Property Tax Levels of 340 Suburbs, 1962–72

Change Variable	r	β	R^2
Land area density	.77	.11	.59
Fertility ratio	.62	.35	.70
Females in labor force	-.47	-.27	.73
Functional responsibilities	.64	.27	.75
Median family income	-.41	-.25	.77
Race	.38	-.20	.79
Mortality rate	-.32	.41	.81
Poverty rate	.18	.17	.83
Residential crowding	.63	.86	.85
Homeownership	.12	-.28	.86
Room crowding	.27	-.17	.88

Source: Compiled by the author.

Relatedly, declining income levels, homeownership, and increasing room crowding are predictors of the need for increased expenditures and the need to increase property tax levels.

Determinants of Change in Nonproperty Tax Levels

As the figures shown in Table 8.12 indicate, measures of suburban demographic and socioeconomic change are good predictors of changes in nonproperty tax levels. Changes in land area density, fertility ratios, functional responsibilities, median family income, race, mobility, mortality, working females, poverty, residential crowding, homeownership, room crowding, and white-collar occupations can explain 86 percent of the variance in changes in nonproperty tax levels.

Recalling that the most commonly used nonproperty taxes are sales taxes (general and selective or excise), it is not surprising that increases in density, income, in-migration, working females, and homeownership are good predictors of increases in nonproperty tax levels. Relatedly, decreases in social pathologies (fertility ratios, mortality rates, poverty rates, and so on) help explain increases in nonproperty tax levels.

TABLE 8.12: Determinants of Changes in Nonproperty Tax Levels of 340 Suburbs, 1962-72

Change Variable	r	β	R^2
Land area density	-.67	.12	.45
Fertility ratio	-.57	-.37	.56
Functional responsibilities	-.65	-.40	.62
Median family income	.36	.25	.66
Race	-.28	.31	.71
Mobility	-.24	.15	.74
Mortality rate	.29	-.60	.75
Females in labor force	.42	.27	.77
Poverty rate	-.13	-.19	.79
Residential crowding	-.62	-1.06	.81
Homeownership	-.12	.35	.84
Room crowding	-.26	.19	.85
White-collar occupations	-.17	-.13	.86

Source: Compiled by the author.

TABLE 8.13: Determinants of Changes in Nontax Revenue Levels of 340 Suburbs, 1962–72

Change Variables	r	β	R^2
Land area density	-.61	-.56	.38
College-educated persons	.42	.23	.47
Crime rate	-.13	.88	.57
Mortality rate	.31	.53	.64
Race	-.54	-.25	.68
Median family income	.33	.12	.70
Run-down housing	.17	.16	.71
Housing value	-.32	-.17	.72
Mobility	-.21	-.22	.73
Functional responsibilities	-.27	.26	.74
Population size	.30	-.08	.74
Fertility ratio	-.39	.10	.75

Source: Compiled by the author.

Determinants of Change in Nontax Revenue Levels

Changes in nontax revenue levels (Table 8.13), like changes in tax revenues, can largely be explained by changes in land area density, college-educated citizens, crime rate, mortality rate, race, median family income, run-down housing, housing value, mobility, functional responsibilities, population size, and fertility ratios ($R^2 = .75$).

Nontax revenues (charges and special assessments) are more efficiency-related revenues; there is a direct linkage between use and assessment. Thus there is very little evidence of redistribution of resources in service delivery patterns. Such revenue patterns are more likely to be characteristic of smaller, wealthier, older, stable communities.

As expected, changes in nontax revenue levels are associated with increases in college-educated persons, income levels, and fertility ratios (family measures). Relatedly, measures showing increasing population stability (mortality rate, run-down housing, crime rate) are also related to increases in nontax revenue levels. This pattern also accounts for the negative relationship between change in nontax revenue levels and density, race, and mobility—all measures of population growth.

Determinants of Change in Suburban Revenue
Reliance Patterns

The patterns of determinants of change in suburban revenue reliance differ from those patterns of change in revenue levels. Changes in suburban demographic, socioeconomic, and governmental conditions are not consistently superior predictors of changes in locally raised revenue reliance patterns (tax and nontax revenues), as contrasted with intergovernmental revenue reliance patterns. While suburban environmental change indicators can explain the greatest variance in changes in nonproperty tax reliance (67 percent) and nontax revenue reliance (61 percent), they can explain only 41 percent of the variance in changes in property tax revenue reliance. On the other hand, they can account for 59 percent of the variance in changes in federal aid reliance. The least predictable changes in revenue reliance are changes in state aid revenues.

Determinants of Change in Suburban Federal Aid Reliance

The suburban environmental change measures that are significant predictors of change in reliance upon federal aid are residential crowding, median family income, females in the labor force, land area density, poverty rates, room crowding, median educational levels, functional responsibilities, fertility rates, race (percent blacks), median age, population size, college-educated persons, and mortality rates.

At first glance, many of the results appear to be contradictory to most theories regarding determinants of increased reliance on federal aid. This is largely the result of the fact that it is impossible to determine which types of federal monies are being used by which types of suburbs. If federal monies are being solicited primarily for funding services and facilities likely to benefit the needs of the poor, elderly, minorities (such as welfare, housing and urban renewal projects, hospitals and health services), then this would explain the finding that increases in reliance on federal aid are related to increases in working females, density of population, room crowding, blacks, population size, mortality rates, and fertility ratios. If, however, federal monies are sought by suburbs to construct capital improvements for traditional service functions (sanitation, sewerage), a pattern that is likely to be more characteristic of smaller, efficiency-oriented suburbs, then it seems plausible that increases in reliance on federal aid would be related to increases in median family income but to decreases in the poverty rate—as the results show.

TABLE 8.14: Determinants of Changes in Federal Intergovernmental Revenue Reliance Patterns of 340 Suburbs, 1962-72

Change Variables	r	β	R^2
Residential crowding	-.51	-.48	.26
Median family income	.32	.80	.36
Females in labor force	.37	.34	.41
Land area density	-.35	.28	.45
Poverty rate	-.25	-.30	.49
Room crowding	-.23	.06	.51
Median school years completed	.22	-.27	.53
Functional responsibilities	-.37	-.33	.54
Fertility ratio	-.28	.28	.55
Race	-.27	.15	.57
Median age	-.02	-.05	.58
Population size	.27	.07	.58
College-educated persons	.26	-.15	.58
Mortality rate	.50	.33	.59

Source: Compiled by the author.

Determinants of Change in Suburban State Aid Reliance

The figures shown in Table 8.15 indicate that only 36 percent of the variance in changes in suburban reliance on state aid can be explained by changes in suburban environmental conditions. The change indicators that are found to be significant determinants are land area density, white-collar occupations, poverty rate, residential crowding, crime rate, homeownership, birthrate, functional responsibilities, median age, mortality rate, run-down housing, and females in the labor force.

Again, the fact that not much variance in changes in reliance on state aid can be explained is likely to be a function of the fact that there is no distinction between increased reliance on shared taxes and increased reliance on state grants-in-aid.

Specifically, it is impossible to determine whether the increase in reliance on state aid was more attributable to increased reliance on shared tax revenues or state grants-in-aid. Increased reliance on state shared tax revenues (such as sales, alcoholic beverage, motor fuels, and tobacco) would largely depend on whether the allocation formulas were constructed on the basis of need or origin. If constructed on the basis of need, then it is easily explainable why increases in poverty rate, birthrate, age, and mortality rate, but decreases in homeownership, are good predictors of increased reliance on state

TABLE 8.15: Determinants of Changes in State Intergovernmental Revenue Reliance Patterns of 340 Suburbs, 1962-72

Change Variables	r	β	R^2
Land area density	-.37	-.56	.14
White-collar occupations	.21	.21	.22
Poverty rate	.11	.26	.26
Residential crowding	-.13	1.15	.27
Crime rate	-.21	-.12	.28
Homeownership	.11	-.43	.30
Birthrate	.31	.18	.32
Functional responsibilities	-.24	-.45	.33
Median age	.23	.28	.34
Mortality rate	.13	.34	.34
Run-down housing	.12	-.10	.35
Females in labor force	.26	-.05	.36

Source: Compiled by the author.

aid. If, on the other hand, distribution of shared taxes is on the basis of origin (point of collection), then it follows that increases in white-collar occupations and residential crowding, but decreases in functional responsibilities, are related to increased reliance on state aid, since these are characteristics of wealthier communities that would naturally contribute larger portions of sales-type taxes and would thus receive larger portions in return.

If increased reliance on state aid is more attributable to increased use of grants-in-aid instead of shared taxes, the same problems exist. Again, the particular type and purpose of such aid would be an important consideration. In fact, the same determinant patterns would be likely to apply to grants-in-aid for equity (redistributive) purposes as would apply to shared taxes returned on the basis of need. Similarly, determinant patterns would likely be similar for efficiency-oriented suburbs—those increasing reliance on shared taxes returned on the basis of origin or on grants-in-aid for capital improvement projects.

Determinants of Change in Suburban Property Tax Reliance

Surprisingly, suburban demographic, socioeconomic, and governmental change indicators cannot account for more than 41 percent of the variance in suburban property tax reliance changes (Table 8.16). On the basis of earlier findings of this study, it appears that the factors most affecting changes in reliance on property taxes are state

TABLE 8.16: Determinants of Changes in Property Tax Reliance Patterns of 340 Suburbs, 1962–72

Change Variables	r	β	R^2
White-collar occupations	.61	.41	.37
Median age	.59	.21	.39
Median family income	.25	.06	.39
Run-down housing	.26	.01	.39
Birthrate	.19	.09	.40
Functional responsibilities	.18	.15	.40
Females in labor force	.19	.10	.41
Homeownership	.24	-.06	.40
Mobility	.49	-.10	.41

Source: Compiled by the author.

legal restrictions on local use of the property tax or political constraints making such changes highly unlikely.

Whereas the overall predictive power is not great, those change indicators that are nevertheless significant predictors of change in reliance on property taxes are white-collar occupations, median age, median family income, run-down housing, birthrate, functional responsibilities, females in the labor force, homeownership, and mobility.

The results of the comparison-of-means analysis indicated that increased reliance on property taxes was more characteristic of smaller, more economically specialized suburbs primarily because of legal restrictions on, or eligibility constraints prohibiting use of, types of revenue other than the property tax. This, then, probably accounts for the finding here that increases in proportions of white-collar workers, middle-aged persons, higher income levels, and lower birthrates (characteristics likely to be associated with wealthier, more homogeneously populated suburbs) are related to increased reliance on property taxes.

Determinants of Change in Suburban Nonproperty Tax Reliance

The figures shown in Table 8.17 indicate that changes in suburban residential crowding, proportions of females in the work force, homeownership, blacks, aged, and college-educated persons, and changes in income levels and poverty rates can account for 67 percent of the variance in changes in nonproperty tax reliance.

The most commonly used types of nonproperty taxes are income taxes and sales taxes (general and selective). The wealth-based na-

TABLE 8.17: Determinants of Changes in Nonproperty Tax Reliance Patterns of 340 Suburbs, 1962-72

Change Variables	r	β	R^2
Residential crowding	-.70	-.95	.49
Females in labor force	.46	.23	.59
Homeownership	-.13	.24	.61
Race	-.29	.25	.64
Median family income	.17	.12	.65
Aged	-.16	-.09	.66
Poverty rate	-.23	-.09	.66
College-educated persons	.33	.08	.67

Source: Compiled by the author.

ture of nonproperty taxes explains why increases in homeownership, income levels, educational levels, and females in the work force, but decreases in poverty rates and proportions of elderly citizens, predict increases in nonproperty tax reliance among suburban municipalities.

Determinants of Change in Suburban Nontax Revenue Reliance

Changes in suburban environmental conditions are powerful predictors of changes in suburban nontax revenue reliance patterns (Table 8.18).

Land area density, crime rate, females in the labor force, birthrate, median family income, race, residential crowding, college education, median age, functional responsibilities, and run-down housing change measures explain 61 percent of the variation in suburban nontax revenue reliance changes.

It will be recalled that nontax revenues are typically charges and special assessment revenues (efficiency-related revenues). The results of the comparison-of-means analysis indicated that while suburban reliance on nontax revenues has generally declined, it has declined the least among the older, larger suburbs, charged with a variety of functional responsibilities, many of which are, in fact, financed directly by such user assessments. The findings shown in Table 8.18 are consistent with the earlier findings. Increase in reliance on nontax revenues is related to increase in land area density, crime rates, residential crowding, proportions of run-down housing, and functional responsibilities.

TABLE 8.18: Determinants of Changes in Nontax Revenue Reliance Patterns of 340 Suburbs, 1962-72

Change Variables	r	β	R^2
Land area density	.59	.10	.35
Crime rate	.59	.06	.46
Females in labor force	-.53	-.25	.51
Birthrate	-.56	-.15	.55
Median family income	-.23	-.16	.56
Race	.29	-.23	.58
Residential crowding	.56	.30	.59
College-educated persons	-.37	-.05	.60
Median age	-.15	-.14	.60
Functional responsibilities	.51	.16	.61
Run-down housing	-.32	.09	.61

Source: Compiled by the author.

SIGNIFICANCE OF THE FINDINGS

The results of the descriptive comparison-of-means analysis utilizing regional, population size, economic base, governmental character (reformism), and functional responsibility classification schemes indicate that some U.S. suburbs are beginning to show signs of fiscal strain. Fiscal strain is best evidenced by increasing reliance upon intergovernmental monies (federal and state) and on nonproperty taxes, both of which are usually brought about by the particular government's tax structure, which itself is likely nearing its limits—fiscally, legally, and/or politically.

Changes in demographic, socioeconomic, and governmental conditions are generally good predictors of changes in revenue levels and reliance patterns among these 340 suburbs. Changes in suburban environmental conditions, however, can explain more of the variance in changes in locally raised revenue structures (tax and nontax) than in intergovernmental, or externally raised, revenue structures (federal and state). This suggests that federal and state aid may not be as responsive to the changing needs of municipal governments, particularly suburban governments, as is commonly thought to be the case.

The potential for fiscal crises has been found to exist among certain types of suburbs—usually those further along in the maturation process. Pressure on suburban revenue structures begins with change in the demographic, socioeconomic, and governmental make-up of suburbs. Such changes usually force the abandonment of efficiency-oriented fiscal structures and the adoption of more equity-oriented fiscal structures.

NOTES

1. See Glenn W. Fisher, "Revenue and Expenditure Patterns in Five Large Cities," Quarterly Review of Economics and Business 3 (Autumn 1963): 61-72; S. R. Johnson and P. E. Junk, "Sources of Tax Revenues and Expenditures in Large U.S. Cities," Quarterly Review of Economics and Business 10 (Winter 1970): 7-15; Mordecai S. Feinberg, "The Implications of Core City Decline for the Fiscal Structure of the Core City," National Tax Journal 17 (September 1964): 213-31; J. W. Jack and P. C. Reuss, "Financing Municipal Government: Fiscal Challenge of the Seventies," Municipal Finance (February 1971): 141-48; and G. W. Sazama, "Equalization of Property Taxes for the Nation's Largest Central Cities," National Tax Journal 18 (June 1965): 151-74.

2. Robert B. Pettengill and Jogindar S. Uppal, Can Cities Survive? The Fiscal Plight of American Cities (New York: St. Martin's Press, 1974).

3. Seymour Sacks and John Callahan, "Central City Suburban Fiscal Disparity," in Advisory Commission on Intergovernmental Relations, City Financial Emergencies (Washington, D.C.: Government Printing Office, 1973), p. 48.

4. Pettengill and Uppal, op. cit.; and L. L. Moak and A. M. Hillhouse, Concepts and Practices in Local Government Finances (Chicago: Municipal Finance Officers Association, 1975).

5. See Dick Netzer, Economics of the Property Tax (Washington, D.C.: The Brookings Institution, 1966); A. K. Campbell and Seymour Sacks, Metropolitan America: Fiscal Patterns and Governmental Systems (New York: The Free Press, 1967); John Pazour, "Local Government Fiscal Conditions," The Municipal Yearbook 1972 (Chicago: International City Management Association, 1973); Sacks and Callahan, op. cit.; and Pettengill and Uppal, op. cit.

6. See J. Margolis, "Metropolitan Finance Problems: Territories, Functions, and Growth," in Public Finance: Needs, Sources, Utilization, ed. J. Buchanan (Princeton, N.J.: National Bureau of Economic Research Symposium, 1961), pp. 229-93; Jesse Burkhead, "Uniformity in Governmental Expenditures and Resources in a Metropolitan Area: Cuyahoga County," National Tax Journal 14 (December 1961): 337-48; Morris Beck, "Determinants of the Property Tax Level: A Case Study of Northeastern New Jersey," National Tax Journal 18 (March 1965): 74-77; Oliver P. Williams et al., Suburban Differences and Metropolitan Policies: A Philadelphia Story (Philadelphia, Pa.: University of Pennsylvania Press, 1965); Oliver Oldman and Henry Aaron, "Assessment-Sales Ratios under the Boston Property Tax," National Tax Journal 18 (March 1965): 36-49; Mark Haskell and Stephen Leshinski, "Fiscal Influence on Residential

Choice: A Study of the New York Region," Quarterly Review of Economics and Business 9 (Winter 1969): 47-56; W. E. Oates, "The Dual Impact of Federal Aid on State and Local Expenditures: A Comment," National Tax Journal 21 (June 1968): 220-23; Donald J. Curran, Metropolitan Financing: The Milwaukee Experience, 1920-1970 (Madison, Wis.: The University of Wisconsin Press, 1973); George E. Peterson and A. Solomon, "Property Taxes and Populist Reform," The Public Interest 30 (Winter 1973): 60-75; and H. O. Pollakowski, "The Effect of Property Taxes and Local Public Spending on Property Values: A Comment and Further Results," Journal of Political Economy 81 (July/August 1973): 994-1003.

7. See A. G. Holtmann, "Migration to the Suburbs, Human Capital, and City Income Tax Losses: A Case Study," National Tax Journal 21 (September 1968): 326-31; Henry S. Terrell, "The Fiscal Impact of Nonwhites," in Fiscal Pressures on the Central City: The Impact of Commuters, Nonwhites, and Overlapping Governments, ed. Werner Z. Hirsch, et al. (New York: Praeger, 1971); D. F. Bradford and H. Kelejian, "An Econometric Model of the Flight to the Suburbs," Journal of Political Economy 81 (May/June 1973): 566-89; Haskell and Leshinski, op. cit.; and Peterson and Solomon, op. cit.

8. See Amos Hawley, "Metropolitan Population and Municipal Government Expenditures in 'Central Cities,'" Journal of Social Issues 7 (1951): 100-08; J. D. Kasarda, "The Impact of Suburban Population Growth on Central City Service Functions," American Journal of Sociology 77 (May 1972): 1111-24; P. E. Vincent, "The Fiscal Impacts of Commuters," in Hirsch et al., eds., op. cit.; Margolis, op. cit.; Harvey E. Brazer, City Expenditures in the U.S. (New York: National Bureau of Economic Research, 1959); Woo Sik Kee, "State and Local Fiscal Systems and Municipal Expenditures," Public Administration Review 27 (March 1967): 39-41; D. F. Bradford and W. E. Oates, "Suburban Exploitation of Central Cities and Governmental Structure," in Redistribution through Public Choice, ed. H. Hochman and G. Peterson (New York: Columbia University Press, 1973); J. M. Banovetz, Government Cost Burdens and Service Benefits in the Twin Cities Metropolitan Area (Minneapolis, Minn.: University of Minnesota, Public Administration Center, 1965); William B. Neenan, "Suburban-Central City Exploitation Thesis: One City's Tale," National Tax Journal 23 (June 1970): 117-39; R. S. Smith, "Are Nonresidents Contributing Their Share to Core City Revenue?" Land Economics (August 1972): 240-47; R. Boelaert, "Political Fragmentation and Inequality of Fiscal Capacity in the Milwaukee SMSA," National Tax Journal 23 (March 1970): 83-88; and K. V. Greene, W. B. Neenan, and C. Scott, Fiscal Interaction in a Metropolitan Area (Lexington, Mass.: Lexington Books, 1974).

9. Campbell and Sacks, op. cit.; Pazour, op. cit.; Sacks and Callahan, op. cit.; and Pettengill and Uppal, op. cit.

10. Jack and Reuss, op. cit., p. 143.

11. G. R. Stephens and H. J. Schmandt, "Revenue Patterns of Local Government," National Tax Journal 15 (December 1962): 423-37.

12. Robert C. Wood, 1400 Governments (Cambridge, Mass.: Harvard University Press, 1961).

13. Robert L. Lineberry and Ira Sharkansky, Urban Politics and Public Policy, 2d ed. (New York: Harper & Row, 1974).

14. Moak and Hillhouse, op. cit., p. 139.

15. Ibid., p. 163.

16. Ibid., p. 156.

17. Pettengill and Uppal, op. cit., p. 35.

18. Brian J. L. Berry, City Classification Handbook: Methods and Applications (New York: Wiley, 1972), p. 2.

19. Thomas R. Dye, "Population Density and Social Pathology, Urban Affairs Quarterly 11 (December 1975): 265-75.

Selected Bibliography

BOOKS

Adrian, Charles R., and Charles Press. Governing Urban America. 3d ed. New York: Mcgraw-Hill, 1968.

Advisory Commission on Intergovernmental Relations. A Circuit-Breaker on Property Tax Overload. Washington, D.C.: U.S. Government Printing Office, 1971.

_____. City Financial Emergencies: The Intergovernmental Dimension. Washington, D.C.: U.S. Government Printing Office, July 1973.

_____. The Commuter and the Municipal Income Tax. Washington, D.C.: U.S. Government Printing Office, April 1970.

_____. Federal Approaches to Aid State and Local Capital Financing. Washington, D.C.: U.S. Government Printing Office, September 1970.

_____. Federal-State-Local Finances: Significant Features of Fiscal Federalism. Washington, D.C.: U.S. Government Printing Office, February 1974.

_____. Financing Schools and Property Tax Relief—A State Responsibility. Washington, D.C.: U.S. Government Printing Office, January 1973.

_____. Fiscal Balance in the American Federal System. Vol. 1. Washington, D.C.: U.S. Government Printing Office, October 1967.

_____. Fiscal Balance in the American Federal System—Metropolitan Fiscal Disparities. Vol. 2. Washington, D.C.: U.S. Government Printing Office, October 1967.

_____. Intergovernmental Cooperation in Tax Administration. Washington, D.C.: U.S. Government Printing Office, June 1961.

_____. Intergovernmental Responsibilities for Water Supply and Sewage Disposal in Metropolitan Areas. Washington, D.C.: U.S. Government Printing Office, October 1962.

_____. Local Nonproperty Taxes and the Coordinating Role of the State. Washington, D.C.: U.S. Government Printing Office, September 1961.

_____. Measures of State and Local Fiscal Capacity and Tax Effort, 1962. Washington, D.C.: U.S. Government Printing Office, 1963.

_____. Measuring the Fiscal Capacity and Effort of State and Local Areas. Washington, D.C.: U.S. Government Printing Office, March 1971.

_____. Metropolitan Social and Economic Disparities: Implications for Intergovernmental Relations in Central Cities and Suburbs. Washington, D.C.: U.S. Government Printing Office, January 1965.

_____. Performance of Urban Functions: Local and Areawide. Washington, D.C.: U.S. Government Printing Office, September 1963.

_____. Public Opinion and Taxes. Washington, D.C.: U.S. Government Printing Office, May 1972.

_____. The Role of Equalization in Federal Grants. Washington, D.C.: U.S. Government Printing Office, January 1964.

_____. The Role of the States in Strengthening the Property Tax. Washington, D.C.: U.S. Government Printing Office, June 1963.

_____. State Aid to Local Government. Springfield, Va.: National Technical Information Service, October 1969.

_____. State and Local Finances 1967–1970. Washington, D.C.: U.S. Government Printing Office, 1969.

_____. State Constitutional and Statutory Restrictions on Local Taxing Powers. Washington, D.C.: U.S. Government Printing Office, 1962.

_____. State-Local Taxation and Industrial Location. Washington, D.C.: U.S. Government Printing Office, April 1967.

_____. State Technical Assistance to Local Debt Management. Washington, D.C.: U.S. Government Printing Office, January 1965.

_____. Tax Overlapping in the U.S. Washington, D.C.: Government Printing Office, 1964.

_____. Urban America and the Fiscal System. Springfield, Va.: National Technical Information Service, October 1969.

Anderson, Nels. The Industrial Urban Community: Historical and Comparative Perspectives. New York: Appleton-Century-Crofts, 1971.

Anderson, Nels, ed. Urbanism and Urbanization. Leiden: Brill, 1964.

Andersson, Gunnar Alex. The Industrial Structure of American Cities. Lincoln: University of Nebraska Press, 1956.

Bahl, Roy W., Jr. Metropolitan City Expenditures: A Comparative Analysis. Lexington: University of Kentucky Press, 1969.

Baker, John H. Urban Politics in America. New York: Scribner's, 1971.

Banfield, Edward C. The Unheavenly City. Boston: Little, Brown, 1970.

Banfield, Edward C., ed. Urban Government. New York: The Free Press, 1969.

Banfield, Edward C., and James Q. Wilson. City Politics. Cambridge, Mass.: Harvard University Press, 1963.

Banovetz, James M. Government Cost Burdens and Service Benefits in the Twin Cities Metropolitan Area. Minneapolis: Public Administration Center, University of Minnesota, 1965.

Bator, Francis M. The Question of Government Spending. New York: Harper, 1960.

Becker, Gary. Human Capital: A Theoretical and Empirical Analysis. New York: Columbia University Press, 1964.

Bell, Carolyn Shaw. The Economics of the Ghetto. New York: Pegasus, 1970.

Benson, George C. S., Sumner Benson, Harold McClelland, and Proctor Thomson. The American Property Tax: Its History, Administration, and Economic Impact. Claremont, Calif.: Claremont College, 1965.

Berger, Bennett. Working Class Suburb. Berkeley: University of California Press, 1960.

Bernard, Jessie. The Future of Motherhood. New York: Dial, 1974.

_____. Women and the Public Interest, An Essay on Policy and Protest. Chicago: Atherton, 1971.

Berry, Brian J. L. City Classification Handbook: Methods and Applications. New York: Wiley, 1972.

_____. Metropolitan Area Definition: A Reevaluation of Concept and Statistical Practice. Washington, D.C.: U.S. Department of Commerce, Bureau of the Census, 1968.

Berry, Brian J. L., and Frank E. Horton, eds. Geographic Perspectives on Urban Systems. Englewood Cliffs, N.J.: Prentice-Hall, 1970.

Birch, David L. The Economic Future of City and Suburb. New York: Committee of Economic Development, 1970.

Bird, Frederick L. The General Property Tax: Findings of the 1957 Census of Government. Chicago: Public Administrative Service, 1960.

Birkhead, Gutherie, ed. Metropolitan Issues: Social, Governmental, Fiscal. Syracuse, N.Y.: Maxwell Graduate School of Public Affairs, 1962.

Bish, Robert L. The Public Economy of Metropolitan Areas. Chicago: Markham, 1971.

Blalock, Hubert M., Jr. Causal Inference in Nonexperimental Research. New York: Norton, 1964.

_____. An Introduction to Social Research. Englewood Cliffs, N.J.: Prentice-Hall, 1970.

_____. Social Statistics. 2d ed. New York: McGraw-Hill, 1972.

Blaug, M. An Introduction to the Economics of Education. Baltimore, Md.: Penguin Books, 1972.

Bloomberg, Warner, and Morris Sunshine. Suburban Power Structures and Public Education: A Study of Values, Influence, and Tax Effort. Syracuse, N.Y.: Syracuse University Press, 1963.

Bollens, John, and Henry Schmandt. The Metropolis: Its People, Politics and Economic Life. New York: Harper & Row, 1965.

Boulding, Kenneth, and Martin Plaff, eds. Redistribution to the Rich and Poor. Belmont, Calif.: Wadsworth, 1971.

Boulding, Kenneth, Martin Plaff, and Anita Plaff, eds. Transfers in an Urbanized Economy. Belmont, Calif.: Wadsworth, 1973.

Brazer, Harvey E. City Expenditures in the U.S. New York: National Bureau of Economic Research, 1959.

Break, George F. Intergovernmental Fiscal Relations in the United States. Washington, D.C.: The Brookings Institution, 1967.

Buchanan, James M. Fiscal Theory and Political Economy. Chapel Hill: University of North Carolina Press, 1960.

Buchanan, James M., ed. The Demand and Supply of Public Goods. New York: Rand McNally, 1968.

_____. Public Finance: Needs, Sources, Utilization. Princeton, N.J.: National Bureau of Economic Research Symposium, 1961.

Buchanan, James M., and Robert D. Tollison, eds. Theory of Public Choice: Political Applications of Economics. Ann Arbor: University of Michigan Press, 1972.

Buchanan, James, and Gordon Tullock. The Calculus of Consent. Ann Arbor: University of Michigan Press, 1962.

Bureau of Business Research. America's Cities. Ann Arbor: University of Michigan Press, 1970.

Burkhead, Jesse. State and Local Taxes for Public Education. Syracuse, N.Y.: Syracuse University Press, 1963.

Burkhead, Jesse, and Jerry Miner. Public Expenditure. Chicago: Aldine-Atherton, 1971.

Campbell, Alan K., and Seymour Sacks. Metropolitan America: Fiscal Patterns and Governmental Systems. New York: The Free Press, 1967.

Campbell, Donald T., and Julian C. Stanley. Experimental and Quasi-Experimental Design for Research. Chicago: Rand McNally, 1963.

Chase, Samuel B., Jr., ed. Problems in Public Expenditure Analysis. Washington, D.C.: The Brookings Institution, 1968.

Chinitz, Benjamin, ed. City and Suburb: The Economics of Metropolitan Growth. Englewood Cliffs, N.J.: Prentice-Hall, 1964.

Clark, Samuel D. The Suburban Society. Toronto: University of Toronto Press, 1966.

Clawson, Marion. Suburban Land Conversion in the U.S. Baltimore, Md.: John Hopkins Press, 1971.

Committee for Economic Development. Fiscal Issues in the Future of Federalism. New York: Committee for Economic Development, 1968.

Conant, James. Slums and Suburbs. New York: McGraw-Hill, 1961.

The Conference Board. Government Services in Major Metropolitan Areas. New York: The Conference Board, 1972.

Connery, Robert, ed. Municipal Income Taxes. New York: Academy of Political Science, Columbia University, 1968.

Crecine, John. Financing the Metropolis: Public Policy in Urban Economics. Beverly Hills, Calif.: Sage Publications, 1970.

Curran, Donald J. Metropolitan Financing: The Milwaukee Experience, 1920-1970. Madison: The University of Wisconsin Press, 1973.

Danielson, Michael N., ed. Metropolitan Politics: A Reader. Boston: Little, Brown, 1966.

David, Stephen M., and Paul E. Peterson, eds. Urban Politics and Public Policy: The City in Crisis. New York: Praeger, 1973.

Dean, Lois R. Five Towns, A Comparative Community Study. New York: Random House, 1967.

Dentler, Robert A. American Community Problems. New York: McGraw-Hill, 1968.

Department of Finance and Revenue, Government of the District of Columbia. Comparison of Major State and Local Tax Burdens in Selected Washington Metropolitan Area Jurisdictions. Washington, D.C., 1973.

_____. Major State and Local Tax Burdens in Washington Compared with Those in the 30 Larger Cities. Washington, D.C., 1973.

Dobriner, William M. Class in Suburbia. Englewood Cliffs, N.J.: Prentice-Hall, 1963.

Dobriner, William M., ed. The Suburban Community. New York: Putnam, 1958.

Dogan, Mathi, and Rokkan Stein, eds. Quantitative Ecological Analysis in the Social Sciences. Cambridge, Mass.: MIT Press, 1969.

Donaldson, Scott. The Suburban Myth. New York: Columbia University Press, 1969.

Douglass, H. Paul. The Suburban Trend. New York: Century, 1926.

Downes, Bryan T. Cities and Suburbs: Selected Readings in Local Politics and Public Policy. Belmont, Calif.: Wadsworth, 1971.

Downs, Anthony. An Economic Theory of Democracy. New York: Harper & Row, 1957.

_____. Urban Problems and Prospects. Chicago: Markham, 1970.

Draper, N. R., and H. Smith. Applied Regression Analysis. New York: Wiley, 1967.

Due, John F., ed. State and Local Sales Taxes. Chicago: Public Administration Service, 1971.

Duncan, Otis D., and Albert J. Reiss, Jr. Social Characteristics of Urban and Rural Communities, 1950. New York: Wiley, 1956.

Duncan, Otis D., W. Richard Scott, Stanley Lieberson, Beverly Duncan, and Hal H. Winsborough. Metropolis and Region. Baltimore, Md.: The Johns Hopkins Press, 1960.

Dye, Thomas R. Politics in States and Communities. 2d ed. Englewood Cliffs, N.J.: Prentice-Hall, 1969.

Ecker-Racz, L. L. The Politics and Economics of State-Local Finances. Englewood Cliffs, N.J.: Prentice-Hall, 1970.

The Editors of Fortune. The Exploding Metropolis. Garden City, N.Y.: Doubleday Anchor Books, 1958.

Eisenstein, Louis. The Ideologies of Taxation. New York: Ronald Press, 1961.

Elazar, David J. American Federalism: A View from the States. New York: Crowell, 1966.

Eulau, Heinz, and Kenneth Prewitt. Labyrinths of Democracy: Adaptations, Linkages, Representation, and Politics in Urban Politics. Indianapolis: Bobbs-Merrill, 1973.

Eyestone, Robert. Political Economy: Politics and Policy Analysis. Chicago: Markham, 1972.

Fabricant, Solomon. The Trend of Government Activity in the U.S. since 1900. New York: National Bureau of Economic Research, 1952.

Fellman, David, and Kenyon E. Poole. The Costs of American Governments: Facts, Trends, Myths. New York: Dodd, Mead, 1969.

Fiser, Webb S. Mastery of the Metropolis. Englewood Cliffs, N.J.: Prentice-Hall, 1962.

Forrester, Jay W. Urban Dynamics. Cambridge, Mass.: MIT Press, 1969.

Garson, G. David. Handbook of Political Science Methods. Boston: Holbrook Press, 1971.

Gibbs, Jack P., ed. Urban Research Methods. New York: Van Nostrand, 1962.

Gilbert, Charles E. Governing the Suburbs. Bloomington: Indiana University Press, 1967.

Glazer, Nathan, ed. Cities in Trouble. Chicago: Quadrangle Books, 1970.

Goldwin, Robert A., ed. A Nation of Cities: Essays on America's Urban Problems. Chicago: Rand McNally, 1966, 1968.

Goodall, Leonard E. The American Metropolis. Columbus, Ohio: Merrill, 1968.

Greene, Kenneth V., William B. Neenan, and Claudia Scott. Fiscal Interaction in a Metropolitan Area. Lexington, Mass.: Lexington Books, D. C. Heath, 1974.

Greer, Scott. The Emerging City. New York: Free Press of Glencoe, 1962.

_____. Governing the Metropolis. New York: Wiley, 1962.

_____. Metropolitics. New York: Wiley, 1963.

_____. Urban Renewal and American Cities. Indianapolis: Bobbs-Merrill, 1965.

Groves, Harold. Financing Government. New York: Holt, Rinehart, and Winston, 1964.

Hadden, Jeffrey K., and E. F. Borgatta. American Cities: Their Social Characteristics. Chicago: Rand McNally, 1965.

Hadden, Jeffrey K., Louis H. Masotti, and Calvin J. Larson, eds. Metropolis in Crisis: Social and Political Perspectives. Ithaca, Ill.: Peacock, 1971.

Hansen, Alvin H., and Harvey S. Perloff. State and Local Finance in the National Economy. New York: Norton, 1944.

Hansen, Niles M. The Future of Nonmetropolitan America: Studies in the Reversal of Rural and Small Town Population Decline. Lexington, Mass.: Lexington Books, 1973.

_____. Rural Poverty and the Urban Crisis: A Strategy for Regional Development. Bloomington: Indiana University Press, 1970.

Hansen, W. Lee, and Burton A. Weisberg. Benefits, Costs, and Finance of Public Higher Education. Chicago: Markham, 1969.

Hatry, Harry P., and Donald M. Fisk. Improving Productivity and Productivity Measurement in Local Government. Washington, D.C.: National Commission on Productivity, June, 1971.

Hatt, Paul K., and Albert J. Reiss, eds. Cities and Society. Glencoe, Ill.: Free Press, 1957.

Hauser, Phillip and Leo F. Schnore, eds. The Study of Suburbanization. New York: Wiley, 1965.

Haveman, Robert Henry. The Economics of the Public Sector. New York: Wiley, 1970.

Haveman, Robert H., and Julius Margolis, eds. Public Expenditure and Policy Analysis. Chicago: Markham, 1970.

Heilbroner, Robert L., and Peter L. Bernstein. Primer on Government Spending. New York: Random House, 1963.

Heilbrun, James. Urban Economics and Public Policy. New York: St. Martin's Press, 1973.

Heller, Walter, Lyle C. Ruggles, Donald C. Fitch, and Brazer Shoup. Revenue Sharing and the City. Baltimore, Md.: Published for Resources for the Future by The Johns Hopkins Press, 1968.

Hellerstein, Jerome R. State and Local Taxation: Cases and Materials. St. Paul: West, 1961.

_____. Taxes, Loopholes, and Morals. New York: McGraw-Hill, 1963.

Hempel, George. The Postwar Quality of State and Local Debt. New York: Columbia University Press, National Bureau of Economic Research: General Services, no. 54, 1971.

Hirsch, Werner Z. The Economics of State and Local Government. New York: McGraw-Hill, 1970.

_____. Measuring Factors Affecting Expenditure Levels for Local Government Services. St. Louis: Metropolitan St. Louis Survey, 1957.

_____. Urban Economic Analysis. New York: McGraw-Hill, 1973.

Hirsch, Werner, Z., ed. Urban Life and Form. New York: Holt, Rinehart and Winston, 1963.

Hirsch, Werner, and Sidney Sonenblum. Governing Urban America in the 1970's. New York: Praeger, 1973.

Hirsch, Werner, Phillip E. Vincent, Henry S. Terrell, Donald C. Shoup, and Arthur Rosett. Fiscal Pressures on the Central City: The Impact of Commuters, Nonwhites, and Overlapping Governments. New York: Praeger, 1971.

Holland, Daniel, ed. The Assessment of Land Values. Madison: University of Wisconsin Press, 1970.

Hoover, J. Edgar, and Raymond Vernon. Anatomy of a Metropolis. Cambridge, Mass.: Harvard University Press, 1959.

Housing and Home Finance Agency. Metropolis in Transition: Local Government Adaptation to Changing Urban Needs. Washington, D.C., September 1, 1963.

Isard, Walter, and Robert E. Coughlin. Municipal Costs and Revenues. Wellesley, Mass.: Chandler-Davis, 1957.

Iverson, Gudmund R. Applied Statistics. Ann Arbor, Mich.: Inter-University Consortium for Political Research, 1971.

Jacobs, Jane. The Economy of Cities. New York: Random House, 1969.

Johnson, Harry L., ed. State and Local Tax Problems. Knoxville: University of Tennessee Press, 1969.

Johnson, J. Econometric Methods. 2d ed. New York: McGraw-Hill, 1963.

Kerlinger, Fred N. Foundations of Behavioral Research. New York: Holt, Rinehart and Winston, 1964.

Kimmel, Lewis H. Taxes and Economic Incentives. Washington, D.C.: The Brookings Institution, 1950.

Kramer, John, ed. North American Suburbs: Politics, Universality, and Change. Berkeley, Calif.: Glenodessy Press, 1972.

Kreps, Juanita. Sex in the Marketplace: American Women at Work. Baltimore, Md.: Johns Hopkins University Press, 1971.

Leege, David C., and Wayne L. Francis. Political Research. New York: Basic Books, 1974.

Lineberry, Robert L., and Ira Sharkansky. Urban Politics and Public Policy. 2d ed. New York: Harper & Row, 1974.

Lynn, Arthur D. The Property Tax and Its Administration. Madison: University of Wisconsin Press, 1969.

Mace, Ruth L. Municipal Cost-Revenues Research in the U.S. Chapel Hill: Institute of Government, University of North Carolina, 1961.

McKelvey, Blake. The Emergence of Metropolitan America, 1915-1966. New Brunswick, N.J.: Rutgers University Press, 1968.

McKinley, J. P. Local Revenue Problems and Trends. Berkeley: Bureau of Public Administration, University of California, 1949.

Margolis, Julius, ed. The Analysis of Public Output. New York: National Bureau of Economic Research, 1970.

_____. The Public Economy of Urban Communities. Baltimore, Md.: Johns Hopkins Press, 1965.

Margolis, Julius, and Henri Gritton, eds. Public Economics. New York: Macmillan, 1969.

Masotti, Louis. Education and Politics in Suburbia. Cleveland: Press of Western Reserve University, 1967.

Masotti, Louis H., and Jeffery K. Hadden, eds. Suburbia in Transition. New York: New Viewpoints, 1974.

_____. Suburbs, Suburbia, and Suburbanization: A Bibliography. Monticello, Ill.: Council of Planning Librarians, 1972.

_____. The Urbanization of the Suburbs. Beverly Hills, Calif.: Sage Publications, 1973.

Maxwell, James A. Financing State and Local Governments. Washington, D.C.: The Brookings Institution, 1965.

Meadows, Paul, and Ephraim Mizruchi, eds. Urbanism, Urbanization, and Change: Comparative Perspectives. Reading, Mass.: Addison Wesley, 1969.

Moak, L. L., and A. M. Hillhouse. Concepts and Practices in Local Government Finance. Chicago: Municipal Finance Officers Association, 1975.

Morgan, David R., and Samuel A. Kirkpatrick, eds. Urban Political Analysis: A Systems Approach. New York: The Free Press, 1972.

Mosher, Frederick C., and Orville F. Poland. The Costs of American Governments: Facts, Trends, Myths. New York: Dodd, Mead, 1969.

Musgrave, Richard A. Essays in Fiscal Federalism. Washington, D.C.: The Brookings Institution, 1965.

_____. Fiscal Systems. New Haven, Conn.: Yale University Press, 1969.

_____. The Theory of Public Finance. New York: McGraw-Hill, 1959.

Musgrave, Richard A., and R. Musgrave. Public Finance in Theory and Practice. New York: McGraw-Hill, 1973.

Musgrave, Richard A., and Alan T. Peacock, eds. Classics in the Theory of Public Finance. New York: Macmillan, 1958.

Mushkin, Selma J., and John F. Cotton. Functional Federalism. Washington, D.C.: George Washington University, 1968.

_____. Sharing Federal Funds for State and Local Needs. New York: Praeger, 1969.

Nathan, Richard P., Allen D. Manvel, and Susannah E. Calkins. Monitoring Revenue Sharing. Washington, D.C.: The Brookings Institution, 1975.

Neenhan, William B. Political Economy of Urban Areas. Chicago: Markham, 1972.

Netzer, Dick. Economics and Urban Problems: Diagnoses and Prescriptions. New York: Basic Books, 1970.

_____. Economics of the Property Tax. Washington, D.C.: The Brookings Institution, 1966.

_____. State-Local Finance and Intergovernmental Fiscal Relations. Washington, D.C.: The Brookings Institution, 1969.

Nie, Norman H., Dale H. Bent, and C. Hadali Hull. SPSS: Statistical Package for the Social Sciences. New York: McGraw-Hill, 1970.

O'Connor, James. The Fiscal Crisis of the State. New York: St. Martin's Press, 1973.

Ogburn, William F. Social Characteristics of Cities. Chicago: International City Managers Association, 1973.

Pechman, Joseph A., and Benjamin A. Okner. Who Bears the Tax Burden? Washington, D.C.: The Brookings Institution, 1974.

Perloff, Harvey S. Regions, Resources, and Economic Growth. Baltimore: Published for Resources for the Future by the Johns Hopkins Press, 1960.

Perloff, Harvey S., and Loudon Wingo, Jr., eds. Issues in Urban Economics. Baltimore: Johns Hopkins Press, 1968.

Peterson, George E., Arthur P. Solomon, Hadi Madjid, and William C. Apgar, Jr. Property Taxes, Housing and the Cities. Lexington, Mass.: Lexington Books, 1973.

Pettengill, Robert B., and Jogindar S. Uppal. Can Cities Survive? The Fiscal Plight of American Cities. New York: St. Martin's Press, 1974.

Phares, Donald. State-Local Tax Equity: An Empirical Analysis of the Fifty States. Lexington, Mass.: Heath, 1973.

Rabinowitz, Alan. Municipal Bond Finance and Administration. New York: Wiley-Interscience, 1969.

Ratcliff, Richard. Urban Land Economics. New York: McGraw-Hill, 1949.

Reiss, Albert J., ed. On Cities and Social Life. Chicago: University of Chicago Press, 1964.

Riedel, James A., ed. New Perspectives in State and Local Politics. Waltham, Mass.: Xerox College Printing, 1971.

Rodwin, Lloyd. The Future Metropolis. New York: Braziller, 1961.

Rossi, Peter Henry, and Robert A. Dentler. The Politics of Urban Renewal. New York: Free Press of Glencoe, 1961.

Ruskay, Joseph A., and Richard A. Osserman. Half Way to Tax Reform. Bloomington: Indiana University Press, 1970.

Sacks, Seymour, and William F. Hellmuth, Jr. Financing Government in a Metropolitan Area: The Cleveland Experience. New York: The Free Press, 1961.

Schaller, Howard, ed. Public Expenditure Decisions in the Urban Community. Washington, D.C.: Resources for the Future, Inc., 1965.

Schnore, Leo F. Class and Race in Cities and Suburbs. Chicago: Markham, 1972.

_____. Social Sciences and the City: A Survey of Urban Research. New York: Praeger, 1968.

_____. The Urban Scene: Human Ecology and Demography. New York: The Free Press, 1965.

Schultze, Charles L. The Politics and Economics of Public Spending. Washington, D.C.: The Brookings Institution, 1968.

Schultze, William A. Urban and Community Politics. North Scituate, Mass.: Duxbury Press, 1974.

Scott, Claudia D. Forecasting Local Government Spending. Washington, D.C.: Urban Institute, 1972.

Scott, Stanley, and Edward Feder. Factors Associated with Variations in Municipal Expenditure Levels. Berkeley: University of California, Bureau of Public Administration, 1957.

Sharkansky, Ira. The Politics of Taxing and Spending. New York: Bobbs-Merrill, 1969.

Sigafoos, Robert A. The Municipal Income Tax: Its History and Problems. Chicago: Public Administrative Service, 1954.

Smith, Wilson. Cities of Our Past and Present: A Descriptive Reader. New York: Wiley, 1964.

Sobin, Dennis P. The Future of the American Suburbs: Survival or Extinction? Port Washington, N.Y.: National University Publications, 1971.

Spectorsky, A. C. The Exurbanites. Philadelphia: Lippincott, 1955.

Stanley, David T. Managing Local Government under Union Pressure. Washington, D.C.: The Brookings Institution, 1972.

Sussman, Marvin B., ed. Community Structure and Analysis. New York: Crowell, 1959.

Swanson, Bert E. The Concern for Community in Urban America. New York: Odyssey Press, 1970.

Sweeney, Stephen B., ed. Metropolitan Analysis: Important Elements of Study and Action. Philadelphia: University of Pennsylvania Press, 1958.

Tax Foundation. Big City Revenue Structures in Transition. New York: Tax Foundation, 1972.

_____. The Financial Outlook for State-Local Government to 1980— A Summary. New York: Tax Foundation, 1972.

_____. Fiscal Outlook for State and Local Governments to 1975. New York: Tax Foundation, 1966.

_____. Research Bibliography: Financing Municipal Government. New York: Tax Foundation, 1960.

Taylor, Graham R. Satellite Cities. New York: Appleton, 1915.

Thomlinson, Ralph. Urban Structure. New York: Random House, 1969.

Thompson, Wilbur R. A Preface to Urban Economics. Baltimore: Published for Resources for the Future by Johns Hopkins Press, 1965.

Thurow, Lester C. The Impact of Taxes on the American Economy. New York: Praeger, 1971.

Tietze, Frederick J., and James E. McKeown, eds. The Changing Metropolis. Boston: Houghton Mifflin, 1964.

Tufte, Edward R. Data Analysis for Politics and Policy. Englewood Cliffs, N.J.: Prentice-Hall, 1974.

Twentieth Century Fund Task Force on Women and Employment. Exploitation from 9 to 5. Lexington, Mass.: Lexington, 1975.

U.S. Bureau of the Census. Census of Governments: 1972. Vol. 2, Taxable Property Values and Assessment—Sales Price Ratios and Tax Rates. Washington, D.C.: Bureau of the Census, 1973.

_____. City Government Finances in 1971–72. Washington, D.C.: Bureau of the Census, 1973.

_____. General Demographic Trends for Metropolitan Areas 1960–1970. Washington, D.C.: Bureau of the Census, 1972.

_____. Historical Statistics on State and Local Government Finances. Washington, D.C.: Bureau of the Census, 1955.

_____. Local Government Finances in Selected Metropolitan Statistical Areas. Washington, D.C.: Bureau of the Census, 1966.

U.S. Congress, Joint Economic Committee. Impact of the Property Tax: Its Economic Implications for Urban Problems. Washington, D.C.: Government Printing Office, 1968.

U.S. Congress, Subcommittee on Economic Programs, Joint Economic Committee. Financial Municipal Facilities. Washington, D.C.: Government Printing Office, 1968.

U.S. Department of Commerce. Trends in Assessed Valuations and Sales Ratios 1956–1966. Washington, D.C.: Government Printing Office, March 1970.

U.S. Department of Labor. Economic Report of the President. Washington, D.C.: Government Printing Office, 1973.

U.S. Department of Labor, Manpower Administration. Manpower Report of the President. Washington, D.C.: Government Printing Office, 1971.

U.S. Women's Bureau. 1969 Handbook on Women Workers. Washington, D.C.: Government Printing Office, 1969.

Vernon, Raymond. The Changing Economic Function of the Central City. New York: Committee for Economic Development, 1960.

_____. Metropolis 1985. Cambridge, Mass.: Harvard University Press, 1960.

Warner, Sam. Streetcar Suburbs. Cambridge, Mass.: Harvard University Press, 1967.

Warren, Robert O. Government in Metropolitan Regions. Davis, Calif.: Institute of Governmental Affairs, 1966.

Watts, William, and Lloyd A. Free. State of the Union. New York: Universe Books, 1973.

Weintraub, Robert E. Options for Meeting the Revenue Needs of City Governments. Santa Barbara, Calif.: TEMPO, General Electric, 1967.

Whitelaw, W. E. An Econometric Analysis of a Municipal Budgetary Process Based on Time Series Data. Cambridge, Mass.: Harvard Program on Regional and Urban Economics, September 1968.

Wildavsky, Aaron. The Politics of the Budgetary Process. Boston: Little, Brown, 1964.

Williams, Oliver P., and Charles R. Adrian. Four Cities. Philadelphia: University of Pennsylvania Press, 1963.

Williams, Oliver P., Harold Herman, Charles S. Liebman, and Thomas R. Dye. Suburban Differences and Metropolitan Policies: A Philadelphia Story. Philadelphia: University of Pennsylvania Press, 1965.

Williams, Oliver P., and Charles Press, eds. Democracy in Urban America. 2d ed. Chicago: Rand McNally, 1961.

Wirt, Frederick M., Benjamin Walker, Frances F. Rabinovitz, and Deborah R. Hensler. On the City's Rim: Politics and Policy in Suburbia. Lexington, Mass.: Heath, 1972.

Wonnacott, Ronald J., and Thomas H. Wonnacott. Econometrics. New York: Wiley, 1970.

Wood, Robert, and Vladimir V. Almendinger. 1400 Governments. Cambridge, Mass.: Harvard University Press, 1961.

Wood, Robert C. Suburbia: Its People and Their Politics. Boston: Houghton Mifflin, 1959.

Woodbury, Coleman, ed. The Future of Cities and Urban Redevelopment. Chicago: University of Chicago Press, 1953.

Wright, Deil S. Federal Grants-in-Aid: Perspectives and Alternatives. Washington, D.C.: American Enterprise Institute, June 1968.

Zimmer, Basil G. Metropolitan Area Schools: Resistance to District Reorganization. Beverly Hills, Calif.: Sage Publications, 1968.

Zimmerman, Joseph Francis. Government of the Metropolis. New York: Holt, Rinehart and Winston, 1968.

Zisk, Betty H. Local Interest Politics: A One-Way Street. Indianapolis: Bobbs-Merrill, 1973.

ARTICLES

Aaron, Henry, and Martin McGuire. "Public Goods and Income Distribution." Econometrica 38 (November 1970): 908-20.

Adams, Robert F. "Fiscal Response to Intergovernmental Transfer." The Review of Economics and Statistics 48 (August 1966): 308-13.

_____. "On the Variation in the Consumption of Public Services." Review of Economics and Statistics 47 (November 1965): 400-05.

Advisory Commission on Intergovernmental Relations. Intergovernmental Perspective 3 (1977): 8–9.

Aiken, Michael. "Comparative Urban Research and Community Decision-Making." New Atlantis 1 (Winter 1970): 85–110.

Aiken, Michael, and Robert Alford. "Community Structure and Innovation: The Case of Public Housing." American Political Science Review 64 (September 1970): 843–64.

Albin, Peter S. "Unbalanced Growth and Intensification of the Urban Crisis." Urban Studies 8 (June 1971): 139–46.

Alford, Robert R., and Harry M. Scoble. "Political and Socioeconomic Characteristics of American Cities." In The Municipal Yearbook 1968, pp. 82–97. Chicago: ICMA, 1969.

Andrews, R. B., and Jerome J. Dasso. "The Influence of Annexation on Property Tax Burdens." National Tax Journal 14 (March 1961): 88–97.

Aronson, J. Richard, and Eli Schwartz. "Financing Public Goods and the Distribution of Population in a System of Local Governments." National Tax Journal 26 (June 1973): 137–59.

Atchley, Robert C. "A Size-Function Typology of Cities." Demography 4 (1967): 721–33.

Bahl, Roy W. "Public Policy and the Urban Fiscal Problem: Piecemeal versus Aggregate Solutions." Land Economics 46 (February 1970): 41–50.

_____. "Studies on Determinants of Public Expenditure." In Functional Federalism, edited by Selma J. Mushkin and John Cotton. Washington, D.C.: George Washington University, 1968.

Bahl, Roy W., and J. J. Warford. "Interstate Distribution of Benefits from the Federal Budgetary Process." National Tax Journal 24 (June 1971): 169–76.

Bahl, Roy W., Jr., and Robert J. Saunders. "Determinants of Changes in State and Local Government Expenditures." National Tax Journal 18 (March 1965): 50–57.

Baird, Robert N., and John H. Landon. "Political Fragmentation, Income Distribution, and the Demand for Government Services." Nebraska Journal of Economics and Business 11 (Autumn 1972): 171-84.

Barlev, Benzion. "Location Effects of Intra-Area Tax Differentials." Land Economics 69 (February 1973): 86-89.

Barlowe, Raleigh, James G. Ahl, and Gordon Backman. "Use-Value Assessment Legislation in the U.S." Land Economics 49 (May 1973): 206-12.

Barr, J. L., and O. A. Davis. "An Elementary Political and Economic Theory of Local Government." Southern Economic Journal 33 (October 1966): 149-65.

Bateman, Worth, and Harold M. Hochman. "Social Problems and the Urban Crisis: Can Public Policy Make a Difference?" American Economic Review 61 (May 1971): 346-53.

Baumol, William. "Urban Services: Interactions of Public and Private Decisions." In Public Expenditure Decisions in the Urban Community, edited by Howard Schaller, pp. 1-18. Washington, D.C.: Resources for the Future, Inc., 1965.

Beagle, Dan, Al Haber, and David Wellman. "Turf Power and the Taxman: Urban Renewal, Reorganization, and the Limits of Community Control." Leviathan, April 1969.

Bean, Frank D., Dudley L. Poston, Jr., and Halliman H. Winsborough. "Size, Functional Specialization, and the Classification of Cities." Social Science Quarterly 53 (June 1972): 20-32.

Beck, Morris. "Determinants of the Property Tax Level: A Case Study of Northeastern New Jersey." National Tax Journal 18 (March 1965): 74-77.

Bergmann, Barbara, and Irman Adelman. "The 1973 Report of the Council of Economic Advisers: The Economic Role of Women." American Economic Review 63 (September 1973): 509-14.

Berk, Richard A. "Performance Measures: Half Full or Half Empty?" Social Science Quarterly 54 (March 1974): 762-64.

Berle, Adolf A., Jr. "Reflections on Financing Governmental Functions of the Metropolis." Proceedings of the Academy of Political Science 27 (May 1960): 66-79.

Black, David E. "The Nature and Extent of Effective Property Tax Rate Variation within the City of Boston." National Tax Journal 25 (June 1972): 203-10.

Blalock, Hubert M., Jr. "Correlated Independent Variables: The Problem of Multicollinearity." Social Forces 42 (December 1963): 233-38.

Boelaert, Remi. "Political Fragmentation and Inequality of Fiscal Capacity in the Milwaukee SMSA." National Tax Journal 23 (March 1970): 83-88.

Bollens, John. "Factors Affecting Local Government Expenditure Levels." In Exploring the Metropolitan Community, edited by John C. Bollens. Berkeley: University of California Press, 1961.

Booms, Bernard H. "City Governmental Form and Public Expenditure Levels." National Tax Journal 19 (June 1966): 187-99.

Borcherding, Thomas E., and Robert T. Deacon. "The Demand for the Services of Non-Federal Governments." American Economic Review 62 (September 1972): 891-901.

Boskin, M. "Local Government Tax and Product Competition and the Optimal Provision of Public Goods." Journal of Political Economy 81 (January/February 1973): 203-10.

Bowman, John H. "City-Suburban Differentials in Local Government Fiscal Effort: A Comment." National Tax Journal 22 (September 1969): 418-21.

Bradford, David F., and Harry H. Kelejiian. "An Econometric Model of the Flight to the Suburbs." Journal of Political Economy 81 (May/June 1973): 566-89.

Brainard, William C., and F. Trenery Dolbear, Jr. "The Possibility of Oversupply of Local 'Public' Goods: A Critical Note." Journal of Political Economy 75 (February 1967): 86-90.

Brazer, Harvey E. "The Federal Government and State-Local Finances." National Tax Journal 20 (June 1967): 155-64.

_____. "The Role of Major Metropolitan Centers in State and Local Finances." American Economic Review 47 (May 1958): 305-16.

_____. "Some Fiscal Implications of Metropolitanism." In City and Suburb, edited by Benjamin Chinitz, pp. 127-50. Englewood Cliffs, N.J.: Prentice-Hall, 1964.

Brazer, Marjorie C. "Economic and Social Disparities between Central Cities and Their Suburbs." Land Economics 43 (November 1967): 394-402.

Breton, Albert. "A Theory of Government Grants." Canadian Journal of Economics and Political Science 31 (May 1965): 175-87.

Bridges, Benjamin, Jr. "Income Elasticity of the Property Tax." National Tax Journal 17 (September 1964): 253-64.

Buchanan, James M. "Federalism and Fiscal Equity." American Economic Review 40 (September 1950): 583-99.

_____. "Principles of Urban Fiscal Strategy." Public Choice 11 (Fall 1971): 1-16.

Buchanan, James M., and Charles J. Goetz. "Efficiency Limits of Fiscal Mobility: An Assessment of the Tiebout Model." Journal of Public Economics 1 (April 1972): 25-43.

Buckler, Alfred G. "Problems Presented by Proliferation of Municipal Nonproperty Taxes." Municipal Finance 34 (February 1962): 106-11.

Burkhead, Jesse. "Uniformity in Governmental Expenditures and Resources in a Metropolitan Area: Cuyahoga County." National Tax Journal 14 (December 1961): 337-48.

Cho, Young H. "The Effect of Local Governmental Systems on Local Policy Outcomes in the United States." Public Administration Review 27 (March 1967): 31-38.

Clark, Colin. "The Economic Functions of a City in Relation to Its Size." Econometrica 13 (April 1945): 97-113.

Clarke, James W. "Environment, Process, and Policy: A Reconsideration." American Political Science Review 63 (December 1969): 1172-82.

Coke, James, and Charles Liebman. "Political Values and Population Density Control." Land Economics 37 (November 1961): 347-62.

Cole, Richard L. "The Urban Policy Process: A Note on Structural and Regional Influences." Social Science Quarterly 52 (December 1971): 646-55.

Colon, Gerhard, Lucy Edelberg, Arthur L. Horniker, Berthold Kaufmann, and Charles D. Stewart. "Public Expenditures and Economic Structures." Social Research 3 (February 1936): 57-77.

Dajani, Jarir S. "Cost Studies of Urban Public Services." Land Economics 69 (November 1973): 479-83.

Daland, Robert T. "Political Science and the Study of Urbanism." American Political Science Review 51 (June 1957): 491-509.

Davies, David. "Financing Urban Functions and Services." Law and Contemporary Problems 30 (Winter 1965): 127-67.

Davis, Kingsley. "The Urbanization of the Human Population." Scientific American 213 (September 1965): 40-53.

Davis, Otto, and Kenneth Wertz. "The Consistency of the Assessment of Property: Some Empirical Results and Managerial Suggestions." Applied Economics 1 (May 1969): 151-57.

Davis, Otto A., and George H. Haines, Jr. "A Political Approach to a Theory of Public Expenditure: The Case of Municipalities." National Tax Journal 19 (September 1966): 259-75.

Denton, Frank T., and Byron G. Spencer. "A Simulation Analysis of the Effects of Population Change on a Neoclassical Economy." Journal of Political Economy 81 (March/April 1973): 356-75.

Deran, Elizabeth. "Tax Structure in Cities Using the Income Tax." National Tax Journal 21 (June 1968): 147-52.

Downes, Bryan T. "Suburban Differentiation and Municipal Policy Choices: A Comparative Analysis of Suburban Political Systems."

In Community Structure and Decision Making, edited by Terry N. Clark. San Francisco: Chandler, 1968.

Duncan, Beverly. "Intra-Urban Population Movement." In Cities and Society, edited by Paul K. Hatt and Albert G. Reiss, pp. 297-309. Glencoe, Ill.: The Free Press, 1957.

Duncan, Otis Dudley. "Community Size and the Rural-Urban Continuum." In Cities and Society, edited by Paul K. Hatt and Albert J. Reiss, Jr., pp. 35-45. Glencoe, Ill.: The Free Press, 1957.

_____. "Research on Metropolitan Population: Evaluation of Data." Journal of the American Statistical Association 51 (December 1956): 591-96.

Dye, Thomas R. "City-Suburban Social Distance and Public Policy." Social Forces 44 (September 1965): 100-06.

_____. "Governmental Structure, Urban Environment, and Educational Policy." Midwest Journal of Political Science 11 (August 1967): 353-80.

_____. "Population Density and Social Pathology." Urban Affairs Quarterly 11 (December 1975): 265-75.

_____. "Urban Political Integration: Conditions Associated with Annexation in American Cities." Midwest Journal of Political Science 8 (November 1964): 430-46.

Dye, Thomas R., and Susan A. MacManus. "Predicting City Government Structure." American Journal of Political Science 20 (May 1976): 257-71.

Dye, Thomas R., Oliver P. Williams, Harold Herman, and Charles Liebman. "Differentiation and Cooperation in a Metropolitan Area." Midwest Journal of Political Science 7 (May 1963): 145-55.

Elazar, Daniel J. "'Fragmentation' and Local Organizational Response to Federal-City Programs." Urban Affairs Quarterly 4 (June 1967): 30-46.

Ellickson, B. "Jurisdictional Fragmentation and Residential Choice." American Economic Review, Papers and Proceedings 61 (1971): 334-40.

Epstein, Cynthia Fuchs. "Positive Effects of the Multiple Negative: Explaining the Success of Black Professional Women." In Women in a Changing Society, edited by Joan Huber, pp. 150-73. Chicago: University of Chicago Press, 1973.

Fava, Sylvia Fleis. "Suburbanism as a Way of Life." American Sociological Review 21 (February 1956): 34-37.

Fefferman, Arthur S. "The State and Local Fiscal Assistance Act of 1972." National Tax Journal 25 (September 1972): 473-78.

Feinberg, Mordecai S. "The Implications of Core-City Decline for the Fiscal Structure of the Core City." National Tax Journal 17 (September 1964): 213-31.

Fischer, Claude S. "Urbanism as a Way of Life." Sociological Methods and Research 1 (November 1972): 187-242.

Fisher, Glenn W. "Determinants of State and Local Government Expenditures: A Preliminary Analysis." National Tax Journal 14 (December 1965): 349-55.

_____. "Interstate Variation in State and Local Government Expenditure." National Tax Journal 17 (March 1964): 57-74.

_____. "Revenue and Expenditure Patterns in Five Large Cities." Quarterly Review of Economics and Business 3 (Autumn 1963): 61-72.

Fisk, Donald M., and Richard E. Winnie. "Output Measurement in Urban Government: Current Status and Likely Prospects." Social Science Quarterly 54 (March 1974): 725-40.

Fitch, Lyle C. "Metropolitan Financial Problems." The Annals of the American Academy of Political and Social Science 314 (November 1957): 66-73.

Forstall, Richard L. "Application of the New Social and Economic Grouping of Cities." Urban Data Service. Washington, D.C.: ICMA, 1971.

_____. "Economic Classifications of Places over 10,000, 1960-1963." In The Municipal Yearbook 1967, pp. 30-48. Chicago: ICMA, 1967.

_____. "A New Social and Economic Grouping of Cities." In The Municipal Yearbook 1970, pp. 102-59. Chicago: ICMA, 1970.

Fortune, Peter. "The Impact of Taxable Municipal Bonds: Policy Simulations with a Large Econometric Model." National Tax Journal 26 (March 1973): 29-42.

Frey, Bruno S. "Why Do High Income People Participate More in Politics." Public Choice, vol. 11 (1971).

Froman, Lewis A., Jr. "An Analysis of Public Policies in Cities." Journal of Politics 29 (February 1967): 94-108.

Fuchs, Victor. "Differences in Hourly Earnings between Men and Women." Monthly Labor Review 94 (May 1971): 9-15.

Galle, Omer R. "Occupational Composition and the Metropolitan Hierarchy: The Inter- and Intro-Metropolitan Division of Labor." American Journal of Sociology 69 (November 1963): 260-69.

Gans, Herbert T. "Urbanism and Suburbanism as a Way of Life." In Human Behavior and Social Processes, edited by Arnold Rose. Boston: Houghton Mifflin, 1962.

_____. "The White Exodus to Suburbia Steps Up." In Urban Politics and Problems, edited by H. R. Mahood and Edward L. Angus, pp. 163-74. New York: Scribner's, 1969.

Gayer, David. "The Effects of Medicaid on State and Local Government Finances." National Tax Journal 25 (December 1972): 511-19.

Gillespie, W. Irwin. "Effect of Public Expenditures on the Distribution of Income." In Essays in Fiscal Federalism, edited by Richard A. Musgrove, pp. 122-86. Washington, D.C.: The Brookings Institution, 1965.

Goodman, L. A. "A Modified Multiple Regression Approach to the Analysis of Dichotomous Variables." American Sociological Review 37 (1972): 28-46.

Gordon, Daniel N. "Immigrants and Urban Governmental Form in American Cities, 1933-1960." American Journal of Sociology 35 (August 1970): 665-81.

Gramlich, Edward M. "Alternative Federal Policies for Stimulating State and Local Expenditures: A Comparison of Their Effects." National Tax Journal 21 (June 1968): 119-29.

Graves, Frank M. "Fiscal Disparities between the Atlanta and Non-Atlanta Areas of Fulton County, Georgia." National Tax Journal 23 (December 1970); 449-55.

Greene, Kenneth V. "Collective Decision-Making Models and the Measurement of Benefits in Fiscal Incidence Studies." National Tax Journal 26 (June 1973): 177-88.

Greene, Kenneth V., and Claudia D. Scott. "Suburban-Central City Spillovers of Tax Burdens and Expenditure Benefits." Northeast Regional Science Review, vol. 3 (1973).

Greer, Scott. "The Social Structure and Political Process of Suburbia." American Sociological Review 25 (August 1960): 514-26.

Groves, Harold M. "New Sources of Light on Intergovernmental Fiscal Relations." National Tax Journal 5 (September 1952): 234-38.

Grunfeld, Y. "The Interpretation of Cross-Section Estimates in a Dynamic Model." Econometrica 29 (July 1961): 397-404.

Hanoch, Giora. "An Economic Analysis of Earnings and Schooling." Journal of Human Resources 2 (Summer 1967): 310-29.

Harris, C. Lowell. "State-Local Taxation: An Overview." Taxes 50 (April 1972): 232-50.

Harris, Chauncy D. "A Functional Classification of Cities in the U.S." Geographical Review 30 (January 1943): 86-99.

_____. "The Functions of Metropolitan Suburbs." American Sociological Review 5 (April 1957): 165-73.

Haskell, Mark A. "Federal Grants-in-Aid: Their Influence on State and Local Expenditures." Canadian Journal of Economic and Political Science 30 (November 1964): 585-90.

Haskell, Mark A., and Stephen Leshinski. "Fiscal Influences on Residential Choice: A Study of the New York Region." Quarterly Review of Economics and Business 9 (Winter 1969): 47-56.

Hawley, Amos. "Metropolitan Population and Municipal Government Expenditures in 'Central Cities." Journal of Social Issues 7 (1951): 100–08.

Heinberg, J. D., and Wallace E. Oates. "The Incidence of Differential Property Taxes on Urban Housing: A Comment and Some Further Evidence." National Tax Journal 23 (March 1970): 92–101.

Henderson, James M. "Local Government Expenditures: A Social Welfare Analysis." Review of Economics and Statistics 50 (May 1968): 156–63.

Hibbs, Douglas A., Jr. "Problems of Statistical Estimation and Causal Inference in Time-Series Regression Models." In Sociological Methodology 1973-1974, edited by H. L. Costner. San Francisco: Jossey-Bass, 1974.

Hill, Richard Child. "Separate and Unequal: Governmental Inequality in the Metropolis." American Political Science Review 68 (December 1974): 1557–68.

Hines, Fred, Luther Tweeten, and Martin Redfern. "Social and Private Rates of Return to Investment in Schooling by Race-Sex Groups and Regions." Journal of Human Resources 5 (Summer 1970): 318–40.

Hirsch, Werner Z. "Determinants of Public Education Expenditures." National Tax Journal 13 (March 1960): 29–40.

_____. "Expenditure Implications of Metropolitan Growth and Consolidation." Review of Economics and Statistics 41 (August 1959): 232–41.

_____. "Local versus Areawide Urban Government Services." National Tax Journal 17 (December 1964): 331–39.

_____. "The Supply of Urban Public Services." In Issues in Urban Economics, edited by Harvey S. Perloff and Lowdon Wingo, Jr. Baltimore: Johns Hopkins University Press, 1968.

Hochman, Harold H., and James D. Rogers. "Pareto Optimal Redistribution." American Economic Review 59 (September 1969): 542–47.

Holtmann, A. G. "Migration to the Suburbs, Human Capital, and City Income Tax Losses: A Case Study." National Tax Journal 21 (September 1968): 326-31.

Horowitz, Ann R. "A Simultaneous-Equation Approach to the Problem of Explaining Interstate Differences in State and Local Government Expenditures." Southern Economic Journal 34 (April 1968): 459-76.

Jack, John W., and Paul C. Reuss. "Financing Municipal Government: Fiscal Challenge of the Seventies." Municipal Finance, February 1971, pp. 141-48.

James, Louis J. "The Stimulation and Substitution Effects of Grants-in-Aid: A General Equilibrium Analysis." National Tax Journal 26 (June 1973): 251-65.

Johnson, Maxine C. "Women and Public Policy: The Search for Equity in the Labor Market." Paper presented at the 1976 Annual Meeting of the Southwestern Political Science Association, Dallas, Texas, April 7-10, 1976.

Johnson, Ronald L., and Edward Knop. "Rural-Urban Differentials in Community Satisfaction." Rural Sociology 35 (December 1970): 544-48.

Johnson, S. R., and Paul E. Junk. "Sources of Tax Revenues and Expenditures in Large U.S. Cities." Quarterly Review of Economics and Business 10 (Winter 1970): 7-15.

Jones, Victor. "Economic Classification of Cities and Metropolitan Areas." In The Municipal Yearbook 1953, pp. 49-69. Chicago: ICMA, 1953.

Jones, Victor, and Andrew Collver. "Economic Classification of Cities and Metropolitan Areas." In The Municipal Yearbook 1960, pp. 67-90. Chicago: ICMA, 1960.

Jones, Victor, and Richard L. Forstall. "Economic and Social Classification of Metropolitan Areas." In The Municipal Yearbook 1963. Chicago: ICMA, 1964.

Jones, Victor, Richard L. Forstall, and Andrew Collver. "Economic and Social Characteristics of Urban Places," and "Economic and Social Classification of Metropolitan Areas." In The Municipal Yearbook 1963, pp. 37-115. Chicago: ICMA, 1963.

Kain, John F. "Housing Segregation, Negro Employment, and Metropolitan Decentralization." Quarterly Journal of Economics 82
(May 1968): 175-97.

Kasarda, John D. "The Impact of Suburban Population Growth on
Central City Service Functions." American Journal of Sociology
77 (May 1972): 1111-24.

Kee, Woo Sik. "Central City Expenditures and Metropolitan Areas."
National Tax Journal 18 (December 1965): 337-53.

_____. "City-Suburban Differentials in Local Government Fiscal Ef-
fort." National Tax Journal 21 (June 1968): 183-89.

_____. "State and Local Fiscal Systems and Municipal Expenditures."
Public Administration Review 27 (March 1967): 39-41.

_____. "Suburban Population Growth and Its Implications for Core
City Finance." Land Economics 43 (May 1967): 202-11.

Keil, Thomas J., and Charles A. Ekstrom. "Municipal Differentiation and Public Policy: Fiscal Support Level in Varying Environ-
ments." Social Forces 52 (March 1974): 384-94.

Kessel, John H. "Governmental Structure and Political Environment."
American Political Science Review 56 (September 1962): 615-20.

King, Leslie J., and Douglas Jeffrey. "City Classification by Oblique
—Factor Analysis of Time Series Data." In City Classification
Handbook: Methods and Applications, edited by Brian J. L.
Berry, pp. 211-24. New York: Wiley, 1972.

Kirschenbaum, Alan B. "A Flight from Suburbia: A Demographic
Analysis." Maxwell Review, October 1967, pp. 17-26.

Kish, Leslie. "Differentiation in Metropolitan Areas." American Sociological Review 19 (August 1954): 388-98.

Kolderie, Ted, John Shannon, Dick Netzer, and Mabel Walker. "The
Quest for Revenues." Municipal Finance 14 (November 1971):
30-55.

Kuh, E. "The Validity of Cross-Sectionally Estimated Behavior in
Time Series Applications." Econometrica 27 (April 1959): 197-
214.

Kurnow, Ernest. "Determinants of State and Local Expenditures Re-examined." National Tax Journal 16 (September 1963): 252-55.

LeMay, Michael. "Expenditure and Nonexpenditure Measures of State Urban Policy Output: A Research Note." American Politics Quarterly 1 (October 1973): 511-28.

Lieberson, Stanley. "Suburbs and Ethnic Residential Patterns." American Journal of Sociology 67 (May 1962): 673-81.

Liebert, Roland J. "Municipal Functions, Structure, and Expenditures: A Reanalysis of Recent Research." Social Science Quarterly 54 (March 1974): 765-83.

Liebman, Charles S. "Functional Differentiation and Political Characteristics of Suburbs." American Journal of Sociology 66 (March 1961): 485-90.

Lile, Stephen E., and Don M. Soule. "Interstate Differences in Family Tax Burdens." National Tax Journal 22 (December 1969): 433-45.

Lindblom, Charles E. "The Science of Muddling Through." Public Administration Review 19 (Spring 1959): 79-88.

Lineberry, Robert L, and Edmund P. Fowler. "Reformism and Public Policy in American Cities." American Political Science Review 58 (September 1967): 701-16.

Lineberry, Robert L., and Robert C. Welch. "Who Gets What: Measuring the Distribution of Urban Public Services." Social Science Quarterly 54 (March 1974): 700-12.

MacManus, Susan A., and Nikki R. Van Hightower. "The Impacts of Local Government Tax Structures on Women: Inefficiencies and Inequalities." Social Science Journal 14 (April 1977): 103-16.

_____. "Municipal Fiscal Structure in a Metropolitan Area." Journal of Political Economy 65 (June 1957): 225-36.

Manvel, Allen D. "Trends in the Value of Real Estate and Land, 1956-1966." In Three Land Research Studies. National Commission on Urban Problems, Research Report no. 12. Washington, D.C.: U.S. Government Printing Office, 1968.

Margolis, Julius. "Metropolitan Finance Problems: Territories, Functions, and Growth." In Public Finance: Needs, Sources, Utilization, edited by James M. Buchanan, pp. 229-93. Princeton, N.J.: National Bureau of Economic Research Symposium, 1961.

Maxwell, James A., and J. Richard Aronson. "Federal Grant Elasticity and Distortion." National Tax Journal 22 (December 1969): 550-51.

_____. "The State and Local Capital Budget in Theory and Practice." National Tax Journal 20 (June 1967): 165-70.

Mayer, Thomas. "The Distribution of the Tax Burden and Permanent Income." National Tax Journal 28 (March 1974): 141-46.

Mazek, Warren F., and William E. Laird. "City-Size References and Population Distribution: The Analytical Context." Quarterly Review of Economics and Business 14 (Spring 1974): 113-21.

Micszkowski, Peter. "The Property Tax: An Excise Tax or a Profits Tax?" Journal of Public Economics 1 (April 1972): 73-96.

Mikesell, John L. "Central Cities and Sales Tax Rate Differentials: The Border City Problem." National Tax Journal 23 (June 1970): 206-13.

Miller, Stephen M., and William K. Tabb. "A New Look at a Pure Theory of Local Expenditures." National Tax Journal 26 (June 1973): 161-76.

Morss, Elliott R. "Federal Activities and Their Regional Impact on the Quality of Life." National Tax Journal 24 (June 1971): 177-92.

_____. "Some Thoughts on the Determinants of State and Local Expenditures." National Tax Journal 19 (March 1966): 95-103.

Musgrave, Richard A. "Economics of Fiscal Federalism." Nebraska Journal of Economics and Business 10 (Autumn 1971): 1-17.

Musgrave, Richard A., J. J. Carroll, L. D. Cook, and L. Franc. "Distribution of Tax Payment by Income Groups: A Case Study for 1947." National Tax Journal 4 (March 1951): 1-53.

Mushkin, Selma J. "Barriers to a System of Federal Grant-in-Aid." National Tax Journal 13 (September 1960): 193-218.

_____. "Intergovernmental Aspects of Local Expenditure Decisions." In Public Expenditure Decisions in the Urban Community, edited by Howard Schaller. Washington, D.C.: Resources for the Future, 1963.

Neenan, William B. "Suburban-Central City Exploitation Thesis: One City's Tale." National Tax Journal 23 (June 1970): 117-39.

Nelson, Howard J. "A Service Classification of American Cities." Economic Geography 31 (July 1955): 189-210.

_____. "Some Characteristics of the Population of Cities in Similar Service Classifications." Economic Geography 33 (April 1957): 95-108.

Netzer, Dick. "Financial Needs and Resources over the Next Decade: State and Local Government." In Public Finances: Needs, Sources, and Utilization. Princeton, N.J.: National Bureau of Economic Research, 1961.

_____. "Financing Urban Government." In Dimensions of State and Urban Policy Making, edited by Richard H. Leach and Timothy G. O'Rourke, pp. 307-20. New York: Macmillan, 1975.

Newcomer, Mabel. "Estimates of the Tax Burden on Different Income Classes." In Studies in Current Tax Problems, pp. 1-52. New York: Twentieth Century, 1937.

Oates, W. E., E. P. Howrey, and W. J. Baumol. "The Analysis of Public Policy in Dynamic Urban Models." Journal of Political Economy 79 (January/February 1971): 142-53.

Oates, Wallace E. "The Dual Impact of Federal Aid on State and Local Government Expenditures: A Comment." National Tax Journal 21 (June 1968): 220-23.

_____. "The Effects of Property Taxes and Local Public Spending on Property Values: An Empirical Study of Tax Capitalization and the Tiebout Hypothesis." Journal of Political Economy 77 (November/December 1969): 957-71.

O'Brien, Thomas. "Grants-in-Aid: Some Further Answers." National Tax Journal 24 (March 1971): 65-77.

Oldman, Oliver, and Henry Aaron. "Assessment-Sales Ratios under the Boston Property Tax." National Tax Journal 18 (March 1965): 36-49.

Olson, Grace Kneedler. "Economic Classification of Cities." In The Municipal Yearbook 1945, pp. 30-38. Chicago: ICMA, 1945.

Orr, Larry L. "The Incidence of Differential Property Taxes on Urban Housing." National Tax Journal 21 (September 1968): 253-62.

Osman, Jack W. "The Dual Impact of Federal Aid on State and Local Government Expenditures." National Tax Journal 19 (December 1966): 362-72.

_____. "On the Use of Intergovernmental Aid as an Expenditure Determinant." National Tax Journal 21 (December 1968): 437-47.

Ostrom, Elinor. "Metropolitan Reform: Propositions Derived from Two Traditions." Social Science Quarterly 53 (December 1972): 424-93.

Ostrom, Vincent. "Operational Federalism: Organization of Public Service in the American Federal System." Public Choice 7 (Spring 1969): 1-17.

Pauly, Mark V. "Income Redistribution as a Local Public Good." Journal of Public Economics 2 (February 1973): 35-58.

_____. "Optimality, 'Public' Goods, and Local Government: A General Theoretical Analysis." Journal of Political Economy 78 (May/June 1970): 572-85.

Pazour, John. "Local Government Fiscal Conditions." In The Municipal Yearbook, 1972, pp. 281-90. Chicago: ICMA, 1973.

Pechman, Joseph A. "The Rich, the Poor and the Taxes They Pay." Public Interest 17 (Fall 1969): 21-43.

Peterson, George. "The Regressivity of the Residential Property Tax." Journal of Public Economics.

Peterson, George E., and Arthur P. Solomon. "Property Taxes and Populist Reform." Public Interest 30 (Winter 1973): 60-75.

Phalen, J. John, and Leo F. Schnore. "Color Composition and City-Suburban Status Differences: A Replication." Land Economics 41 (February 1965): 87-91.

Pidot, George B., Jr. "A Principal Components Analysis of the Determinants of Local Government Fiscal Patterns." Review of Economics and Statistics 51 (May 1969): 176-88.

Pinkerton, James R. "The Changing Class Composition of Cities and Suburbs." Land Economics 59 (November 1973): 462-69.

Pogue, Thomas F., and L. G. Sgontz. "The Effect of Grants-in-Aid on State and Local Spending." National Tax Journal 21 (June 1968): 190-99.

Pollakowski, Henry O. "The Effect of Property Taxes and Local Public Spending on Property Values: A Comment and Further Results." Journal of Political Economy 81 (July/August 1973): 994-1003.

Prescott, James R., and William C. Lewis. "State and Municipal Locational Incentives: A Discriminant Analysis." National Tax Journal 22 (September 1969): 399-407.

Ridker, R., and J. J. Henning. "The Determinants of Residential Property Values with Special Reference to Air Pollution." Review of Economics and Statistics 49 (May 1967): 246-57.

Riesman, David. "The Suburban Dislocation." Annals of the American Academy of Political and Social Science 314 (November 1953): 123-46.

Ritchey, P. Neal. "Urban Poverty and Rural to Urban Migration." Rural Sociology 39 (Spring 1974): 12-27.

Rogers, Chester B. "Environment, System and Output: The Consideration of a Model." Social Forces 48 (September 1969): 72-87.

Ross, Heather. "Poverty: Women and Children Last." In Economic Independence for Women: The Foundation for Equal Rights, edited by Jane Roberts Chapman. Beverly Hills, Calif.: Sage Publications, 1976.

Sacks, Seymour, and John Callahan. "Central City Suburban Fiscal Disparity." In City Financial Emergencies: The Intergovernmental Dimension, pp. 91-152. Washington, D.C.: U.S. Government Printing Office, 1973.

Sacks, Seymour, and Robert Harris. "The Determinants of State and Local Government Expenditures and Intergovernmental Flows of Funds." National Tax Journal 17 (March 1964): 75-85.

Sanders, Heywood T. "Cities, Politics, and Elections: Partisanship in Nonpartisan Elections." In The Municipal Yearbook 1971, pp. 16-20. Chicago: ICMA, 1972.

_____. "Policies, Populations, and Governmental Structures." In The Municipal Yearbook 1972, pp. 160-64. Chicago: ICMA, 1973.

Sawicki, David S. "Studies of Aggregated Areal Data: Problems of Statistical Inference." Land Economics 69 (February 1973): 109-14.

Sazama, Gerald W. "Equalization of Property Taxes for the Nation's Largest Central Cities." National Tax Journal 18 (June 1965): 151-74.

Schmandt, Henry J., and G. Ross Stephens. "Local Government Expenditure Patterns in the United States." Land Economics 34 (November 1963): 397-406.

_____. "Measuring Municipal Output." National Tax Journal 8 (December 1960): 369-75.

Schnore, Leo F. "Components of Population Change in Large Metropolitan Suburbs." American Sociological Review 23 (October 1958): 570-73.

_____. "The Functions of Metropolitan Suburbs." American Journal of Sociology 61 (March 1956): 453-58.

_____. "The Growth of Metropolitan Suburbs." American Sociological Review 22 (April 1957): 165-73.

_____. "Municipal Annexations and the Growth of Metropolitan Suburbs, 1950-1960." American Journal of Sociology 67 (January 1962): 406-17.

_____. "Satellites and Suburbs." Social Forces 36 (December 1957): 121-27.

_____. "The Social and Economic Characteristics of American Suburbs." In Cities and Suburbs, edited by Brian T. Downes, pp. 49-59. Belmont, Calif.: Wadsworth, 1971.

_____. "The Socio-Economic Status of Cities and Suburbs." American Sociological Review 28 (February 1963): 76-85.

_____. "Urban Form: The Case of the Metropolitan Community." In Urban Life and Form, edited by Werner Z. Hirsch, pp. 167-93. New York: Holt, Rinehart and Winston, 1963.

_____. "Urban Structure and Suburban Selectivity." Demography 1 (1964): 164-76.

_____. "The Use of Public Transportation in Urban Areas." Traffic Quarterly 16 (October 1962): 488-98.

Schnore, Leo F., and Robert R. Alford. "Forms of Government and Socioeconomic Characteristics of Suburbs." Administrative Science Quarterly 6-7 (June 1963): 1-17.

Schnore, Leo F., and Vivian Felig Klaff. "Suburbanization in the Sixties: A Preliminary Analysis." Land Economics 68 (February 1972): 23-33.

Schnore, Leo F., and Hal H. Winsborough. "Functional Classification and the Residential Location of Social Classes." In City Classification Handbook: Methods and Applications, edited by Brian J. L. Berry, pp. 124-51. New York: Wiley, 1972.

Shannon, John. "Residential Property Tax Relief—A Federal Responsibility?" National Tax Journal 26 (September 1973): 499-573.

Shapiro, Harvey. "Economies of Scale and Local Government Finance." Land Economics 39 (May 1963): 135-86.

Sharkansky, Ira. "Some More Thoughts about the Determinants of Government Expenditures." National Tax Journal 21 (June 1967): 171-79.

Sharp, A. "The Behavior of Selected State and Local Government Fiscal Variables During the Phases of the Cycle 1949-1961." National Tax Association Proceedings, 1965.

Sherbenou, Edgar. "Class, Participation, and the Council-Manager Plan." Public Administration Review 21 (Summer 1961): 131-35.

Simmons, James M. "Changing Residence in the City: A Review of Intraurban Mobility." Geographical Review 63 (October 1968): 622-25.

Smith, David L. "Federal Grant Elasticity and Distortion: A Reply." National Tax Journal 22 (December 1969): 552-53.

_____. "The Response of State and Local Governments to Federal Grants." National Tax Journal 21 (September 1968): 349-57.

Smith, R. S. "Are Nonresidents Contributing Their Share to Core City Revenues?" Land Economics 68 (August 1972): 240-47.

Smyth, David J. "Tax Changes Linked to Government Expenditure Changes and the Magnitude of Fluctuations in National Income." Journal of Political Economy 78 (January/February 1970): 60-67.

Stephens, G. Ross, and Henry J. Schmandt. "Revenue Patterns of Local Government." National Tax Journal 15 (December 1962): 423-37.

Stewart, Charles T., and Virginia Benson. "Job Migration Linkages between Smaller SMSAs and Their Hinterlands." Land Economics 69 (November 1973): 432-39.

Stigler, George J. "Tenable Range of Functions of Local Government." In Joint Economic Committee, Subcommittee on Fiscal Policy, Federal Expenditure Policy for Economic Growth and Stability, pp. 213-19. Washington, D.C.: U.S. Government Printing Office, 1957.

Stinson, Thomas F. "Population Changes and Shifts in Local Government Finance." Municipal Finance 42 (August 1969): 134-39.

Suits, D. "The Use of Dummy Variables in Regression Equations." Journal of the American Statistical Association 52 (December 1957): 548-51.

Sussna, Stephen. "Residential Densities or a Fool's Paradise." Land Economics 69 (February 1973): 1-3.

Teeples, Ronald. "A Model of a Matching Grant-in-Aid Program with External Tax Effects." National Tax Journal 22 (December 1969): 486-95.

Terrell, Henry S. "The Fiscal Impact of Nonwhites." In Fiscal Pressures on the Central City: The Impact of Commuters, Nonwhites, and Overlapping Governments, edited by Werner Z. Hirsch, Philip E. Vincent, Henry S. Terrell, Donald C. Shoup, and Arthur Rosett. New York: Praeger, 1971.

Thompson, Wilbur R. "Intergovernmental Income Inequality within Metropolitan Areas." In A Preface to Urban Economics, edited by Wilbur R. Thompson, pp. 115-21. Baltimore: Johns Hopkins Press, 1965.

Thurow, Lester C. "The Theory of Grants-in-Aid." National Tax Journal 19 (December 1966): 373-77.

Tiebout, Charles. "An Economic Theory of Fiscal Decentralization." In Public Expenditure Decisions in the Urban Community, edited by Howard Schallfer. Washington, D.C.: Resources for the Future, Inc., 1963.

_____. "A Pure Theory of Local Expenditures." Journal of Political Economy 64 (October 1956): 416-24.

Tropman, John E. "Critical Dimensions of Community Structure: A Reexamination of the Hadden-Borgatta Findings." Urban Affairs Quarterly 5 (December 1969): 215-32.

Tullock, Gordon. "Federalism: Problems of Scale." Public Choice 6 (Spring 1969).

Vernon, Raymond. "The Economics and Finances of the Large Metropolis." Daedalus 90 (Winter 1961): 31-47.

Vincent, Phillip E. "The Fiscal Impact of Commuters." In Fiscal Pressures on the Central City: The Impact of Commuters, Nonwhites and Overlapping Governments, edited by Werner Z. Hirsch, Philip E. Vincent, Henry S. Terrell, Donald C. Shoup, and Arthur Rosett, pp. 41-143. New York: Praeger, 1971.

Waldauer, Charles. "Fiscal Interdependence among Tax Base-Sharing Local Governments: The External Effects of School Aid." National Tax Journal 23 (December 1970): 457-62.

_____. "Grant Structures and Their Effects on Aided Government Expenditures: An Indifference Curve Analysis." Public Finance 28 (1973): 212-25.

Walker, Mabel. "Major Impacts on the Property Tax." Municipal Finance, February 1971, pp. 117-25.

Walter, Benjamin, and Frederick M. Wirt. "Social and Political Dimensions of American Suburbs." In City Classification Handbook: Methods and Applications, edited by Brian J. L. Berry, pp. 97-123. New York: Wiley, 1972.

Warren, Robert O. "A Municipal Services Market Model of Metropolitan Organization." Journal of the American Institute of Planners 30 (August 1964): 193-204.

Weicher, John C. "Aid, Expenditures, and Local Government Structure." National Tax Journal 25 (December 1972): 473-584.

_____. "Determinants of Central City Expenditures: Some Overlooked Factors and Problems." National Tax Journal 23 (December 1970): 379-96.

_____. "The Effect of Urban Renewal on Municipal Service Expenditures." Journal of Political Economy 80 (January/February 1972): 86-101.

Weicher, John C., and R. J. Emerine II. "Econometric Analysis of State and Local Aggregate Expenditure Functions." Public Finance 28 (1973): 69-83.

Weisbrod, Burton. "An Expected Income Measure of Economic Welfare." Journal of Political Economy 70 (August 1962): 355-67.

Welch, Ronald B. "Some Observations on Assessment Ratio Measurement." National Tax Journal 17 (March 1964): 13-21.

Wicks, John H., and Michael N. Killworth. "Administrative and Compliance Costs of State and Local Taxes." National Tax Journal 20 (September 1967): 309-15.

Wilde, James A. "The Expenditure Effects of Grant-in-Aid Programs." National Tax Journal 21 (September 1968): 340-47.

_____. "Grants-in-Aid: The Analysis of Design and Response." National Tax Journal 24 (June 1971): 143-55.

Will, Robert E. "Scalar Economics and Urban Service Requirements." Yale Economic Essays 5 (Spring 1965): 1-62.

Williams, Alan. "The Optimal Provision of Public Goods in a System of Local Government." Journal of Political Economy 74 (February 1966): 18-33.

Williams, Oliver P. "A Typology for Comparative Local Government." Midwest Journal of Political Science 5 (May 1961): 150-64.

Winsborough, Hal H. "City Growth and City Structure." Journal of Regional Science 4 (Winter 1962): 35-49.

_____. "An Ecological Approach to the Theory of Suburbanization." American Journal of Sociology 68 (March 1963): 565-70.

Wirt, Frederick M. "The Political Sociology of American Suburbia: A Reinterpretation." In Urban Politics and Problems, edited by H. R. Mahood and Edward L. Angus, pp. 175-92. New York: Scribner's, 1969.

Wirth, Louis. "Urbanism as a Way of Life." American Journal of Sociology 44 (July 1938): 1-24.

Woodbury, Coleman. "Suburbanization and Suburbia." In Politics of Metropolitan Areas, edited by Philip B. Coulter, pp. 169-80. New York: Crowell, 1967.

Wood, Robert C. "The Local Government Response to the Urban Economy." In City Politics and Public Policy, edited by Edward Banfield and James Q. Wilson, pp. 69-96. New York: Wiley, 1968.

Wright, Deil S. "A Half-Century of Trends in Municipal Property Taxes: 1910-1960." Municipal Finance 37 (May 1965): 149-55.

Wright, Deil S., and Robert M. Marker. "A Half-Century of Local Finances." National Tax Journal 3 (September 1964): 274-91.

Wright, Deil S., and David E. Stephenson. "Inflexible Finances." National Cities Review 59 (December 1970): 578-85.

Ziegler, Joseph A. "Interurban Cycle Differentials and Fiscal Behavior." _National Tax Journal_ 25 (March 1972): 91-95.

Zikmund, Joseph. "A Comparison of Political Attitude and Activity Patterns in Central Cities and Suburbs." _Public Opinion Quarterly_ 31 (Spring 1967): 69-75.

Zimmerman, Dennis. "Expenditure-Tax Incidence Studies, Public Higher Education, and Equity." _National Tax Journal_ 26 (March 1973): 65-70.

Index

Aaron, Henry, 131
ACIR (see Advisory Commission on Intergovernmental Relations)
Advisory Commission on Intergovernmental Relations (ACIR), 64, 123, 150
Andrews, R. B., 105-6
areas outside the central city (OCC), 11, 64, 97, 98, 188
assessment levels, property tax, 122, 125, 141
average unit costs (AUC), 150

Bahl, Roy, 145
Baird, Robert N., 54
Baumol, William, 145
Beck, Morris, 125-26
Black, David, 125, 133
blacks, 167, 207, 210, 213; racial income inequalities, 172; sex income differentials among, 170; and tax burdens, 174-76, 179; and tax efficiency, 179, 181-83
Boston, 67, 125

Callahan, John, 28-29, 64, 65-66, 67, 119
Campbell, Alan K., 55
Census, Bureau of, 7, 8, 10, 11, 13, 32, 35, 56, 57, 98, 122, 123, 126, 168-69, 200
Census of Governments, 11, 14-15, 17, 20, 127
Census of Housing, 16
Census of Population, 14, 16
central cities, 11, 29, 30-31, 32, 34, 35-37, 38-39, 43, 45-48, 49, 50-51, 52, 53, 55-56, 58, 59, 63, 64, 65, 66, 67, 68, 71, 72, 73, 76-78, 79-82, 83, 84-85, 86, 88, 89, 90-91, 92, 96, 97, 98, 99, 100, 101, 102, 103, 104-5, 106, 107-9, 110, 111-17, 119, 126, 128-29, 130-33, 134, 137, 138, 139, 141-42, 143, 144, 145-50, 151, 153-58, 159-60, 186-87, 188
City Finances, 11, 15, 17, 20
Civil Rights Act (1964), Title VII, 167
comparison-of-means analysis, 20-21, 29, 83, 89-90, 111, 160, 189, 197, 202, 213, 214, 215

competition, in gaining federal grants, 6
correlational analysis, 21, 160, 205

Dasso, Jerome J., 105-6
descriptive analysis (see comparison-of-means analysis)
Detroit, 3, 120, 186
differential employment, 170
dynamic deterioration, process of, 145

effective property tax rates, 10, 14-15, 123-42; for all types real property, 126, 128, 129, 130, 131, 133-34, 141 [determinants, central city, 137; determinants, suburban, 138-39]; calculation of, 10; determinants, 137-41; earlier studies on, 124-26; for fully taxable single-family residential property, 123, 126, 129, 130-31, 133, 134, 137, 141 [determinants, central city, 139; determinants, suburban, 139-41]; general patterns, 126-37 [population variations, 129-31; progressivity, 126-27, 129, 137; regional variations, 127-29; variations by economic bases, 131-33; variations by functional responsibility, 133-37; variations by governmental character, 133]
Equal Pay Act (1963), 167
equity versus efficiency, 144, 159
externalities (spillovers), 14, 146

FBI Uniform Crime Reports, 16
federal (aid) grants, 5-6, 12, 30-32, 43, 50-52, 64, 69, 71, 72, 73, 76, 78, 79, 82, 84-86, 92-93, 194, 198, 199, 205-6, 210, 215; categorical, 5, 93; competition in obtaining, 6; formula, 6, 12; project, 5-6, 12
Feinberg, Mordecai, 63-64, 65
fiscal irresponsibility, 3
1400 Governments, 38, 105
Fowler, Edmund P., 55
functional responsibilities, 17, 21, 27, 29, 43, 44-48, 49, 52-58 passim, 63, 67, 76-78, 79-83, 84, 86-92 passim, 96, 107-10, 111-17 passim, 126, 128, 133-37, 141, 151, 153-54, 159, 189, 194-202 passim, 205-15 passim

grants-in-aid, 5, 6, 12-13, 52, 64, 78, 86, 96, 194, 200, 206, 211, 212

Haskell, Mark A., 148
heads of household, 168-69
Hirsch, Werner Z., 146, 150, 151-53, 154
household status, 169-70, 172, 173-74 179, 183

intergovernmental revenues, 4-6, 10, 11, 12, 13, 30-32, 34, 35, 38, 57, 62, 63, 64, 65, 66, 67, 69, 71, 72, 73, 76, 78, 79-82, 90, 187, 201, 215; federal, 5-6, 12, 35, 65, 67, 69, 71, 72, 73, 76, 78, 82, 187; state, 6, 12-13, 35, 65, 67, 69, 71, 72, 73, 76, 78, 79, 82, 187; level determinants, 50-54, 205 [federal, 50-52, 84; state, 52-54, 84]; reliance determinants, 83-88, 210 [federal, 84-86, 92-93; state, 86-88, 92-93]; suburban, changes in, 188-89, 194-95 [federal, 189, 194; state, 188-89, 195]
intergovernmental transfer payments, 146

Jack, John W., 64, 194
Johnson, S. R., 28
Junk, Paul E., 28

Kasarda, John, 145
Kee, Woo Sik, 44, 98-99, 111, 112, 147

land area density, 111, 115, 125-26, 154-58, 207, 208, 209, 210, 211, 214
Landon, John H., 54
Leshinski, Stephen, 148
Lineberry, Robert L., 39, 55, 106
local government tax structures: and economic position of women and blacks, 167, 183; efficiency of, 179, 181-83; inequities of, 167, 173, 174, 176, 179, 181, 183
Los Angeles, 67

Mieszkowski, Peter, 124, 134
Miller, Stephen M., 145, 148
multiple regressional analysis, 21, 49, 63, 205
municipal revenue data, weaknesses of current, 11-16
municipal revenues: intergovernmental, 4-6; nontax, 7-8; tax, 7; types of, 4
Municipal Yearbook, The, 17, 37

Netzer, Dick, 181
New Jersey, 125
New York City, 3, 44, 120, 124, 186

OCC (see areas outside the central city)
Oldman, Oliver, 131

Pazour, John, 64-65
per capita incomes, 9, 95, 98, 145, 167; calculation of, 169; higher for female household heads, 170-71; and household status, 170, 183; racial inequalities in, 172, 183; sex and inequality of, 169-70, 183; tax burdens and, 172
Peterson, George E., 125, 140-41
Pettengill, Robert B., 29, 67, 71, 96, 202
Philadelphia, 186
policy determinant research, 48-59, 83-92; stepwise multiple regression, 49
population mobility, 11, 58, 89, 111, 114, 154, 158, 159, 160
property tax rates, 122-23, 141; actual, 122; effective, 123-42; nominal, 122, 123, 141; statutory, 122, 141
property tax rates, effective (see effective property tax rates)
property taxes, 7, 13, 14, 34-39 passim, 43; 48, 54, 62-69 passim, 71, 72, 73, 78, 79, 82, 83, 88, 92, 97-106 passim, 109-15, 116, 118, 167, 173, 187, 196-201 passim, 207-8, 212-13; regressivity of, 167, 173, 197

real property, definitions of, 122
redistribution, of income, 5, 6, 31, 50, 52, 86, 194, 207, 212
reform, governmental, 39, 76, 106, 118, 151
residential crowding, 118, 159, 205-6, 207, 208, 210, 211, 212, 213, 214
Reuss, Paul C., 64, 194
revenue levels, 8-9, 27-59, 62, 187; calculation of, 8, 27; general, 29-48, 59, 71 [higher in central cities, 29-32; population variations, 35-37; regional variations, 32-35; variations by economic bases, 37-39; variations by functional responsibility, 44-48; variations by governmental character, 39-44]; previous studies of, 28-29, 30; suburban, changes in, 188-98 [determinants, 205-9 (federal aid, 205-6; nonproperty tax, 208; nontax, 209; property tax, 207-8; state aid, 206-7)]

revenue patterns, changes as predictors of financial crises, 187, 198, 215
revenue reliance, 9, 62-93; calculation of, 9, 62; general patterns, 65-83, 187 [population variations, 69-72, 78; regional variations, 67-69; variations by economic bases, 72-76; variations by functional responsibility, 76-78, 79-83; variations by governmental character, 76-79]; previous studies of, 63-65; suburban patterns, changes in, 198-202[determinants, 210-14 (federal aid, 210; nonproperty tax, 212-13; state aid, 211-12); intergovernmental, 198, 199-200, 210 (federal, 199, 200 210; state, 200, 210); nontax, 198, 202, 210; tax, 198, 200-2 (property, 200-1, 210; nonproperty, 201-2, 210)]

revenue usage, measures of, 8-11, 62; effective property tax rate, 10, 14-15; revenue level, 8-9; revenue reliance, 9; tax burden, 9-10, 14; tax efficiency, 10-11, 14, 15
revenues, nontax, 7-8, 11, 15, 16, 30, 34, 37, 43, 44, 48, 57, 63, 64, 65, 67, 69, 71, 72, 73, 76, 78, 79, 82, 83, 88, 90, 118, 187, 188; level determinants, 57-59 [central city, 58; suburban, 58-59, 205]; reliance determinants, 89-92 [central city, 90-91, 93; suburban, 91-92, 93, 202]; suburban, changes in, 197-98, 209
revenues, tax, 9, 15, 30, 32, 63, 64, 65, 71, 76, 82-83, 90, 95, 172, 173; comparisons, limitations of, 11-15; level determinants, 54-56 [central city, 55-56; suburban, 56, 205]; nonproperty, 7, 32, 34, 43, 44, 48, 65, 66, 67, 69, 71, 73, 78, 79, 82-83, 92, 187, 189, 197; property, 7, 15, 32, 34, 43, 44, 48, 55-56, 65, 66, 67, 71, 72, 73, 78, 79, 82-83, 88-89, 91, 92, 187, 189, 195-96; reliance determinants, 88-89 [central city, 88, 89, 92, 93; suburban, 89, 92, 93]; suburban, changes in, 188, 189, 195-97
Ross, Heather, 183-84

Sacks, Seymour, 28-29, 61, 64, 65-66, 67, 119
Sanders, Heywood T., 99, 111
Schmandt, Henry J., 28, 44
Seattle, 67
service/tax burden ratios, 147, 154, 179 (see also tax-service ratios)
sex, and income inequality, 169-70
Shapiro, Harvey, 148-49, 181

shared taxes, 6, 12, 52, 78, 86, 88, 200, 206, 211, 212
Sharkansky, Ira, 39, 106
SMSA (see Standard Metropolitan Statistical Areas)
Solomon, Arthur P., 125, 141
spillovers (see externalities)
Standard Metropolitan Statistical Areas (SMSA), 3, 11, 16, 29, 51, 55, 63, 64, 65, 88, 97, 98, 114-15, 124, 125, 168, 169, 173, 176, 181, 186, 188
state aid, 6, 12-13, 30, 31-32, 34, 43, 44, 45, 48, 52-54, 64, 65, 69, 71, 72, 73, 76, 78, 79, 82, 84, 86, 92-93, 195, 198, 200, 211-12, 215
Stephens, G. Ross, 28, 44
Stinson, Thomas, 44, 63-64
suburban revenue patterns, changing, 186-215; earlier studies, 187-88; revenue levels, 188-98 [determinants, 205-9; intergovernmental, 188-89, 194-95; nontax, 188, 197-98; tax, 188, 189, 195-97]; revenue reliance, 198-202 [determinants, 210-14; intergovernmental, 198, 199-200 (federal, 199, 200; state, 200); nontax, 198, 202; tax, 198, 200-2 (property, 200-1; nonproperty, 201-2)]
suburbs, 11-12, 28-29, 30-32, 34-35, 37, 38, 39, 43-44, 48, 51-52, 53-54, 56, 58-59, 63, 64, 65-66, 67, 69, 72, 73-76, 78-79, 82-83, 84, 85-88, 89, 91-92, 96, 97, 98, 99, 101, 102-3, 105-7, 109-10, 114-15, 117-19, 126-27, 129, 131, 133, 134-37, 138-41, 142, 143, 144, 145-48, 150, 151, 153-54, 158-60; maturation processes of, 186-87, 188

Tabb, William K., 145, 148
tax burdens, 9-10, 14, 143; calculation of, 9, 173; comparing, reasons for, 96; definition of, 9, 95, 172; earlier studies on, 97-99, 111 [weaknesses, 97-98]; general patterns, 98-111, 172-76 [by household status, 173-74, 176; nonproperty taxes, 173; population variations, 102-3, 176; property taxes, 173; by race, 174-76; regional variations, 100-1, 176; by sex, 174; variations by economic bases, 104-6; variations by functional responsibility, 107-10; variations by governmental character, 106-7]; nonproperty tax determinants, 115-19]central city, 115-17; suburban, 117-19]; property tax determinants, 111-15 [central city, 111-14; suburban, 114-15]

tax efficiency, 10-11, 14, 15, 143-62; calculation of, 10-11; central city correlates, 154-58 [demographic, 154-58; governmental, 158; socioeconomic, 158]; central city/ suburban differences, 146, 154, 159-60, 161-62; and citizen locational decisions, 143-46, 154-58, 160; defined, 143, 176-79; determinants [central city, 160; suburban, 160]; general patterns, 146-54, 176-83 [for all services, 179-81; by economic bases, 151; by functional responsibility, 153-54; by governmental character, 151-53; by population size, 148-50, 181; for poverty-linked services, 181-83; regional, 148, 181]; previous studies on, 144-47; suburban correlates, 158-59
tax effort, 99
tax levels, municipal, 30, 35-37, 38-39, 43, 44, 45, 48, 55-56
taxes, 9-10, 31; income, 7, 13, 97, 173, 201, 213; nonproperty, 7, 13-14, 34, 35-37, 39, 43, 48, 62, 64, 66, 67, 71, 72, 73, 78, 79, 82, 83, 88, 92, 97, 98, 99, 100, 101, 102-3, 105, 106, 109-11, 115-19, 131, 197, 198, 200, 201, 202, 208, 213-14, 215; piggyback, 6; privilege, 7,

34; property (see property taxes); sales, 6, 7, 13, 34, 86, 97, 115, 173, 197, 201, 208, 213; shared, 6, 12, 52, 78, 86, 88, 200, 206, 211, 212
tax-service ratios, 145, 146 (see also service/tax burden ratios)
Tiebout, Charles, 144, 181
Tiebout consumer-choice model of residential location, 96, 98, 133, 154
Tufte, Edward R., 49
Twentieth Century Fund Task Force on Women and Employment, 169

Uppal, Jogindar S., 29, 67, 71, 96, 202

Vital Statistics of the U.S., 16

Will, Robert E., 150
Williams, Alan, 146
Wirt, Frederick, 38
women, 167, 210, 211, 213, 214; higher income by household status, 170-71; household status of, 168-69; lower earnings by, 169-70, 183; and tax burdens, 174, 176, 179, 183; and tax efficiency, 179-83
women's movement, 167
Wood, Robert, 38, 105, 196

About the Author

SUSAN A. MACMANUS is an Assistant Professor of Political Science at the University of Houston. She also serves as a consultant to many Texas cities regarding plans of electing council members (at-large, single-member district schemes), annexation, and other aspects of municipal government. In addition, she is a research associate for The Brookings Institution in its monitoring study of Public Service Employment programs.

Dr. MacManus has published in the areas of municipal finance and local governmental structure. Her articles have appeared in the American Journal of Political Science, the Western Political Quarterly, and Social Science Journal.

Dr. MacManus holds a B.A. from Florida State University, an M.A. from the University of Michigan, and a Ph.D. from Florida State University.

Related Titles

Published by
Praeger Special Studies

FEDERAL GRANTS-IN-AID: Maximizing Benefits to the States
Anita S. Harbert

*THE POLITICS OF RAISING STATE AND LOCAL REVENUE
Richard D. Bingham
Brett W. Hawkins
F. Ted Hebert

THE PROPERTY TAX AND ALTERNATIVE LOCAL TAXES:
An Economic Analysis
Larry D. Schroeder
David L. Sjoquist

REGIONAL ECONOMIC DIVERSIFICATION
Michael E. Conroy

*Also available in paperback as a PSS Student Edition